6.85

Hail Mary?

D0023785

Hail Mary?

The Struggle for Ultimate Womanhood in Catholicism

Maurice Hamington

ROUTLEDGE

New York and London

Published in 1995 by

Routledge
29 West 35TH Street
New York, NY 10001

Published in Great Britain in 1995 by

Routledge
11 New Fetter Lane
London EC4P 4EE

Copyright © 1995 by Routledge

Printed in the United States of America
Design: Jack Donner

All rights reserved. No part of this book may be reprinted or reproduced or utilized in any form or by any electronic, mechanical, or other means, now known or hereafter invented, including photocopying and recording, or in any information storage or retrieval system without permission in writing from the publishers.

All scripture quotations are taken from the Scholars Version translation. *The Complete Gospels: Annotated Scholars Version.* Copyright © 1992, 1994 by Polebridge Press. Used with permission. All rights reserved.

Library of Congress Cataloging-in-Publications Data

Hamington, Maurice, 1960 –
     Hail Mary? : the struggle for ultimate womanhood in Catholicism / Maurice Hamington.
     p. cm.
     Includes bibliographical references and index.
     ISBN 0–415–91303–9 — ISBN 0–415–91304–7 (pbk.)
     1. Mary, Blessed Virgin, Saint—Theology—Controversial literature. 2. Mary, Blessed Virgin, Saint—Cult—Controversial literature. 3. Catholic Church—Doctrines Controversial literature. 4. Catholic Church—Doctrines—History—20th century. 5. Feminist theology. 6. Women in the Catholic Church. I. Title.

BT614.H35 1995
232.91—dc20

95-11985
CIP

To Stephanie and Rosemary
with love.

Contents

Acknowledgments   ix

Introduction   1

Chapter 1
The History and Social Construction of Mary   9

Chapter 2
The Struggle to Control Mary   31

Chapter 3
Catholic Sexual Morality and the Blessed Virgin Mary   53

Chapter 4
Mary, the Mediatrix and Asymmetrical Gender Power   89

Chapter 5
Women and Evil / Mary and Eve   125

Chapter 6
The Recasting of Marian Imagery   157

Notes   181

Index   211

Acknowledgments

Many generous and insightful individuals assisted in the development of this book. I am grateful to John Orr, Barrie Thorne, and Ron Hock, who guided my research when this was a dissertation project. I couldn't have asked for a more supportive group of scholars to assist me in this venture. Barrie Thorne in particular taught me the power of feminist consciousness and I owe her a great debt for helping bring this publication to fruition as a mentor and a friend.

I would also like to express my appreciation to those who read portions of the manuscript including Wanda Teays and Jackie Rodgers. Others who made significant contributions were Marv Meyer, Sheila Briggs, and Stephanie Hamington.

Because this book is part of a greater trajectory of academic pursuit, I would be remiss if I did not express my appreciation to two key mentors, Marie Egan and Alexis Navarro, without whose scholarship and friendship I would not have left a business career to pursue academia. They are part of Mount St. Mary's College in Los Angeles, which has provided me with a supportive community. Other key mentors who modeled progressive Christian approaches to me include Marv Meyer, Frank Ponnet, and Dan Jiru.

I would also like to praise the professional and personable staff at Routledge including Kimberly Herald, Andrew Rubin, Mary Carol De Zutter, and most of all Marlie Wasserman. Their expertise has left its mark throughout this book.

In an era when social services are under attack, it is important to mention that this book would not have been possible without the availability of both public and private libraries as well as affordable day care (thank you everyone at the Allegra Center!). Of course, this is ultimately a family project. Stephanie now knows more about Mary than anyone would care to, and Rosemary inspired this work—perhaps in a decade or so she will be able to read it.

Finally, I would like to express gratitude to pioneering Christian feminists, and in particular to Rosemary Radford Ruether, whose writing has inspired a generation of scholars, including this profeminist male.

Introduction

The old saying, "As Mary goes, so goes the Church," should be reversed. Rather we have learned: "As the Church goes so goes Mary."

—Barbara Corrado Pope[1]

The single most significant female religious figure in Western civilization, Mary, the mother of Jesus, is at the center of an ideological struggle within Catholicism. This struggle centers upon the modern meaning of Mary for the faithful, and particularly for Catholic women. Mary is a potent religious symbol with deep-rooted moral implications for the relationship of Catholic men and women in a number of areas, including sexuality, power, and concepts of evil. While volumes have been written about Mary, and she has been the subject of much recent feminist analysis, little has been said about the moral implications of Marian imagery. This book will specifically explore how evolving Marian images fit into a feminist religious ethic.

The conservative male hierarchy of Roman Catholicism has a vested interest in maintaining the traditional imagery that permeates the Cult of Mary. A radical change in the traditional portrayal of Mary could have implications for change in Catholic theology, moral teaching, and the structure of the Church. Many feminist theologians who view the Cult of

Mary as a paradigm for patriarchal social control and the oppression of women would welcome such change. Modern developments in biblical scholarship and social construction theory have fueled this feminist critique of Mariology. These developments make the present era a crucial period for reexamining religious symbolism such as that associated with Mary. This book describes the development of the traditional images of Mary, and the modern reinterpretation by Christian feminists within an ethical framework. The essential issue to be explored is the moral implication of traditional Marian imagery, given feminist analysis and the Catholic phenomenological framework that has created Mary.

Rosemary Radford Ruether, Andrew Greeley, and others have argued that Mary is much more than a theological symbol for women.[2] Mary is a living metaphor for women and the feminine spirit. To control the theological understanding of Mary is to exert influence over women in the analogical imagination of the religious faithful. Catholic feminist theologian Elizabeth Johnson makes an explicit connection between the fate of the Cult of Mary and that of Christian women:

> It seems a sure judgment to say that the future of the Marian tradition is closely tied with the future history of women in the church, and that it will be regenerated or remain collapsed of its own weight depending in large measure on what happens in that history. A renewed Marian tradition will be credible only in a church which recognizes and embodies in theory and practice the full dimensions of the dignity of women. . . . Ultimately, what is at stake in this question is not only the redirection of the tradition about Mary, but the search for our common humanity: the essence of woman, of man, and of redeemed humanity, the church itself.[3]

In the view of many Christian feminists, Mary's traditional portrayal has had misogynist overtones. She is venerated in Catholic doctrine and encyclicals for her humility, her lowliness in the sight of God, and her lack of sexuality. However, Mary historically has resisted being under complete control, and the woman-spirit within her imagery has often risen beyond its patriarchically established boundaries. She carries an undeniable popular power, as witnessed in the ongoing "Cult of Mary" that includes claims of Marian apparitions, and the faith of millions who make an annual pilgrimage to the locations of her sightings. Nevertheless, Christian feminists are not satisfied with Mary's popularity because her traditional portrayal perpetuates feminine stereotypes that fuel oppression. Feminist scholars have drawn from sociology and biblical studies, historically male-dominated disciplines, to develop their analysis. These disciplines point to the lack of historical data on Mary, which makes her virtually anonymous from an objective standpoint and renders her traditional images as projections placed upon her by a patriarchal Church. The Cult of Mary has a historically specific basis that has been molded over time by the Catholic hierarchy's social and theological agenda.

Women are relative newcomers to theology, moral theology, and biblical studies because of a tradition of male exclusivity in these fields. However, Christian feminist scholars such as Rosemary Radford Ruether, Elisabeth Schussler Fiorenza, Mary Daly, Elizabeth Johnson, Els Maeckelberghe, and others are using these disciplinary frameworks to replace the traditional construction of the compliant, humble Mary with a strong, independent image. This struggle to renegotiate Marian imagery is interwoven with the fight for equality of women in the systems of power within Christian churches. This book reviews and assesses the struggle for image control, analyzing a history of varied social constructions. It views the Marian tradition as more of a human projection than an objective, historically verifiable reality. Given Mary's created and recreated nature, many feminist scholars contend that she can be "deconstructed," and subsequently "reimaged."

Chapter One sets forth the historical context for the Cult of Mary. This background establishes the roots of this popular phenomenon with an eye to the constructed nature of its beginnings. Every significant event and turn in history that the Cult of Mary makes has a political or theological rationale beyond devotion to Mary. Understanding the origins of the Cult of Mary is a significant factor in advancing alternative histories such as those in the work of Rosemary Radford Ruether, Jane Schaberg, Mary Daly, and Elizabeth Johnson, which are considered later. Marian history also demonstrates the nature of Mariology as central to the theology of the Catholic Church and its perspective on the relationship of men and women. Chapter One concludes by fitting the history of Mary into a sociological understanding of religious reality and its human creation.

Chapter Two defines the three-way relationship of constituencies that have influenced Marian imagery: the hierarchical Catholic Church, the theological Catholic Church, and the popular Catholic Church. A monolithic understanding of Mary and her tradition does not exist within Catholicism. Each faction tells its own story of Mary, and the various renditions are often quite dissimilar. Historically, Church documents, theological writings, and popular piety have yielded differing perspectives on Mary and her implications for faith. This difference in perspective has varied from subtlety to polar opposition. To a certain extent, each position influences the others while also balancing extreme views. Of these factions within the Church, theology is the locus of ethical critique, giving voice to modern feminist analyses. This chapter defines feminist theology and feminist religious ethics, and explains the theory of social construction developed in the first chapter by describing who is involved in building the modern Cult of Mary, the gendered nature of the construction, and, most importantly, the moral nature of the construction. This book views Mary as a model of the Church's moral control over Catholic women, and therefore as the linchpin in any movement for change.

Chapters Three, Four, and Five explore specific images of Mary and their implications in feminist ethical analysis. Each reviews the historical background of a particular Marian image, presents a historical and ethical feminist critique, and finally explores the implications of the image for modern Catholic women. In the final section of each chapter, I attempt to contribute new insight into the connection of Marian imagery to the broader issues of sexism within Catholic theology.

Chapter Three takes up the Catholic doctrine of Mary's perpetual virginity, which originated in canonical and noncanonical texts, Gnosticism, and the writings of Church "fathers," specifically St. Jerome. Modern biblical analysis provides serious questions as to a scriptural basis for Mary's perpetual virginity. Feminist scholarship takes this analysis and extends its implications. Ruether, utilizing biblical exegesis, argues for recognition that Jesus had brothers and thereby casts doubt on Mary's perpetual virginity. Schaberg meticulously develops an alternative scriptural theme that concludes Jesus was an illegitimate child. Both authors point out that alternative histories concerning Mary and the birth of Jesus are just as plausible, if not more so, than the traditionally accepted history. Despite such evidence, Mary remains the Catholic model of sexuality, particularly as it pertains to women. A review of statements made by bishops in official church documents and in statements made by the pope reveal a model of human sexuality that places virginity as its highest value, and Mary as the zenith of that value. Pope John Paul II speaks of women taking part in the natural "spousal order" through virginity. In a fascinating convolution of sexuality, Mary's virginity, or perceived asexuality, has been transformed into a model of heterosexuality. Mary's role in a feminist ethic of sexuality will be explored.

Chapter Four explores the issue of power. Mary's role as "mediatrix" establishes her as wielding significant divine influence in human salvation. The origins of this title have been developed with particular attention to the role Marian apparitions play in perpetuating the concept of Mary's power. The feminist analysis poses questions as to the authenticity of this power. Does Mary exemplify independent female power as a Goddess or is her influence only a result of her relationship to other divine figures? There is a parallel between the movement to interpret Mary as the Christian Goddess and the attempt by women to obtain ordination in the Catholic Church. In both cases theological restrictions prevent male and female expressions of spiritual equality. The concluding focus on ethical implications demonstrates how Mary's "false power" perpetuates gender inequality, particularly in family relationships. Mary is touted by the Church as the perfect mother, but what are the implications of this form of motherhood for Catholic familial dynamics?

In Chapter Five, the long-standing tradition of Mary as the New Eve is explored as it pertains to concepts of feminine evil. For this exploration, not only is Mary's title as the New Eve plumbed for its traditional development, but the Christian tradition of Eve is also sought because of its companion role in Mary's elevation. Over years of Catholic teaching, Mary's goodness became absolute; however this goodness was juxtaposed to the evil of Eve, creating a tremendous dualism as the model of womanhood. This moral dualism meant that women were considered either good or evil by standards impossible to emulate. Christianity created a gendered moral framework. The feminist analysis in this area attempts to recover the entire myth of Eve or to reinterpret the Eve tradition. The moral implication of the Eve/Mary dualism in perpetuating violence and the abuse of vilified women is discussed in the conclusion of this chapter.

The final chapter of this book discusses approaches to reversing or altering the pattern of Mary's religious construction in order to mitigate the destructive alienation of women that emanates from the Cult of Mary. A dialogue with the work of Catholic feminist scholars provides parameters for a new approach. The synthesis of this dialogue is a backdrop for the suggested direction of "low Mariology," personified in the figure of "Mary Everywoman." This imagery attempts to recover the ancient concept of every woman's participation in the divinity of the "triple Mary." Transcendence, as opposed to divination, is suggested as a means to overcome constructed religious alienation.

Before proceeding, a brief review of Marian terminology as it pertains to Mariology, Mariolatry, and the Cult of Mary is offered. The terms "Cult of Mary," "Mariology," and "Mariolatry" have been used to describe the phenomenon of Mary's popular potency. In common conversation, the term "cult" has taken on a pejorative connotation, conjuring images of mysterious, unscrupulous religious groups that spur fanaticism and prey upon the young and weak of society for membership. Sociologist Howard Becker, in the tradition of Max Weber and Ernest Troeltsch, describes a cult as an "ideal type" of religion (other types being church, sect, and denomination). As such, a cult resembles a sect, but is more informal and transient. Clear membership is not distinguished, and participants do not necessarily give up their formal religious connection. Personal experience is the centerpiece of the cult, and it usually draws people around an inspirational figure.[4]

The Cult of Mary does not easily fit the sociological typology. It is as old as Christianity and can hardly be termed transient, although in each age it reemerges with certain changes in character. The charisma of its leader also must be questioned. In Mary's case, the available picture of her personality or force of character is so scant it is difficult to view her as a charismatic leader. Nevertheless, personal experience in the form of apparitions, special prayers, and rituals do suggest a sociological sort of cult.

"Mariology" can be termed a type of pseudoscience that purports to study Mary in an objective sense; its works range from earnestly scholarly to overtly devotional. Although numerous authors attempt to study and analyze Mary dispassionately, there are many works of Mariology that cannot escape an underlying piety toward her. It is almost as if Mariologists are speaking of their own mothers and cannot help expressing their devotion. Perhaps an analogical critique can be levied at some feminist analyses that loathe Mariology and are quick to dismiss Mary as a purely misogynist result of patriarchal religion. This may represent misplaced rage, just as the opposite represents misplaced devotion. Nevertheless, the historical nature of Mariology has been unselfcritical with a bias toward an underlying adoration of Mary.

"Mariolatry" is difficult to define because it is a relational term that finds worship of Mary out of proportion to Catholic orthodoxy. The potentially subjective nature of what constitutes Catholic orthodoxy will be discussed later, but generally Mary is not officially considered divine—her role is to bring greater faith to Jesus. Mariolatry results in Mary becoming thought of as a type of goddess, worshipped above or equal to Jesus and/or

God. Perspective is critical to an understanding of Mariolatry. Those outside the Catholic faith might place all devotion to Mary under the category of Mariolatry, while Catholics would only find some of the extreme practices to be idolatrous. Marian historian Hilda Graef finds that the first great rise of Mariolatry occurred in the prereformation era, which at least in part fueled the Great Schism in the Church.[5] Martin Luther, while retaining a certain amount of Marian piety, did dramatically reduce the perceived excesses.[6] Perhaps Mariolatry can best be described as the point at which Mariology becomes "Christotypical" rather than "ecclesiatypical." In the former case, claims surrounding Mary are analogous to those claims usually reserved for Christ (e.g., a sinless nature, redeeming the world and ascending into heaven, etc.). Mary is considered a type of Christ. If Mary is viewed as a conduit of devotion that leads to greater worship of Jesus and God, then she is "a type of the Church." However, Mariolatry requires a Christotypical perspective. This phenomenon was particularly present during points in history in which Jesus, given his strictly divine qualities, was depicted as thoroughly removed from humanity. Mary filled the void to represent humanity as a mediator with heaven.[7] The more of a role Mary was given, the easier it was to extend divine powers to her.

The tension between Mariology and Mariolatry within the Catholic Cult of Mary depicts the potency of this religious figure. Mary can be a tool of patriarchal power, "studied" for her insight into true womanhood. Yet the popular fervor for Mary carries her beyond the bounds established by the Church. This typifies the problematic nature of all of Mary's imagery. Whether it be her sexuality, power, or goodness, for Mary there is one overriding description: enigma.

Hail Mary? seeks to illuminate the moral significance of Mary by applying theories of the social construction of Marian imagery, including a consideration of its history and modern ethical implication. These moral implications will be explored by connecting Marian imagery to its role in a variety of issues, including sexuality, women's ordination, goddess worship, parenting roles, and woman hating. In addition, this book articulates and analyzes the feminist critique of the Cult of Mary in an effort to demonstrate how a deconstruction, and subsequent reconstruction, of Mary is inevitable in the work of Catholic feminists. The elements of the deconstruction process provide a framework for recasting Marian imagery.

1

The History and Social Construction of Mary

"Mary": the product of a tug of war lasting centuries.
—Els Maeckelberghe[1]

Understanding the history of the Cult of Mary is the key to unlocking the evolution of Marian images and, subsequently, their implication for modern Catholics. Whatever the role-defined image—Mary, the Virgin; Mary, the Mediatrix; or Mary, the New Eve—there is a particular historical setting, a set of social values, and a theological logic behind its origins. Time and social perspective may add layers of complexity to the rationale for each image, but an unraveling of the history is crucial for even a modicum of comprehension of Mary's complexity. Part of the task of feminist analysis is to question the traditional interpretation of historically specific events and ideas. Therefore, a feminist analysis of Marian imagery must begin with its origins.

Subsequent chapters will focus upon significant events in the history of particular Marian images as they impact current symbolic interpretation, but this chapter will provide the sweeping historical pageant of the Cult of Mary. The general history of Marian devotion provides an important framework for the theoretical and analytical presuppositions of this book. The Marian tradition is a complex weaving of theological logic, medieval Christian devotion, psychology, sexual morality, and politics. However, little in the Marian tradition is based on "facts" known about the life of Mary. I will conclude this chapter by demonstrating that Mary is the ultimate model of a religious social construction of reality.

The history of the Cult of Mary also demonstrates the stratified nature of Catholic theology. It is an error to assume that a unified Catholic perspective concerning the life and meaning of Mary has been preserved for two thousand years. Popular beliefs about Mary have risen from the masses who look upon her with beloved adoration. Church pronouncements and dogma about Mary serve the Christology at the heart of Catholicism. Outside the control of the Church hierarchy, independent theologians provide reflections upon Mary that include ethical analyses and symbolic implications. For Catholics, the symbolism of Mary integrates these various perspectives with another layer of complexity determined by culture and social values. All that Mary represents is bound together in the myths and legends that have been preserved. Feminist theologian Els Maeckelberghe describes Mary as a "patchwork quilt," with every century adding another patch of cloth.[2] If the modern understanding of Mary is considered the finished or latest quilt, one must gain knowledge of the historical pieces before the current quilt can be fully conceptualized. Therefore, viewing Mary in a historical perspective enables us to understand the evolution of Marian images into the multivariate symbol that is the Madonna today. These images involve an abundance of contradictions—handmaiden/queen, virgin/mother, role model/unattainable purity. Nevertheless, Mary continues to be a dominant force in Catholic tradition and theology, particularly for neo-conservative forces in the hierarchy.[3]

While the thesis of this book is that Mary is the linchpin for the future of Catholic feminists, and perhaps the Roman Catholic Church itself, it should be noted that she is a significant figure for other Christian denominations as well.[4] Much has been written about Mary in the past several years by non-Catholic Christian feminists who discuss the role she should play in their theology and spirituality.[5] Nevertheless Mary is primarily a Catholic phenomenon, although the negation of her role in Protestantism did not exonerate non-Catholic Christians from patriarchal behavior. For example, Rosemary Radford Ruether states that while liberal Protestantism has ordained women for several decades, there has been resistance to the commensurate rethinking of theological symbolism and ecclesiastical organization. Ordained Protestant women still appear in token numbers and are relegated to low-paid, marginal positions.[6] The ecumenical search for female expression and experience of the divine that is harmonious with women's experience fuels the feminist analysis of Mary.

While this book focuses upon Catholic feminism, the range of influence religion has in this society gives Mary's impact a wider social significance. Mary is part of western civilization's cultural experience, and she informs the social relations of men and women as they reflect upon religion and history. Nevertheless, this book centers upon Catholic experiences.

The Growth of the Cult of Mary

Overwhelming evidence exists that the early Cult of Mary was in continuity with the worship of ancient earth mothers and fertility goddesses of the pre-Christian era. Thus, in one sense, Mary's history actually predates the Christian movement. Historians such as E. Ann Matter, for example, find that the Christianity of the first centuries denied the possibility of a feminine deity that was previously worshipped in ancient Europe in the forms of Epona, Freya, Herth, Mokosh, and others.[7] As the followers of Christianity increased, and it was later mandated as a state religion, previous goddess worshippers merely supplanted or infused their spirituality with the Christian Mary. Antiquity scholar Stephen Benko refers to Marian piety as a direct continuation of the ancient goddess cult.[8]

There is evidence that some early Christian communities, such as the Collyridians, practiced rituals that honored Mary over Jesus.[9] The Collyridian sect (some translate as "Collyrians" or "Kollyridians") was recorded in the *Panarion*, or Medicine Chest, of St. Epiphanius of Salamis as the 79th heresy of the Church. He denounced the cult as "foolish, crazy idolatry and the work of the devil," consisting of women who praise Mary "more than they ought."[10] The Collyridians worshipped Mary as a goddess and ordained women into their priesthood, although there is some evidence that they were antihierarchical. Geoffrey Ashe speculates that this community can be likened to early Christian feminists.[11] The Collyridians appear to have had a lasting and widespread following. Reports of the sect spread from the south and west of the Black Sea to Arabia. Stephen Benko translates St. Epiphanius's description of a Collyridian ceremony:

> For some women decorate a carriage or a square chair by covering
> it with fine linen, and on a certain definite day of the year they set
> forth bread and offer it as a sacrifice in the name of Mary.[12]

The bread or small cake referred to is a "collris," thus giving the group its name. However, like most sects of the era, members probably simply referred to themselves as Christians.[13] Benko speculates that the Collyridians were another example of goddess worship being absorbed into Christianity. Early Christian scholar Vasiliki Limberis supports this view because the locations of Collyridian devotion were long-standing places of worship to Rhea and Demeter. Many Collyridian practices paralleled Demeter cult rituals.[14] Because of its extension of pre-Christian goddess religion, Collyridian devotion to Mary was elevated to the level of formal deity worship rather than subordinated to Christology.

This goddess assimilation was actually encouraged by the Church because it was an excellent missionary marketing strategy to pagan populations. In exchange for tolerating widespread devotion to Mary, the Church received a greater following. However, for the convert, the exchange was not always equal. Mary was not officially a Christian deity, although she replaced goddesses. Nevertheless, in the minds of the new Christians, Marian identification with the goddess remained.[15] Many temples, titles, and iconography previously dedicated to popular goddesses were transferred over to Mary. For example, the image of Isis with Horus, the infant God-King on her lap was replaced by the Madonna imagery in artistic representations.[16] Other examples of Goddess transference to Mary can be drawn from the cultural history of Christianized nations. In an analysis of female religious tradition in Celtic Ireland, for example, Mary Condren describes the historical transition of devotion from the powerful Irish goddess Brigit to the Christian Mary.[17] Like Mary, Brigit was a complex multivariate figure (Triple Goddess, Virgin Mother, Lawmaker, and Virgin Saint) who represented a number of pre-Christian traditions in Ireland. Over time, Mary supplanted Brigit, but the transformation required some ecclesial intervention. In the seventh century, Pope Sergius ordered that feast days dedicated to the Virgin Mary be held on pagan holy days formerly dedicated to Brigit. Although Brigit faded into the religious background, she was not entirely forgotten. Brigit's final manifestation was as a fifth-century saint of Christianity.[18]

A belief in the goddess has existed as long as religion has been recorded in human civilization.[19] The history of goddess worship made Mary's assumption of various goddess legends anything but a simple transition occurring upon the dawn of Christianity. Faith in the ancient goddesses was strong and pervasive, with a variety of manifestations. In certain instances, Mary did not become associated with goddess legends until the Marian revival of the Middle Ages. Pamela Berger, for example, describes the myth of the "Grain Protectoress," which had existed since the beginning of agriculture. Under a variety of names, and in many different cultures, the grain protectoress had been a goddess who, according to legend, at one time had been responsible for a miraculous growth of grain. Annual rituals of worship and honor developed around the Grain Protectoress. During the early middle ages, rural communities in Europe began to Christianize the grain goddess by associating Mary with this role; an apocryphal story described Mary as responsible for a grain miracle during her exile to Egypt.[20] The Grain Protectoress is but one manifestation of the goddess tradition in the evolving Cult of Mary. This manifestation demonstrates another contradiction that is part of Mary's enigmatic tradition. Mary replaced pagan goddesses, but she never gained their status. There is no sanctioned goddess in the monotheism of Christianity. However, in actual practice, Mary was revered as a goddess much more than the ecclesial authorities would have liked.[21] This issue will be explored in Chapter Four in an examination of Mary's religious power. From the beginning, the sublime Mary provided the Church with a means of consolidating power. Mary was a transitional figure for goddess worship who helped to bring non-Christians into the fold.[22]

The popular veneration of Mary is almost as old as Christianity itself. Mary is mentioned in the gospels, but always in a small and limited role. She only appears in a handful of passages of the Second Testament,[23] and even these few passages are of questionable historical origin and display the characteristics of a mythologized Mary.[24] While specific scriptural analysis will be offered later, there are two significant implications for the rise of the Cult of Mary found in the first-century historical data. The first is that the Cult of Mary drew little from biblical information about the life of Mary. Her historical life remains a mystery that will probably never be solved; indeed a number of scholars have commented on the lack of information on which Mariology was built. Bruce Malina notes that "nearly everything claimed about Mary over the past two thousand years is simply not to be found in the Second Testament."[25] Elizabeth Johnson reduces what is known about Mary to the fact that she was the Jewish mother of Jesus who misunderstood and then believed in him.[26] Karl Rahner aptly stated, "The Church does not know Mary's life story."[27] Finally, Geoffrey Ashe has quipped, "If Christ himself existed, Christ's mother did; but a skeptic who questioned whether we know any more would have a case."[28]

The second important implication of Marian origins is that factual data, or lack of it, did not impede the mercurial rise of the Cult of Mary. The gospel writers working in the late first century were already privy to a growing Marian legendary. The earliest known artistic representation of Mary comes from a fresco of the virgin and child painted circa 150 C.E.* in the catacombs of Priscilla in Rome. The first known prayer to Mary, *Sub Tuum Praesidium*, is dated from the late third to fourth century.[29] This prayer was the first instance of public expression of Mary's intercessory powers.[30] Mary was the subject of serious theological meditation as early as the late second century, in works circulated by Justin, Tertullian, and Irenaeus that depicted her as the New Eve (see Chapter Five). The majority of second century "Apostolic Fathers" made no reference to Mary;[31] however, those who did write of Mary had Christological and soteriological concerns. During the fourth century, the number of special Marian feast days increased and new myths arose. These feast days celebrated traditional aspects of Mary's life such as her virginity and her motherhood. Nevertheless, the subsequent dark ages were a period of maintenance, not growth for the Church and for Mary. It was not until the rise of asceticism in the fifth century, however, that a widespread outpouring of devotion to Mary occurred. Drawing upon the work of Ashe, Michael Carroll speculates that a conciliation occurred in the fifth century between an independent Marian Church and the Christian Church.[32] Carroll admits there is little direct historical evidence for such a linkage. Instead, he cites circumstantial events, such as the merging of Christianity with many other quasi Christian groups during this period. One significant reason for advocating such a claim is that it helps to explain the sudden rise in the Marian cult in the fifth century.[33]

In 431 C.E. the Bishops at the Council of Ephesus gave Mary an ancient eastern title, *Theotokos*, or "the Bearer of God," to counter the arguments of the Patriarch of Constantinople, Nestorius, who believed that there were two natures in Jesus—a human Jesus and a mythic divinity, Christ.[34] Nestorius favored the title *Christotokos* to suggest that Mary bore Jesus in his humanity only. Nestorius proclaimed, "I have learned from scripture that God passed through the Virgin Mother of Christ; That God was born of her I have never learned."[35] Nestorius believed that *Theotokos* exaggerated Mary's significance, and correctly predicted that

---

*In the spirit of religious inclusiveness, dates will be represented with B.C.E. or Before Common Era (rather than B.C.) and C.E. or Common Era (rather than A.D.).

this title would provoke greater Marian goddess worship.[36] Ultimately, the title *Theotokos* was officially accepted after a heated conciliar debate. Nestorius was subsequently excommunicated.

The proclamation of Mary as God-bearer demonstrated that she was the mother of a unified Jesus (a mother of both the human and the divine), and thus squelched the controversy over Jesus' nature. Lacking theological training to understand the nuanced difference, common Catholics often understood "The Bearer of God" to mean "The Mother of God" (a title not officially declared until Pope Paul VI did so during the last session of the Second Vatican Council in 1965). This widespread misunderstanding of her title directly implied Mary's divinity, thus giving more impetus to the growth of her cult. The struggle over the title *Theotokos* is an early example of the Church's inherent pluralism, which reflects the split between the ecclesial church and the popular church. Church Fathers wrestled with a theological concept and its interpretation. Their motivation to use this title included theological consistency and potential political gain—they were not centrally concerned with Mary. However, to defend their Christology, they used Mary's name more frequently until she usurped the focus of their discussion.[37] The less educated populace was already devoted to Mary, and merely sought greater official justification for its beliefs. The hierarchy of the Church and the faithful had different interests and different perspectives on Mary: One was theological, one was devotional.[38]

The Council of Ephesus did not apparently settle the "nature of Jesus" issue for all Church theologians, because the Council of Chalcedon reaffirmed the two natures of Jesus in 451. At Chalcedon, Mary was also declared *Aeiparthenos,* or ever-Virgin. Her supporters among the Church theologians were increasingly victorious in their struggle to increase her influence. Two hundred years after Chalcedon, at the Fourth Lateran Council, Mary's perpetual virginity reached the status of church dogma.

In the eighth century, the idea that Mary had maternal influence over God and served as a "mediatrix" who could temper God's anger and vengeance circulated widely. Mary's role as the compassionate counterforce to a stern judge/god grew to the point that she became known as the "co-redemptrix" of the human race. This title put her on par with Jesus in the theology of salvation put forth by the Christian religion. This "Christo-typical," or Christ-like, attribution contributed to the "Mariolatry" of the era. The image of Mary as a powerful intercessor has persisted until the modern day, and will be the subject of Chapter Four of this book.

A strong revival of interest in Mary came in the eleventh and twelfth centuries. Between 1170 and 1270 in France alone, over 100 churches and 80 cathedrals were dedicated to Mary.[39] The medieval period brought the concept of courtly love and a new role for Mary as a model of womanhood to be romantically and chivalrously pursued.[40] In the first part of the twelfth century a collection of apocryphal stories titled *The Miracles of the Virgin* appeared.[41] Such writings were part of the burgeoning Cult of Mary. Devotion to Mary grew as miracle stories, previously the exclusive purview of the relics of saints, now became associated with Mary.

The fourteenth century gave rise to the first "modern" claims of visions and apparitions of Mary. During this period, the mystic St. Bridget of Sweden envisioned Mary giving birth to Jesus in a prayerful kneeling position. This image illustrates the popularity of images of Mary depicted in a submissive role. St. Bridget's vision inspired many artistic representations including several Botticellis.[42]

Mary provided protection and righteous religious legitimation for the Spanish and Portuguese in their sixteenth century conquest and colonization of the Americas. The conquest was considered the work of Mary, and therefore, a crusade to which the explorers were religiously dedicated. Resistance by indigenous people was viewed as a declaration of a holy war in which Mary would vindicate the Catholics. Indigenous religion was considered evil and had to be replaced by the more civilized Christianity. Mary was imposed on indigenous Americans, and they assimilated her into their existing worship of the mother-goddess.[43] Ironically, a deep devotion to Mary was subsequently fostered in Latin America, spread by the legendary appearance of Our Lady of Guadalupe near Mexico City in 1531. Mary's significance became so great in this part of the world that liberation theologian Virgil Elizondo states, "[It] is an undeniable fact that devotion to Mary is the most popular, persistent, and original characteristic of Latin American Christianity."[44] The paradox of devotion to Mary coexisting with the cultural *machismo* in this society leads to questions concerning causal or at least complicitory relationships parallelling the Catholic Church's simultaneous elevation of Mary and suppression of women. At least one author has referred to this phenomenom as "Marianismo," or the cult of feminine spiritual superiority that coexists with Latin American machismo.[45]

The European witchhunts of the sixteenth and seventeenth centuries were a peculiar phenomenon because Europe was coming out of the middle ages, and supposedly leaving barbarism behind. However, the rise of Mariolatry during this period intensified the valorization of a higher spirituality over the material world. Women who violated an idealized image of femininity through independence or through the questioning of authority were easy prey for impassioned religious contempt.[46] Consequently, the Cult of Mary contributed to the difficult plight of women in this era, because the unattainable pedestal Mary was placed upon made it easy for those caught up in religious zeal to find fault with ordinary women. Mary's purity was thus used as a weapon against women because it contrasted with the characterization of ordinary women, who were seen as sexually insatiable and easily corrupted. The Eve/Mary dualism, which will be discussed further in Chapter Five, made it easy to find women who did not match Mary's perceived piety and behavior.[47] This alleged "weakness" of women contributed to the accusations of moral susceptibility to satanic activity.[48]

Like the church's leadership, Catholic doctrine has been configured in a hierarchical order asserting levels of truth and authority. From the fifteenth century forward, a number of Marian doctrines, although having no biblical source, were incorporated into the highest levels of Church doctrine. Popular devotion to Mary provided a strong impetus for the Marian dogmas, although papal politics also played a significant role. The "magisterium," or official teaching authority of the church, can acknowledge doctrine or accept the revealed truth that originates from popular tradition as legitimately authoritative once it is recognized by the hierarchy. Francis Sullivan reviews the development of Marian theology in the context of the Church's teaching authority:

> Over the course of the centuries, the conviction grew that Mary could never have been alienated from God by original sin [the immaculate conception]. . . . These conclusions do not follow with metaphysical necessity from what Scripture tells us about Mary. They are seen to be contained in the total mystery of Christ, by a kind of intuition, rather than by a process of logical deduction . . . they are believed not only to be true but to be revealed. . . .[49]

This recognition, that the teaching of the Church is influenced by popular tradition as the work of the Holy Spirit in the whole body of the Church, demonstrates the pluralistic nature of dogmatic development.

The dogma of the Immaculate Conception of Mary is the paradigm of authoritative Catholic teaching developed from nonbiblical tradition.[50] Although only vaguely supported by scripture, it was commonly believed that Mary lived a life untouched by sin.[51] A book written in 1847 by Giovanni Perrone, a Jesuit professor at the University of Rome, provided a theological basis for the dogmatic declaration of the Immaculate Conception. Perrone demonstrated that while scripture could not support the Immaculate Conception, neither did it disprove its occurrence.[52] Even the most tenuous scriptural connection was acceptable if theological momentum existed. At issue was whether Mary was born without original sin (a sin carried forward from the fall of Adam and experienced by all of humanity). In 1476, Pope Sixtus IV approved the Feast of the Immaculate Conception, which states that Mary was the only human conceived without original sin.[53] However, it would take four hundred years for the Immaculate Conception to gain the status of dogma or incontestable Church teaching.[54]

The declaration of *Ineffablis Deus* in 1854 by Pope Pius IX was a landmark event in Catholic ecclesiology because it elevated Mary to a special, almost superhuman status, while at the same time solidified the power of the Pope (a movement referred to as "ultramontanism"). It was the first time a Pope had promulgated an infallible dogma. Pope Pius IX was under political and intellectual siege. During his pontificate, the longest in history (1846-1878), he would be exiled from Rome and ultimately lose the Papal States (1870) which represented the last remaining direct political influence of the Pope.[55] Pius IX became opposed to political change, and sought to consolidate his authority in defense of secular political turbulence. Mary would be the vehicle for the elevation of the pontifical status. Pius IX's declaration of the Immaculate Conception was also a reaction to secular intellectuals who found Church teaching in conflict with science. The dogma drove a wedge between Catholics and secularists.[56] Mary's Immaculate Conception was carefully selected as a precedent-setting issue for papal infallibility, presumably because it would not arouse public outcry. Historians Nicholas Perry and Loreto Echeverria find a significant link between these two dogmas.

> Far from having coincidental gestation, the dogmas are reinforcing and complementary. They are the consummation of an alliance between Rome and "Mary" since earliest times. As the invisible maternal supervisor of the Church becomes equal to God—or as "pure" as the Second Person of the Trinity—so her visible paternal counterpart makes a commensurate advance. When the world questions the Chair of Peter and its prerogatives, celestial confirmation is required. In turn, this supernatural factor can be ratified only by an incontrovertible, superhuman voice: that of infallibility.[57]

With the success of this declaration, Pope Pius IX subsequently called for the First Vatican Council, at which papal infallibility was formally approved. The Immaculate Conception was the first Church dogma defined solely by papal authority. The Pope did ask for the Bishops' input in the letter, *Ubi Primum*, and 546 of 605 Bishops responded favorably to the dogma.[58] Nevertheless, Pius IX's pronouncement made no mention of representing the views of the greater Church.[59] It was a solitary decree. Mary was used as an instrument for solidifying hierarchical power in Catholicism.[60]

The concept of the Immaculate Conception was not held without reservation, despite the conviction of the papacy that even doubt brought separation from the Church.[61] One objection to the dogma was that if Mary had been born without sin, what need did she have of Christ's redemption through the crucifixion and resurrection? The theological reply was that Christ's redemption saved Mary prior to her birth. In this manner, "atonement theology" (the belief that Jesus died to atone for the world's sins) transcended the law of time. For the theologically unsophisticated masses, the idea of Mary's immaculate conception was merely an extension of popular miracle stories concerning her birth and life. While Church bishops debated a theological construction of Marian sinlessness as it flowed from Christological redemption, the common Catholic viewed her purity as another aspect of the special nature of their beloved Mary, and it contributed to goddess-like devotion.[62]

It was Pope Pius XII who in 1950 declared the dogma of the Bodily Assumption of Mary into heaven. While the Immaculate Conception of Mary supported Christology (how could the savior have been born of a womb tainted by original sin?), the dogma of the Bodily Assumption of Mary appears to be more closely associated with an elevation of Mary's theological status at the height of popular Mariology in an effort to uplift the Church. The declaration of the Bodily Assumption came on the heels of two world wars during which the Church and Catholics were groping for a means to provide meaning to a world gone astray.[63] This dogma, being the only other infallible declaration by a pope, had its origins in a late-fourth-century apocryphal body of literature titled *Transitus Marie*, or "The Passing of the Virgin Mary."[64] The early Church had taken Mary's death for granted, as witnessed in the writing of Origen and later reinforced by the work of Augustine.[65] However, Mary's growing popularity in the fourth century brought with it an interest in various aspects of her life and death. The *Transitus Marie* had a fanciful motif and is considered to be legend rather than history.[66] According to the legend, after Mary had passed away, Jesus visited the tomb of Mary. He reinfused her soul into her body, then escorted Mary, now a living person, up to heaven.[67] The *Transitus Marie,* sparked speculation and discussion about Mary's death. By the sixth century, celebrations of Mary's death and resurrection appeared.[68] Belief in Mary's assumption perpetuated a concept of her purity. To complement the idea that Mary could not have been corrupted by original sin, the idea that Mary's body was not corrupted by decay on earth was also advanced. Mary's purity had already removed her from an association with the material world, and this declaration completed that disassociation.

The process of declaring the dogma of Mary's Bodily Assumption into heaven represented a unique dialogue between the Pope and the Catholic faithful. This event is significant for the current process of creating and maintaining Marian images. The century between 1850 and 1950 is sometimes referred to as "the golden age of Mary" because it is bracketed by the two official dogmas of Mary and permeated by numerous Marian apparitions. During this period, over eight million petitions were reportedly sent to the Pope asking for an official declaration of Mary's assumption into heaven. In 1946, the Pope sent an encyclical to bishops around the world, *Deiparae Virginis*, asking whether the Assumption should be declared a dogma of faith and whether such a dogma was the will of the faithful.[69] Of the 1181 bishops polled, only 22 dissented from affirming Mary's assumption. This response resulted in Pope Pius XII's declaration of the dogma of Mary's Assumption on November 1, 1950. As Pius IX had done, a stern warning was issued by Pius XII on the severity of doubting the dogma of Mary's Assumption.

> Wherefore, if anyone—which God forbid—should willfully dare to deny or call in doubt what has been defined by us, let him know that he certainly has abandoned the divine and catholic faith.[70]

With the declaration of the Assumption, Marian ecclesial and popular piety had reached its zenith. The year 1954 was declared the first "Marian Year" by Pius XII, and Mary was given the title "Queen of Heaven."[71] Many theologians believed that more Marian dogmas would emerge following the precedent of the Immaculate Conception and the Bodily Assumption. However, the rise of biblical scholarship, the biblical movement, and the ecumenical movement probably tempered Catholic zeal for more dogmas. Nevertheless, there have been failed attempts at further Marian dogmas, such as declaration of Mary as the "co-redemptrix" of salvation.[72]

The Second Vatican Council (1962-1965), which reformed so many aspects of Catholicism and in many ways modernized the Church, became a focal point for Marian controversy as well.[73] Among the social and theological forces evident at the council were democracy (or at least collegiality), subsidiarity (pushing decision making to the lowest levels of an organization), scientific methods, historical consciousness, and the biblical movement. The reforms were intended to bring the Church into the modern world and reclaim it for the people. A second look, however, reveals that at least one aspect of the reforms was directly detrimental to Mary and women of the Catholic faith.

The Church had been undergoing a transformation in its approach to the bible since the landmark encyclical of Pope Pius XII, *Divino Afflante Spiritu*, in 1943. The bible, as the primary source of divine revelation, received a greater emphasis, placing Catholicism more in harmony with Protestant approaches. This trend was exemplified in an increased use of biblical quotes and references in official Church pronouncements. The biblical movement did not bode well for the Cult of Mary. The essentially nonbiblical nature of Mariology put it in conflict with the biblical renewal. While the biblical movement was praised by many as restoring Catholicism to its roots, those roots are steeped in first-century social relations. Catholicism's nonbiblical valorization of tradition allowed for the development of a powerful female figure in Mary. The Second Vatican Council, in returning to a strong biblical basis, restored a Christology that had less need for the competing figure of Mary. While the Cult of Mary had developed to the point that Mary could never be returned to the literal status of the "Handmaiden of the Lord," the hierarchy now had the necessary theological basis to mitigate her role in salvation history and ultimately diminish her power.

Prior to the Second Vatican Council, Mary had represented at least a sliver of women's experience. She had been alienated from most human experience, but at least she was a woman and religiously significant. Canonical texts rendered Mary insignificant, and placed the emphasis on the incarnation of God. In this sense, the biblical movement represents a neoconservative effort that attempts to place gender relations back in an overtly misogynist past.[74] There is still room for "creative" hermeneutics with regard to egalitarian passages, but it is difficult to escape the biblical *Sitz im Leben* (historical, political, and social environment). Kari Borresen captures the danger in the biblical movement as it affected the Second Vatican Council:

The council's attitude was a result of the return to patristic sources
that has characterized Catholic theology in the twentieth century . . .
its [Dogmatic Constitution on the Church] use of the traditional
sources was still dominated by the androcentric assumptions of the
early fathers. . . .[75]

While feminists disagree on how to appropriate Marian imagery, the
biblical renewal diminished their options by mitigating Mary's stature in
Catholicism.

In the most heated debates and closest votes of the council, it was
decided that the bishops' official statement on Mary would be a part of
the final Chapter of the Council's key document, the *Dogmatic Constitution of the Church*, rather than part of a separate document (passing by only
17 votes out of a total of 2,193 participating bishops).[76] Its words reinforced the central role of Mary in Catholic doctrine but sought a balance
between Marian devotion and spiritual dedication to Jesus. Mary was
clearly described as being human rather than divine, even as the bishops
maintained her sinlessness and her bodily assumption. The eighth Chapter of the *Dogmatic Constitution on the Church* was "ecclesiocentric" and
characterized Mary as a type of the church. Her role in the salvation of
humanity was obscured by the bishops,[77] who recognized the "cult" title
for the followers of Mary in a carefully constructed manner so as to
protect its theological position of maintaining spiritual focus upon Jesus
without alienating Marian devotees. In their definitive statement on
Mary's role in the Church, the bishops specifically used the language of
the cult. The "Cult of Mary" is described as proper veneration and piety
toward Mary. This cult must clearly subordinate itself to the supreme cult
directed toward the trinity. The bishops exhort the faithful to maintain
Marian devotions at a moderate religious fervor:

> This most holy synod . . . admonishes all the sons of the Church that
> the cult, especially the liturgical cult, of the Blessed Virgin, be gener-
> ously fostered. . . . But it exhorts theologians and preachers of the
> divine word to abstain zealously both from false exaggerations as
> well as from a too great narrowness of mind in considering the
> singular dignity of the Mother of God. . . . True devotion consists
> neither in sterile or transitory affection, nor in a certain vain creduli-
> ty, but proceeds from true faith, by which we are led to know the
> excellence of the Mother of God, and we are moved to a filial love
> toward our mother and to the imitation of her virtues.[78]

The term "the Cult of Mary" was used by the bishops to establish
"appropriate" personal piety. The result of the bishops' new emphasis

was a mitigation of Marian devotions, although her image was too powerful to suppress entirely.[79]

The Church could not render a statement about Mary without a response from the masses. In what Michael Novak described as a "vicious assault," the Italian press, particularly its right wing, assailed the Bishops' chapter on Mary. The brunt of the attack was that a new understanding of Mary represented the kind of evil emanating from modern progress.[80] Pope Paul VI placated conservative forces in a speech he delivered at the closing of the third session of the Council. Cloaking the immense controversy, the Pope described the *Dogmatic Constitution of the Church* as a victory for Mary.

> By the promulgation of today's constitution, which has as its crown and summit a whole chapter dedicated to Our Lady, we can rightly affirm that the present session ends as an incomparable hymn of praise in honor of Mary.[81]

However, despite Pope Paul VI's efforts, the damage to the Cult of Mary had been done. The effect of the Second Vatican Council upon Mariology was immense. A "Mariological Crisis," exemplified by a reduction in popular devotion and a dearth of theological writings on Mary, occurred in the post-conciliar decade (1964–1974).[82]

The papacy of John Paul II is symbolic of the ambivalent nature of the Church's attitude toward women and Mary. The Pope is considered unsupportive of women's issues, yet he remains devoted to Mary.[83] This devotion is manifested in his many pilgrimages to Marian shrines and his numerous statements and invocations of Mary.[84] John Paul II declared 1987 to be a "Marian Year" for the renewal of devotion to her, and in the same year issued the encyclical, *The Mother of the Redeemer, Redemptoris Mater*. The encyclical maintained a strict, traditional view of Mary, including a physiological (hymen intact) interpretation of the virgin birth.[85] As one author describes the Pope, "His ideal is living contact with Mary as a loving, supremely caring Mother. John Paul's fundamental ideal is the divine motherhood. . . ."[86] The Pope credits Our Lady of Fatima with saving him from death by the gunshot wound inflicted by Mehemenet Ali Agca on May 13, 1981. The Pope often makes pilgrimages to Fatima, Portugal (where Mary allegedly appeared in 1917) and has given the bullet from the assassination attempt to the shrine at Fatima, where it sits in the crown on the statue of Mary.[87] Historians Perry and Echeverria view the Pope's frequent visits to apparitional shrines as a method of tapping into supernatural power to promote his conservative and sexist agenda.

From these sites of God's "irruptions in the history of humanity," "Mary of Nazareth," recharged by the apostolic presence, regenerates National Catholicism and bolsters priestly celibacy and the traditional subservience of women.[88]

Despite the Pope's great dedication to Mary, he is considered by feminist theologians to be an obstruction to the liberation of Catholic women. Rosemary Radford Ruether, for example, finds the pontiff's conservative social perspective destructive to the efforts of the women's movement within the Church.

> in the Pontificate of John Paul II, [we] have seen increasing evidence of reactionary backlash on all matters having to do with sexuality and the status of women in the Church . . . this personal misogyny of the pontiff makes a vivid impression on women, who increasingly see Catholicism as an agent of evil rather than good.[89]

Ruether's critique represents the position of a new breed of theologian not witnessed in the previous two millennia of the Church. Although feminist theologians draw their origins from the roots of the Judeo-Christian tradition, they are the first generation of women religious scholars to have education, academic access, organization, and networks relatively equal to those of men, and to have a set of critical analytical tools for shaping theology. Therefore, the end of our sweep of Marian history finds a new force in the renegotiation of religious imagery. Feminist theology ushers in a new era in the Church.

Mary as an Ideal Type of Religious Construction

The current status of Catholic Mariology is the result of thousands of years of evolutionary development. Despite the volumes that have been written about Mary, one recurrent theme is that the Cult of Mary did not depend upon historical facts or scriptural data for its advancement. This lack of a historical basis makes the influential, and distinctively Catholic, phenomenon of the Cult of Mary ripe for phenomenological investigation. In appropriating the works of the "fathers of sociology," including Karl Marx and Max Weber, as well as the more contemporary writings of Peter Berger, many feminist scholars such as Mary Daly have found religious imagery such as that associated with Mary to be a "social construction" reflecting the values and wishes of dominant groups in society rather than representing a factual, historical reality.[90] Peter Berger's methodology and terminology will be applied to Mary to demonstrate how she is the ideal type of a religious social construction.

Berger describes two distinct realities that become merged in human consciousness. First, there is the existential world, or objective reality. Second, there is the world created by humans, or subjective reality.[91] Politics, economics, ethics, and religion are realms of human construction. Berger refers to the process of human world building as a dialectic with a series of significant moments.[92] The initial moment is "externalization," when the process of human construction begins; for instance a story is told or an event is invested with meaning or value. Externalizations are additions to objective reality brought into the subjective reality of humanity. The next moment is "objectification," during which the externalization takes on a life of its own and is treated as fact. The human origins of the subjective reality are forgotten. "Internalization" is the personal acceptance of constructs perpetuated by society. Certain social constructs reach a higher level of objectification or validity through the process of "reification" when they are attributed to superhuman or divine sources. The human origins in this case have not only been lost, they have been transferred to a higher authority. Whether reified or not, social constructs require legitimations if they are to be sustained throughout the evolution of time and change. Legitimations defend existing social constructs against challenges.[93] When legitimations fail, humans can become alienated from their social constructs.[94] Berger describes this condition as an "overextension of objectification," when not only is the human origin forgotten but there is a failure to find value or meaning in the construct.[95]

Mary is an excellent example of the type of social construction described by Berger. The history of the Cult of Mary makes evident that her imagery is a collection of externalizations. The factual data on her life are extremely sparse, yet she has an abundance of attributions. Catholic theologian John McKenzie stated it bluntly: "Faith in the Mary of traditional Christian devotion is faith in something that is not true."[96] Mary became an objectified reality of mythic proportions in the early Church. She was subsequently reified on an unofficial level by the faithful who adored her, and was later reified on a dogmatic level through the infallible papal pronouncements. Mary's constructed reality was perpetuated by the internalization of Catholics in their faith education and the abundance of stories that circulated about her. Through Marian apologetics, she has been legitimized in each age by various dogmas and pronouncements. The continuing phenomenon of apparitions serves to further legitimize Mary as an ongoing powerful religious force.

Mary Daly, while finding such analysis helpful in debunking a patriarchal religious construction, points out that Berger is blind to the underlying misogyny of such a social process.[97] It is men who have historically provided the world building or externalization process: women, because of their exclusion from political and religious leadership, have internalized the constructions. Daly describes women as internalizers *par excellence*. This reality makes it difficult to define authentic women's experience because it is always mediated through the dominant male culture. The use of women (in the case of the Cult of Mary) and feminine symbols to further legitimize patriarchal religion has been a historical process used to further oppress women.[98]

Berger's description of alienation illuminates current Marian controversy and suggests a reason for her being at the eye of a theological storm. "Religion has been so powerful an agency of nomization precisely because it has also been a powerful, probably the most powerful, agency of alienation."[99] Modern Catholic women, who for so very long have participated in the internalization of the Marian construct as the model of true Christian womanhood, are finding it difficult to accept the Catholic hierarchy's current legitimations. Catholic theologian Els Maeckelberghe expresses the alienation experienced by modern Christian women:

> As a twentieth-century European woman with a Christian upbringing, I am confronted with the question whether Christianity and the words and the concepts used in the Christian tradition are still meaningful. Is Christianity an outmoded but familiar sweater that any reasonable person would jettison?. . . All these questions and observations come together in the figure of Mary.[100]

The construction is breaking down. The Church no longer can find its social patterns and relationships reflected in society. The social referent for patriarchal gender relationships that once existed is gone or fading.[101] Social understandings of virginity, gender relations, and, ultimately, the significance of religion have evolved. Feminist scholars are revealing the social, rather than the divine, origins of the Cult of Mary, and they are questioning her status and significance.

As Ruether states, "A revelatory tradition remains vital so long as its revelatory pattern can be reproduced generation after generation. . . ."[102] When human experience falls into conflict with religious revelatory patterns, then a crisis of religious tradition occurs. If the contradictions are not rectified, and they are of a serious enough nature, a more radical breakdown, perhaps a revolution or reformation, becomes possible. Marian imagery, because of its vital importance to conservative forces as a model of womanhood and Catholic orthodoxy, is the linchpin in a feminist reformation of Catholicism. Mary is far removed from women's experience, yet her invocation is rampant in Church teaching, a contradiction that tears at the fabric of Catholic spirituality for women.[103] Moderate reformist views of Mary may "save" the Church from a feminist revolt if women can find a "comfort zone" in a Mary that is molded to meet modern women's sensibilities.

While Mary is a perfect example of a religious construction, such analysis does not imply that the Marian cult was part of an organized conspiracy. Mary was thrust upon the Church by popular outpourings that forced theologians to create an explanation or legitimation. The externalization began from the people, and over time was fine-tuned by the hierarchy to serve theological needs. Geoffrey Ashe describes the development:

> Crucial and perplexing, however, is the fact that the official justification of her cult does not hold water. The Gospels do *not* imply what Catholics have claimed they do, a special closeness between Christ and his mother. If anything they imply an estrangement. The cult is a thing that surged in on a democratic tide after the Church had existed without it for more than three hundred years, and then had to be rationalized by male theologians as best they could. They were never wholly successful, because, whatever the ingenuity of their pleading, Mary's near-apotheosis could not be given any adequate basis in their scriptural logic. It had a dynamic of its own, and its advent was mysterious.[104]

Were the Marian cult a conspiracy, it would be easier to address, critique, and alter, if necessary. Although not an organized conspiracy, the Cult of Mary has been utilized in "backlashes" against women through the ages. Whether women sought religious independence through the goddess, or sexual freedom, or political freedom, Mary was a figure that could be used to curb such activity.

There are a number of implications for the social constructionist view of Mary. As a construction, or a subjective reality, Mary can be the subject of a struggle for control or a re-negotiation of traditional religious imagery. There are no "objective" data on which to base the Cult of Mary, and therefore feminists who wish to challenge the imagery and create a more empowering figure in Mary have some sociological room to do so. Therein lies the hope of Catholic feminist scholars: If Mary has been legitimized with particular characteristics and values, there is the possibility of debunking those constructs and building others. However, conclusiveness represents a drawback. As a social construction, it will be difficult for anyone to claim the conclusive definition of Mary. The criteria for a conclusive definition of Mary are unclear since history cannot be the court of final authority. The "official" Catholic Church can claim a conclusive definition of Mary based upon the traditional power and authority invested in it. However, feminists are giving voice to the authority of women's experience, and therefore also laying claim to define Mary. In the next chapter, this struggle to control the theological definition of Mary is further discussed.

While I have attempted to demonstrate that Mary is an ideal type of religious social construction, there is a danger in allowing social construction theory to be absolute in explaining historical phenomena. That danger is the annihilation of the victim or internalizer. Social construction theory can negate the idea of a human will in its creation of a deterministic mega-theory. This determinism can be particularly harmful for women because it perpetuates the idea that men are active externalizers and women are passive and dependent internalizers. History actually reveals a type of balance in which women internalize male constructions, but at times will respond with "countertraditions" and therefore take on the role of externalizer in a relationship subversive to dominant culture. Elisabeth Gossman traces several examples of myths perpetuated to construct a definition of "woman," only to find that a countertradition softened or negated the original construct. Gossman demonstrates, for example, that the construct of woman as passive was countered by Hildegard of Bignen's cosmic anthropology, which characterized men and women as complementary rather than either active or passive. This idea was subsequently adopted by the Franciscans.[105] The idea of counter-traditions is not to mitigate the significance of patriarchal power in religious construction—however, it does support the idea that free-thinking individuals may not always passively accept their socialization. Counter traditions will reemerge as images of Mary are discussed and critiqued.

Another caution about the application of social construction theory to Mary is that an acknowledgment of her created nature does not mitigate her potency. As Catharina Halkes states, symbolic figures are no less important than historical ones, particularly when they have the depth of personal, psychological, and religious meaning that Mary does.[106] The next chapter will demonstrate how images of Mary are crucial to various key segments within the Catholic Church, which are competing to define the role of women.

Finally, it should be noted that Mary is an extremely complex construction—actually, a collection of social constructions. In this book, the images of sexuality, power, and goodness portrayed by Mary will be explored. Each is a separate but related construct. The neatness of Berger's theory makes understanding a social construction like pulling back the layers of an onion. However, the convergence of themes in Mary is more like a knot of several shoelaces, in which it is difficult to distinguish one strand from another.

2

The Struggle to Control Mary

Our Lady is going through the acutest identity crisis, but whatever new
guises she may assume, her cult is likely to remain rooted in apparitions
and at the service of manipulative power.
— Nicholas Perry and Loreto Echeverria[1]

The history of the Cult of Mary reveals the fluidity of this tradition.
Despite the attempt by Catholic conservatives to reify the Marian
imagery and doctrine of the late nineteenth and early twentieth
centuries, the two thousand years of evolution, debate, and disagreement
that have characterized Mary's theological position should not be lost
upon her current status. The Cult of Mary is not a monolithic collection
of images, despite hierarchical efforts to reify them. There are three key
participants in the modern negotiation of Marian imagery and symbolism, although they are far from equal: theologians, hierarchical officials,
and all other Catholics, whom I will lump together under the term
"popular Catholicism." Figure 1, while generalizing the positions of the
various Catholic constituencies, depicts a road map for the analysis in the
rest of this chapter.

The struggle described in this book, and witnessed in each of the
Marian images to be explored, is a conflict between Catholic theology
and ecclesiology. A presupposition of this conflict is the understanding

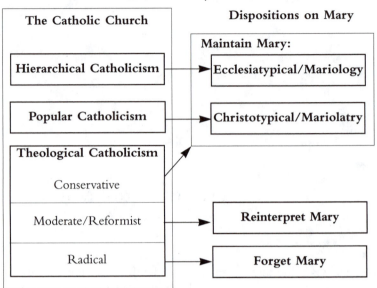

Figure 1: Factions Within Catholicism and
Their General Dispositions on Mary

that a monolithic Catholic position on Mary does not exist. To illuminate the "Catholic" position is to beg for clarification. Which Catholic
position is being presented? The "universal" church is so large, with such
a broad constituency, that unified positions are rare despite a superficial
appearance of solidarity. The official teaching of the Church cannot be
considered the complete reality of Marian devotion. The following
section sketches the key players in the negotiation of Marian images, with
particular attention to characterizing their position and apparent motivation. These categories of Catholicism are significant for two reasons. First,
they illuminate the dynamic complexity of modern Catholicism. Second,
feminist theology has adopted as one of its central themes an acute attention to everyday human experience of spirituality. Therefore, classic
approaches to theology that are negotiated between the work of the hierarchical church and the work of theologians are inadequate. Popular
forms of Catholicism are included in the feminist theological mix.

Popular Catholicism

In the complex scheme of modern Catholic dynamics, popular Catholicism is not an active participant in the struggle to construct Marian
imagery. However, in the broader religious reality of lived spirituality, it is

existentially more significant than either Catholic ecclesiology or Catholic theology. Until the modern era, lay Catholics worldwide were not organized or equipped to enter into a debate over who or what Mary should be. This is not to say that lay Catholics are a passive group that will simply absorb and accept Church teaching. Feminist theologians seek to reinterpret and clarify Mariology, not as a historical or ecclesial exercise but because it has implications for issues that affect real women's lives. Mary's imagery has an impact upon sexual relations, familial power, and church leadership.

Because of the implications Marian images have for Catholics, this study offers an ethical analysis. The underlying assumption is that religious symbolism matters to people because religion is the fundamental institutional vehicle of moral discourse in society. Therefore, what is believed about the great female quasi-deity, Mary, may affect the relationship of men and women in society and in cultures where Catholicism remains a major force. Were there no link to popular Catholicism, this entire analysis of Marian images would merely be an esoteric discussion of religious iconography. As this book progresses and becomes involved in theological debate, it is essential to recall that were it not for popular Catholicism, theological and church officials would not exist. The perception and the religious imagination of the common Catholic is the ultimate judge as to who is "victorious" in the struggle to control Marian imagery.

Mary has a significant ongoing presence in the religious piety of popular Catholicism. Every Roman Catholic church in the world places images of Mary in positions of honor. Often the churches themselves are named for traditional Marian events, apparitions, or devotions (e.g. The Assumption, The Immaculate Conception, Our Lady of Guadalupe, etc.). The churches, statuary, paintings, and stained-glass windows serve as a constant reminder of Mary's presence in the spiritual life of the over 890,000,000 faithful Catholics worldwide.[2] Every Catholic child who receives training in the faith learns the prayer "Hail Mary," which addresses how the grace of Mary reflects the glory of God. Liturgically, gathering to recite the rosary is the most popular devotional ritual after Sunday Mass.[3] The rosary is often recited as a communal prayer in conjunction with mass, during holy seasons, and at funerals. The rosary is also a popular private devotion. The pre-Vatican II image of veiled women kneeling, rosary in hand, as they pray before, during and after mass continues to replay itself on Sunday mornings across the United States and around the world, although this is a dwindling phenomenon.[4] The "Hail Mary" is only one of many prayers and songs dedicated to Mary. She is also celebrated in the spiritual life of the Church through special "feast days" that commemorate significant people and events in the history of the Church. Mary has fourteen feast days devoted to her. On these days Catholics are directed to contemplate various aspects of Mary's life.[5]

The alleged appearances of Mary help create her popularity. Luis Maldonado's definition of popular religion elucidates why apparitions are so important to Mariology: "Popular religion is the quest for (a) more simple, (b) more direct, and (c) more profitable relationships with the divine."[6] These characteristics are all found in Marian apparitions. There have been thousands of reported Marian apparitions through the centuries. Mary has been reported on earth in the form of apparitions far more often than Jesus has. Of these sightings, seven have been "recognized" by the Catholic Church.[7] Many other apparitions (Bayshore, New York and Medjugorje, Yugoslavia, for example) continue to occur, spurring local and sometimes worldwide interest. The most popular of Mary's apparitions was in Lourdes, France, to which the reported number of annual pilgrimages is double that of Mecca.[8]

These sightings portray Mary as delivering a variety of messages for the faithful, including condemnations of miniskirts, a call to retain pre-Vatican II Catholic practices, and apocalyptic warnings against the former communist Soviet Union.[9] The Church considers Marian appearances to be a source of private revelation that should not be seen in conflict with the public revelation of scripture or the revelation found in the tradition of the Church.[10] Despite official Church concern about appropriate piety, millions of people have flocked to the sites of Marian apparitions.[11] Through apparitions, Mary becomes more than a historical figure for believers. She is a "tangible" part of popular religious modernity. The significance of Marian apparitions will be further explored in Chapter Four, which discusses the perception of Mary's power.

John R. Shinners describes three characteristics of popular religion.[12] The first is security. Because the nature of religion is to deal with the divine and mysterious, popular faith tends to seek certainty within the mystical. In the face of the unknown—death, god, the meaning of life—people desire something concrete that can transcend their doubt and fear while providing a sense of purpose. Popular religion tends to support faith unquestioningly. This phenomenon can be observed in the worldwide popularity of fundamentalistic religions that seek solid, objective truth.

Second, popular religions seek to establish tangible proof of the existence of the divine. Miracles, apparitions, and channeling are all seen as manifestations that the divine exists. Once the locus of divine intervention in the material world is established, the faithful tend to want to tap into it. This can be witnessed in pilgrimages to the locations of apparitions, and the blessings associated with those locations. Popular religion establishes a reciprocal relationship with the divine. Personal sacrifices and unwavering faith are offered in return for personal blessings such as physical healing or a happy afterlife. Finally, popular religion is affective. A tremendous emotional response accompanies popular faith and gives it an enduring and defensive quality. Benedict Ashley describes Mariology as a principle example of popular faith.

> The development in the Church of Mariology is a prime example of [a] kind of intuitive, symbolic reflection, and it first of all took place not in the study of theologians but in the devotional life of the people and among the poets, musicians, and artists who invented the liturgy and constructed the churches, as well as among the contemplatives. It is the fruit of meditation, prayer, and human anguish and need.[13]

The Cult of Mary is part of what can be called popular Catholicism. Mary represents a tangible maternal figure that taps into divine power (as witnessed by Marian apparitions) that many people are drawn to.

Sociologist Andrew Greeley argues that for Catholics, Mary is a dense symbol of the religious sacramental imagination.[14] Greeley's surveys indicate that men and women who have a positive response to images of Mary are more likely to pray and have more positive marital relationships.[15] Greeley found that the image of Mary was more powerful for Catholics than the image of Jesus or God. He also believes there are no antiwoman or antifeminist sentiments attached to the popular image of Mary in the United States; for Greeley, Mary represents the feminine face of God. Greeley finds the Church's traditional position of limiting Mary's role to be a self-destructive error, and he argues that the future survival of the Catholic Church depends upon allowing Mary to evolve into the feminine manifestation of God.[16]

Most believers generally have little to do with either theologians or the church hierarchy. For most Catholics, the only contact with ecclesial authority is at Sunday Mass. There is a tendency for Catholics, particularly United States Catholics, to believe that they are, as Greeley has demonstrated, "part-owners" of the Church, and therefore they tend to be somewhat independent in their theology despite conflicts with the hierarchy over issues such as birth control.[17] The devotion found in Popular Catholicism has been a primary force in advancing the Cult of Mary, as documented in the last chapter. However, the popular view of Mary has been much more devotional than ecclesial authorities have wished, and therein lies a tension. Had orthodox Catholicism not placed limits upon Mary's role, it is difficult to tell what status Mary might have achieved in the evolution of the Church. Perhaps she would have become a Catholic goddess.

One of the essential underlying moral issues that should not be ignored in the struggle to control Mary is the extent to which this "struggle" represents a manipulation of popular Catholicism. Neither the hierarchy of the Church nor Catholic theologians would consider their efforts overt manipulation. However, some sensitivity should be shown to the role of the Catholic faithful in the negotiation of Marian imagery between the hierarchical and theological positions. Are the faithful merely spectators prepared to accept the "winners" in the debate over symbolic femininity? Or are they active participants who play an equal part in shaping the images of Mary? If inclusiveness is a worthy value, then consideration must be given not only to the ideologies of the hierarchy or theologians but to the needs and beliefs of the general Catholic laity. This concern for the will of the people is an example of the democratic spirit that underlies U.S. Catholic theology or what has been termed "American Catholic liberalism."[18] Superficially, one would believe that Popular Catholicism, simply by membership identity, must give at least tacit approval of the Marian images put forth by the Church. However, as Greeley has pointed out, a certain element of independence is experienced by the Catholic faithful, particularly in the United States. According to Greeley's research, U.S. Catholics express their opinions concerning the activities of the hierarchy not by leaving the Church but by altering their weekly donations.[19]

Disenchanted with ecclesial authority, some Catholic Christians are identifying with imagery put forth by alternative sources, such as the writings of feminist theologians. Ruether cites an example of the feminist liturgical movement, which is fueled by the growing discontent of women:

> Feminist liturgical communities represent the growing alienation of feminist women (and some men) from the patriarchical paradigm of Christian (and Jewish) religion. For thousands of years males (of the

ruling classes) have claimed a monopoly on the imaging and representation of God and have excluded women from ministry, preaching and theological education (at the university level). This means not only that women have not participated in these leadership roles, but also that the entire patterning of Christianity has been one in which male domination over women has been the model for divine transcendency over the human.[20]

Popular Catholicism cannot be characterized by a pliant, acquiescent, homogeneous, or unsophisticated constituency. Perhaps in a different era this was closer to the truth, but modern Catholics are much more demanding of their religious leaders, particularly within the libertarian orientation of the United States. Nevertheless, the Catholic laity is inconsistently organized in its response to authority, and certainly not uniform in its position on various issues. While popular Catholicism in many respects represents the reality of daily religious experience, it remains theology and the Church hierarchy's task to frame the significant religious questions and dialogue.

Lay Catholics in the United States have formed a number of organizations that seek to make the Church hierarchy more responsive to its membership. These groups typically demand more significant roles for women and changes in the Church's position on reproductive issues. While Mary is not a primary focus for these groups (as she is for the neoconservative lay organizations such as the Blue Army), a shift in Mariological understanding often goes hand in hand with shifts in perspective on women's issues. A few of the more visible progressive lay organizations include:

> *Call to Action.* This organization combines the efforts of theologians such as Charles Curran and Rosemary Radford Ruether with those of lay individuals who seek to democratize the Church in a number of areas.

> *Women Church.* Created by Catholic women, this organization has become an ecumenical movement seeking a feminist spirituality across diverse cultural backgrounds. Women Church, while desiring the transformation of the Catholic Church, independently focuses upon women's spiritual growth in an ongoing redefinition of religion and church.

> *Women's Ordination Conference.* This organization, while sympathetic to other issues of the feminist agenda, primarily seeks the ordination of women, and functions as a network for women who act as priests in Catholic communities removed from the hierarchy.[21]

The existence of lay Catholic organizations notwithstanding, the response of Catholic lay people to feminist concerns runs the gamut. However, every Catholic knows of Mary, the beloved mother figure. John Shinners observes, "In the popular eye, Mary is the perfect friend and mother, for not only is she endeared with every laudable human quality, she is also the all-powerful queen of heaven."[22]

Any renegotiation or reconstruction of Mary must face the challenge of popular Catholicism. Christian feminism offers as one of its critiques of patriarchal religion the lack of responsiveness to the daily experience of the faithful. As Schussler Fiorenza states,

> Feminist theologians maintain that theology has to become again communal and holistic. Feminist theology expresses itself not only in abstract analysis and intellectual discussion, but it employs the whole range of human expression. . . . [23]

However, this creates a challenge for feminists who desire a new imagery for Mary. While there are undercurrents of dissatisfaction with the Church as indicated by the organizations focused on women's issues, Mary remains popular in her current form. It is one thing to write a new theology of Mary; it is quite another to get it widely accepted. Perhaps that is why no comprehensive feminist theology of Mary has been attempted. If Christian feminists truly wish to bring the greater Catholic community into the court of final judgment in the development of theology, a method of inclusion will be necessary.

Hierarchical or Ecclesial Catholicism

Of all the major constituencies in Catholicism, the Church hierarchy is the most organized. The Church has a feudal-like hierarchy of authority and doctrine consisting of the Pope, cardinals, bishops, and priests. However, there are many priests and religious women who are more aligned with the perspective of popular Catholicism or theological Catholicism than with ecclesial Catholicism. The Church hierarchy is by nature conservative and slow to change, although it can and does evolve. Tradition, scripture, and divine command are the tools of the orthodox position.

Through its teaching office, the magisterium, the Church hierarchy views itself as the defender of the faith. In the ecumenical spirit of the Second Vatican Council, the hierarchy has recognized that religious truth is available outside of Catholicism, although the hierarchy is still the "deposit" of the faith.[24] The ecclesial church is the most conservative and reactionary over issues of faith, and many observers claim that the intransigent nature of the Church hierarchy has caused it to lose touch with its popular constituency. In moral matters, the hierarchy of the Church goes to great lengths to demonstrate that it has not erred in the past. Nevertheless, in some areas there has been an evolution of understanding allowing the church to adjust its position. This stance gives the outward impression that the Church has maintained a static position on moral matters, whereas this has not been the case historically.[25] Hierarchical Catholicism represents the most unified front, because public dissent by Church officials evokes serious repercussions.[26]

In terms of Marian imagery, the institutional Church maintains the official teaching that Mary is not a goddess, but that the mother of Jesus, ever virgin, was born without sin and assumed into heaven upon her death. Mary's official status places her in ontological limbo. Official Church teaching prescribes that God should receive *latria*, or adoration. The saints should receive *dulia*, or veneration, and Mary is worthy of *hyperdulia*, or superior veneration.[27] The dogmatic status of Mary's Assumption into heaven, Immaculate Conception, and the virgin birth of Jesus implies that on an official level, to disagree with these dogmas is to remove oneself from what it means to be Catholic.[28] The Church teaches that Mary is worthy of devotion and prayers of intercession. However, to attribute too much or too little to her is akin to heresy. This teaching is consistent with the documents of the Second Vatican Council, and no significant changes in official understanding have occurred since that time.

Official Church documents heap praise upon Mary for her virginity, her faithfulness, and her selflessness. Mary's mediation on behalf of humanity is a common theme even in documents that are not specifically Marian in nature. The invocation of Mary is extremely prevalent in Church teaching. Nevertheless, feminist scholarship identifies the hierarchical imaging as the core of its critique. The dueling opposition that this study documents is one that finds Church teaching defending traditional Marian images against the call for change put forth by feminist theology. Of course, official Church teaching includes an element of history and popular support. However, the extent to which the hierarchy uses Marian images to perpetuate the oppression of women is the key issue. Because the Church remains the final court of authority for tenets of the Catholic faith, it bears the burden of defending the operative religious imagery.

Even under ideal circumstances of absolute theological freedom, there would exist a tension between the theological and hierarchical Church. The ecclesial magisterium establishes boundaries that theologians test, and sometimes extend. A healthy interplay between the two factions would result in the tempering of extreme positions espoused by theologians, while at the same time theologians would prevent the hierarchy from becoming overly staid. However, the last two centuries have witnessed a consolidation of ecclesial authority that has resulted in a sometimes adversarial relationship between the hierarchy and theologians. The hierarchical Church has been challenged by what it has viewed as the misguided theological ideas of "modernism," "American liberalism," and Latin American Liberation Theology. Rather than choosing openly to dialogue with these movements, Church authorities have often selected a posture of retrenchment. The name of Mary is almost universally invoked by the hierarchy when meeting these progressive challenges.[29]

Perhaps the most obvious, singularly significant characteristic of the hierarchical Catholic Church is that it is exclusively male. Were the hierarchy not dominated by men, a feminist analysis of its teaching would not be as forceful. In fact, the Catholic Church is perhaps the world's most enduring and visible institution to maintain overt gender exclusion in its power structure. While previously excluded races and nationalities have risen to prominent positions (including a Polish Pope in 1978), women remain excluded from positions of hierarchical authority such as priest, pastor, monsignor, bishop, cardinal, and Pope. More significantly, women are excluded from the key ritual role of consecrating the eucharist, the core of the Catholic mass and spirituality. Yet, despite this exclusion, the Church of the modern era has often forcibly espoused the social equality or equal dignity of men and women.

The hierarchy of the Catholic Church, unlike theologians, attempts to speak in a single voice and a single leadership through the Vatican. Official Church statements on Mary and on the status of women are numerous. One body of Church teaching representative of recent ecclesial positions on women and Mary is Catholic social teaching.[30] It provides a useful corpus for understanding the motivation, or at least the internal logic, for representing Mary in a particular manner. This teaching demonstrates the evolution of thought on the role of women in society, and contains a conveniently limited number of pronouncements that facilitate examination. I will briefly excerpt and trace some of the social teaching on the role of women, and will indicate the implication of this teaching for the Cult of Mary.

Compared to the history of the Catholic Church, the social teaching of the Church has a brief one hundred year history. Pope Leo XIII's encyclical, *Rerum Novarum,* issued in 1891, provides the Catholic Church's entree to official teachings concerning matters of the world. Of course, the Church was never really unconcerned with social affairs. However, it had never issued a social encyclical prior to this time. Women were regarded in terms of their function as mothers and wives in the social encyclicals.[31] This functionality was determined by roles in the family unit. *Rerum Novarum* supported the theme of women's familial function by applying natural law to the role of women in society:

> it is not right to demand of a woman or a child what a strong adult man is capable of doing or would be willing to do. . . . Certain occupations likewise are less fitted for women, who are intended *by nature* for work of the home—work indeed which especially protects modesty in women and accords *by nature* with the education of children and the well-being of the family. (emphasis added)[32]

This statement reflected the mainstream social consciousness of the era concerning the role of women. The first wave of modern feminism, although it began in the earlier part of the nineteenth century, seemed hardly noticed by the Vatican. Pope Pius XI's statement forty years later (1931) in *Quadragismo Anno* was not counter to popular sentiment.

> It is an intolerable abuse, and to be abolished at all cost, for mothers on account of fathers' low wage to be forced to engage in gainful occupations outside of the home.[33]

These statements are exemplary of what may be termed the "denial phase" of the Church's position on women's rights. Pius XI's words reflect an ongoing tension between declaring the basic human dignity of all people and dividing women and men into distinct labor categories, the labor of child rearing being the exclusive responsibility of women.[34] Ironically, Catholic social teaching, which reinforced the limited options for women in society, was written at the same time Mary was reaching her theological zenith from the middle of the nineteenth to the middle of the twentieth centuries. However, Mary had no political "coattails" for women. Her official elevation did not correspond to Catholic support of women's liberation.

Not until the middle of the twentieth century were the possibilities for different roles for women considered. Pope John XXIII surprised and challenged the hierarchy by recognizing in a 1963 statement that relations between men and women could not remain static:

it is obvious to everyone that women are now taking a part in public life. . . . Since women are becoming ever more conscious of their human dignity, they will not tolerate being treated as mere material instruments, but demand rights befitting a human person both in domestic and public life.[35]

In the *Pastoral Constitution of the Church in the Modern World*, the bishops of the Second Vatican Council echoed the words of Pope John XXIII, "Where they have not yet won it, women claim for themselves an equity with men before the law and in fact."[36] These statements indicate a "recognition phase" for the Church on women's issues.

Beginning in the 1970s, the church moves into an "advocacy stage" in which the promotion of women's rights is espoused. However, this advocacy is always tempered by the lack of gender inclusion in Catholic hierarchical leadership. This dualism creates a credibility problem. As feminists point out, the Church hierarchy can never legitimately uphold ultimate or complete gender equality until it surrenders its exclusionary policy. On the eightieth anniversary of the encyclical *Rerum Novarum*, Pope Paul VI praised egalitarian efforts, but his enthusiasm was partial:

in many countries a charter for women which would put an end to an actual discrimination and would establish relationships of equality in rights and of respect for their dignity is the object of study and time's lively demands. We do not have in mind that false equality which would deny the distinctions laid down by the Creator himself and which would be in contradiction with woman's proper role, which is of such capital importance, at the heart of the family as well as within society. Developments in legislation should on the contrary be directed to protect her proper vocation and at the same time recognize her independence as a person, and her equal rights to participate in cultural, economic, social and political life.[37]

The missing sphere of equal rights listed by Pope Paul VI is participation in the leadership of the Church—such a possibility is not even considered. John Paul II is more precise in his articulation of the role of women. His perspective reflects an understanding of gender equality in human dignity and opportunity, tempered by the maintenance of distinct natures. In Pope John Paul II's 1981 encyclical on labor, *Laborem Exercens*, women's primary role as mother is reinforced,

The true advancement of women requires that labor should be structured in such a way that women do not have to pay for their advancement by abandoning what is specific to them and at the expense of the family, in which women as mothers have an irreplaceable role.[38]

In *Laborem Exercens*, Pope John Paul II appears resigned to the fact that women are working for wages, and he therefore calls on businesses to restructure in order to accommodate women maintaining their most fundamental role as mothers.[39] This position has a number of significant implications, particularly because the role of fathers in parenting is not equally delineated. The accommodation John Paul II calls for appears to validate the idea of the "second shift," during which women must make both economic and domestic labor contributions to the family. The latter contribution is not asked of fathers. The lack of a discussion about fatherhood perpetuates the identification of women with parenting.

In 1988, Pope John Paul II issued an apostolic letter, *Mulieris Dignitatem*, specifically concerning women. What is striking about this document is that if one did not know its title, it could easily be mistaken for a pronouncement about Mary. The number and extent of Marian references and images is overwhelming. The Pontiff makes an overt connection between the vocation of women and Mary as the model for that vocation.[40] The valorization of virgin-motherhood found in the figure of Mary is reinforced to the faithful.

> Virginity and motherhood co-exist in her: they do not mutually exclude each other or place limits on each other. Indeed, the person of the Mother of God helps everyone—especially women—to see how these two dimensions, these two paths in the vocation of women as persons, explain and complete each other.[41]

The praise given to Mary is extensive; she is everything a Christian woman should aspire to be. The Pope is very explicit in defining Mary as the modern role model for women, as in the encyclical *Redemptoris Mater*.

> It can thus be said that women, by looking to Mary, find in her the secret of living their femininity with dignity and of achieving their own advancement. In the light of Mary, the Church sees in the face of women the reflection of a beauty which mirrors the loftiest sentiments in which the human heart is capable: the self-offering totality of love; the strength that is capable of bearing the greatest sorrow; limitless fidelity and tireless devotion to work; the ability to combine penetrating intuition with words of support and encouragement.[42]

Despite her elevation, Mary is clearly not divine. Mary is truly "other"—

other than human, yet other than God. *Mulieris Dignitatem* also praised women for a number of their traditionally attributed qualities and strengths, such as their morality and motherhood. Women share equally in humanity, although they cannot serve the faith community in the Church hierarchy. This caveat, this ultimate "but," in the position of Catholic ecclesiology toward women has helped to prompt the critique of the Church in the only forum available for such analysis—theology.

Theological Catholicism

This section offers a brief sketch of the role of the theologian within Catholicism, with particular focus upon feminist Catholic theologians. In this section, feminist theology will be placed as the key antagonist to the position of the ecclesial Church when it comes to the subject of Mary. A separate theological Catholicism is a relatively new concept in the long history of the Church. While there have always been dissenters, such as Nestorius and Pelagius, they were often part of the ecclesia. The rise of the university with the additional impetus of lay theologians has led to an independent constituency of thinkers and writers free to critique orthodox positions as well as explore new theological perspectives. Of the three segments of Catholicism, theologians have the most divergent outlook from one another. At one extreme there are highly conservative theologians inside and outside the hierarchy who can be strong instruments of orthodoxy. Feminist theologians, deprived of institutional leadership roles because of their gender, suffer fewer repercussions from their public dissent from the hierarchy, except when employed by Catholic universities.

Theologians range from moderate to radical positions concerning theology and Church teaching. Other than professional organizations, theologians have no unified front or forum and wield no official power, although they can be influential through publishing, teaching, and public lecturing. However, the average Catholic seldom has direct access to Catholic theologians. In describing the vocation of the Catholic scholar, Walter Burghardt draws upon the third-century father of the Church, Origen, who believed religious scholarship should include: (1) The recognition of the right of reason, (2) Acquisition of knowledge, (3) Confrontation of old with the new, and (4) The love of truth.[43] Bernard Haring condenses this understanding in his definition of the role of the moral theologian, which he views to be that of the mediator. Haring believes moral theology is a ministry of mediation between the gospel message and the present day and between tradition and change.[44] Feminist theology brings a new perspective to the concept of mediation. It confronts the past and the future by giving voice to the "dangerous memories" of history, and by providing alternative religious paradigms.

As Figure 1 (page 32) indicates, theologians are, by the nature of their profession, less unified in their position than is the Church hierarchy. The self-critical methodology supported by the sciences and fostered in university scholarship creates a range of theological perspectives. Feminist theology is also characterized by a variety of approaches, some of which are considered unorthodox for the field of theology. Carol Christ provides a useful categorization for understanding the various positions of Christian feminists in the Christian tradition. She describes three types on a continuum ranging from mild to substantial criticism. Her rubric can be extrapolated from to obtain a view of Mary.

Feminist Perspectives on Christian Tradition (Christ)	Feminist Perspectives on Mary
Type 1: Proper interpretation will find a nonsexist tradition.	At the core of Marian tradition is female autonomy and power, if interpreted properly.
Type 2: Tradition contains both sexist and nonsexist elements. Nonsexist elements must be affirmed and sexist elements repudiated. Contemporary experience must be included.	Marian tradition contains both positive and negative components. Misogynist elements must be removed.
Type 3: The tradition is essentially sexist, and new traditions must emerge from present experience and nonbiblical sources.	Mary's story is so inherently misogynist that she can't be reimaged.[45]

Despite this divergence, feminist theologians do share a common analytical perspective. Anne E. Carr describes the common ground of feminist religious scholarship:

> Feminist scholarship within the Christian context, for all its variety, is unified in its critical perception of sexism as a massive distortion in the historical and theological tradition that systematically denigrates women, overtly or covertly affirms women's inferiority and subordination to men, and excludes women from full actualization and participation in the church and society. It is unified in its aim of freeing women from restrictive ideologies and institutional structures that

> hinder self-actualization and self-transcendence. And it is unified in
> its attention to the interpreted experience of women as a source of
> religious and theological reflection. . . .[46]

Feminist religious scholarship is able to recognize and celebrate pluralism, particularly as it is informed by women's experience. Christian feminist theology is distinguished from classical theology by its interplay between the past and the present.[47] The past is represented by Christian tradition and the degree of value or truth believed to be inherent in that tradition. Because of its oppressive treatment of women, the entirety of the Christian tradition is not accepted in feminist theology. The present is represented by the religious and social experience of women, particularly viewed in light of the Christian tradition. As Ruether declares, "the present community cannot be ignored."[48]

Two key presuppositions support a feminist approach to theology. One is the obvious lack of positive historical portrayal of women in the Christian tradition. If there were an egalitarian, female-empowering message central to Christian theology, there would be no need for feminist theology or critique. The second presupposition is that the Christian tradition is not a closed system, or, in more theological terms, it is not an exclusive source of divine revelation. Christian feminists recognize women's experiences as an additional source of truth, primarily because of women's relative exclusion from the development of Christian tradition. Elisabeth Schussler Fiorenza's approach is exemplary of the hermeneutical shift sought by Christian feminists.

> A feminist critical interpretation of the Bible cannot take as its point
> of departure the normative authority of the biblical archetype, but
> must begin with women's experience in their struggle for liberation.[49]

The biblical basis of the Judeo-Christian tradition is viewed as a codified depiction of men's religious experience.

In addition to women's experience, non-Christian sources are viewed as legitimate loci of religious truth or insights into the human condition so far as they promote the dignity of all persons. Rosemary Radford Ruether is exemplary in this approach to Christian feminism. In *Sexism and God-Talk: Towards A Feminist Theology*, Ruether describes her methodology as a singular feminist theology amongst many feminist theologies.[50] She recognizes that theology can only be written from a culturally determined perspective, and therefore her approach cannot be reflective of all women's experience. In developing her theology, Ruether employs pre-

Christian pagan resources, liberalism, romanticism, and Marxism, in addition to the Christian biblical tradition.[51] This eclectic approach is indicative of the many feminist theologians who develop new religious paradigms of understanding.

Elizabeth Johnson describes three interrelated tasks of feminist theology. The first is to recognize, criticize, and deconstruct sexism in all aspects of the religious tradition. However, negative critique alone is inadequate. Second, feminist theology must discover the hidden themes of liberation that have been submerged in the tradition. This process includes seeking alternative histories and naming the unnamed of the past. Finally, feminist theology must articulate new religious vision and Christian symbols that recognize the full humanity of women.[52] Feminist theology has an acknowledged bias toward egalitarian, empowering religious expression. Johnson's interconnected goals for feminist theology infuse all of Carol Christ's categories of feminist perspectives. Although Type 1, 2, and 3 scholars exist, feminist theology requires the work of all three types to be an authentically liberating discipline.

Feminists have often criticized traditional theology for its distance from the day to day reality of the lives of the faithful. The construction and manipulation of theology confused by time and various objectives has often removed it from lived experience. Dogma, such as that about the Assumption and Immaculate Conception, employs elaborate justification in its support of Christology. The connection to lived experience is often critiqued for being contrived.[53]

The sharing of ideas that is characteristic of academic freedom has equipped modern feminist theologians with effective tools for criticizing Catholic dogma and tradition. These tools would not have been available in another era. Three of the scholarly analytical tools include biblical scholarship, theories of social construction, and psychoanalytic theory. These tools allow feminist scholars to challenge the source, the interpretation, and the message of Christian traditions. The bible, as the sacred text of Christianity, becomes a cornerstone of feminist analysis. The sacred nature of the bible is called into question because, as Ruether observes, this "objective" truth is very much the codified expression of men's more than women's experience.[54]

Elisabeth Schussler Fiorenza, for example, presents the case for a feminist reinterpretation of scripture against traditional hermeneutical patterns. Schussler Fiorenza recognizes that not only the culture at the time of authorship but also the dominant culture through which interpretation takes place determines the message of scripture. She finds the historical use of the bible to be a mixed bag of interpretations that have resulted in life-giving and death-dealing outcomes.[55] In studying events such as the persecution of Jews and the European witch hunts, the oppressive side of scriptural justification is evident. However, the use of the gospels for liberation from oppression demonstrates a positive interpretation for those concerned with injustices related to race, gender, and class. Shussler Forenza finds a hermeneutical battle waged between patriarchal ethics, with its male-dominated, rule-oriented hierarchies, and the egalitarian ethos that is found in the gospels. She believes the gospel message can transcend hierarchy and oppose the social structures advocated by the dominant culture. Biblical interpretations of the passages that include Mary therefore must include an understanding of the status of women at the time of their authorship, as well as a recognition that later interpretation of the passages includes the biases of each age. Biblical reinterpretations are not historically unconnected, so an interpretation of Mary in one era is not usually negated in the next. Instead, there is an evolution of imagery. Oppressive patriarchal interpretations can have deep historical roots. The greater the tradition, the more historical reification is possible, which makes changing imagery that much more difficult to sort through.

It is difficult to discern which elements of Christian feminism are of a moral concern and which are not. Ronald Green in *Religion and Moral Reason* argues that religion finds its basis "in a process of moral and religious reasoning common to all human beings."[56] While Green is not disputing the serious differences between religions and their significant impact on world history, he does find that moral reasoning makes up the "deep structure" of the world's religions, influencing every ritual, doctrine, and prayer. The fundamental thrust of Christian feminism is a moral one. Fairness, inclusion, justice, equality, nondiscrimination—all the adjectives used in the feminist critique of patriarchal institutions have a moral basis that reflects the ethical standards of modern moral consciousness. Catholic feminist theologian Lisa Cahill expresses the moral basis for feminist ethics as redefining "equality" and "justice" while helping to clarify the criteria for reform.[57]

> Feminist ethics turns to women's experience to challenge women's subordinate status in family, society, and Church and to reconstitute the images, theories and institutions which shape women's and men's gender identities.[58]

Many progressive male theologians welcome the feminist critique and recognize the underlying morality of its mission. David Tracy remarks,

> contemporary Western feminist theory . . . at its best is the most ethically challenging and intellectually sophisticated exposure of the full dilemmas of our pluralistic and ambiguous postmodern moment.[59]

Returning to Green's hypothesis, Mary also fits the model of a fundamentally moral construction within the ethical deep structure of Roman Catholicism. Mary not only transmits the moral theology of the Church, she also plays a key part in the "safety valve" of mercy against harsh justice. Green establishes three elements of religion's deep moral structure:

1. A method of moral reasoning that has a moral point of view.
2. A set of beliefs that affirm the reality of moral retribution.
3. A series of transmoral beliefs that allow for the suspension of moral judgment and retribution when this is needed to overcome moral paralysis and despair.[60]

Green succesfully applies these elements to mainstream world religions and their teachings although the specific outcomes of moral discourse vary. The Catholic establishment of Mary does not violate Green's rubric. Mary is portrayed as having an ethical standpoint that is consistent on sexual matters, papal primacy, ecclesiology, Christology, etc. Mary has been invoked to bear witness to almost every Catholic dogma. The moral view of Mary and the Church are one. She affirms the reality of Christ, as well as God's judgment and punishment of sins. Mary has become a source of popular devotion because of the fear of God's judgment. However, as the eternal Mother, she can intervene on behalf of the repentant who face God's wrath. Mary is not only the archetype of a religious social construction, she epitomizes the deep structure of the Church's moral reasoning.

When Mary's constructed moral aspects are layered upon her psychological significance as reflective of women's experience, it becomes evident why she is at the eye of a theological storm of epic proportions. Christian feminism is fighting a moral battle (a holy war?) to validate women's experience. As Catholic ethicist Margaret Farley states, gender struggles are indeed moral struggles, "The kinds of changes needed in the patterns of relationship between women and men are changes that are finally constituted in and by a moral revolution."[61] Mary is centrally important to both the structure of traditional Catholicism and to the women who wish to be liberated from within that tradition.

A *Gendered* Struggle to Control Mary

The tug of war over Marian imagery would be of great enough import if the discussion simply centered upon the constructed moral values for Catholics. However, the socially constructed Cult of Mary takes on further significance if psychoanalytic dimensions of a gendered struggle are considered. The all-male hierarchy is more than a demographic anomaly in the history of the construction of Mary; gender means the difference between a social construction and a sexist construction in Catholic theology.

In a controversial hypothesis, Michael Carroll meticulously explains the popularity of the Cult of Mary as driven by father-ineffective families.[62] Such families are typified by a strong mother/caretaker in the home and an absent or weak father figure, which creates a setting for stronger childhood sexual attachment to the mother (oedipal complex). Mary becomes an outlet for these heightened feelings of desire. Men channel their desire into devotion for Mary to alleviate surplus sexual energy. This maternal desire may be expressed in violent action, but there is a powerful normative social restraint regarding incest that is perfected in Mary's perpetual virginity. This tension between desire and restraint causes men to feel that they must be punished through what Carroll terms "Marian masochism." Celibacy is seen as a form of this masochism, and Carroll finds the rise of this practice in the life of the clergy directly related to the rise of the Cult of Mary in the fifth century.[63] Men are often driven to exaggerate their maleness (machismo) to clarify their distinction from their mother. Carroll demonstrates that during Marian devotional proliferation, the necessary sociopsychological elements for father-ineffective families were in place.[64]

Maeckelberghe notes that Carroll's hypothesis fails to explain female devotion to Mary.[65] Carroll finds women identifying with Mary to fulfill, or at least placate, the drive of the electra complex. This theory fails to take into account the psychological work of feminist psychoanalytic theorists such as Nancy Chodorow and Dorothy Dinnerstein. These theorists find women (mothers and daughters) much more in continuity with their psychosexual development through the oedipal complex then are men.[66] Women do not ultimately reject their mothers as men do. The same can be said for the idealized experience of mother: Mary. Women experience Mary as identification or in harmony with their own experience, while men experience Mary as other. Mary's virginity and quasi-divinity, however, result in her being experienced as "object" for men. Her unrealistic and unattainable elevation as the ultimate woman (or the ultimate female distortion) creates an objectification ripe for male manipulation, while women treat Mary as a mirror of their own lives and experiences.[67] Mary is not only a social construction, she is a gendered construction with gendered implications.

In considering the popular religion/theology/orthodoxy triad, the images of Mary become sex-typed. Sandra Zimdars-Swartz notes the dichotomous yet intertwined themes of Mary experienced at the personal level versus the social level. At the personal level, Mary is viewed as the nurturing, concerned mother who saves her children from evil and the wrath of God. On a social level, particularly as reflected in her apparitions, Mary is seen as a leader of a mighty army of faithful who will do battle with evil. Zimdars-Swartz notes that this dichotomy has often led to "a militant Marian ideology united with conservative political forces."[68] However, Zimdars-Swartz's observations can be extended through gender analysis. The personal/psychological "hook" of Mary experienced as a heavenly "mama" breeds strong devotion. This phenomenon has little to do with hierarchical intervention and is centered upon the reverence of motherhood projected to the level of divinity. However, the socially militant aspects of Mariology require a definition of evil that must be provided by an organized authority. In this respect, the Catholic male hierarchy has been allowed to set the agenda for "Marian ideology." Modern Catholic feminism questions the morality defined by the Church hierarchy for Mary, and it struggles to influence Marian imagery.

From the psychoanalytic perspective, the struggle to influence these Marian images has divergent implications. For men, the issue is the creation of an ideal woman who satisfies psycho-sexual needs. Because Mary is a woman there is no expectation of personal continuity or identification with her, yet she is elevated beyond reach so that she becomes a male fantasy of the virgin/mother. She is the ultimate other. Her distance from reality is so great that she is truly an object. For women the issue is ontological. Mary is a dynamic projection of every woman's experience and every woman's hope. Therefore, Mary represents simultaneous contradictory religious imagery for men and women. Men are vying for control over a religious fantasy. Women are fighting to control their spiritual soul. Feminist analysis further complicates the dynamics of a Catholic theology of Mary as described in Figure 1 (page 32). Gendered experience must be taken into consideration and is therefore layered onto Catholic perspectives on Mary in Figure 2.

Feminist theology represents an implosion of the "closed system" of

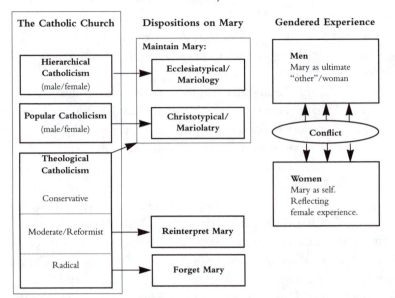

Figure 2: Catholic Factions and the Gendered Filter
of Catholic Perspectives on Mary

historical Catholic theology. The implication of this genre of theology is
as far-reaching as the boundaries of Catholic theology. Feminist theology
has taken aim at the traditional images of Mary, with the goal of freeing
them from ecclesial control. In the following chapters, three such images—
Mary as Virgin, Mary as Mediator, and Mary as the New Eve—and their
accompanying feminist analyses will be explored in light of their significance for ethical issues of sexuality, power relationships, and violence.

3

Catholic Sexual Morality and
the Blessed Virgin Mary

The Lord looked upon the whole of creation, and he saw no one to equal Mary. Therefore he chose her for his mother. If therefore a girl wants to be a virgin, she should resemble Mary.

—Council of Nicaea, 325 C.E.

The tradition of Mary contains a strong sexual message that has contributed to the Catholic Church's static position on sexual morality. Official Catholic sexual morality is perhaps the ecclesial organization's most public and controversial characteristic. It is not surprising that Mary is a central figure in the Church's sexual teaching; the most frequently invoked title for Mary is centered upon her sexuality—The Blessed *Virgin* Mary. The enigma of Mary's virginity transforms her into the great paradox of the ages, the virgin mother. Mary's other images of sinlessness and intercessory power are, in a sense, derived from her virginal motherhood. This unique religious image of virgin motherhood, when coupled with Mary's idealized status, cannot help but have an effect upon Catholic women and men as an unobtainable religious model.

In this chapter the development of Mary's tradition of virginity is traced, including biblical and nonbiblical sources. Analogous to the history of the general Cult of Mary presented in the first chapter, each image of Mary must be regarded as a historical construction with an internal logic in its development and an ultimate moral perspective. The final representation of that historical development and logic is mediated, on an official level, by the current position of the Church. Mary represents the pinnacle of womanhood in Catholic representations of female behavior, and her virginity is also representative of the most sacred form of human sexuality. The feminist theological critique of the hierarchical position deconstructs the "virgin" tradition, while calling into question the complicity of such a tradition in the oppression of women.

The Historical Construction of Mary as the Virgin

The Social Context: Biblical Virginity

The following passage demonstrates the level of significance that virginity held in the second century B.C.E. and the extent to which virgin daughters were prized property.

> A daughter is a treasure that keeps her father wakeful,
>   and worry over her drives away rest:
> Lest she pass her prime unmarried,
>   or when she is married lest she be disliked;
> While unmarried, lest she be seduced,
>   or, as a wife, lest she prove unfaithful;
> Lest she conceive in her father's home,
>   or be sterile in that of her husband.
> Keep a close watch on your daughter,
>   Lest she make you the sport of your enemies,
> A byword in the city, a reproach among the people,
>   an object of derision in public gathers.
> See that there is no lattice in her room,
>   no place that overlooks the approaches to the house.
> Let her not parade her charms before men,
>   or spend her time with married women;
> For just as moths come from garments,
>   so harm to women comes from women;
> Better a man's harshness than a woman's indulgence,
>   and a frightened daughter than any disgrace.
>   Sirach 42:9–14[1]

Fundamental to understanding Mary's virginity is the biblical concept of virginity, which will be explored in the first part of this chapter.[2] Although the theological necessity of making Mary a perpetual virgin appears to be a Christian construction (as the following pages will demonstrate), virginity was also a characteristic of the major goddesses of the pre-Christian era.[3] Cybele, Aphrodite, Demeter, Astrate, Isis, Hathor, Inanna, and Ishtar were all goddess mothers, and many bore half-human, half-divine children who suffered death and subsequent resurrection.[4] Despite these virgin goddesses, virginity was not given the religious valorization or reification found in Christianity. It is the Judeo-Christian tradition that transforms the concept of virginity from an economic consideration to a sacred religious consideration in western culture.

Admonishments of sexual chastity in the Hebrew Scriptures were more often directed toward women rather than men. While men were warned to stay away from adulteresses, there appeared to be no expectation that they be virgins upon their marriage day. The god of the Hebrew scriptures, although portrayed as male, did not participate in sexual activities, as did the deities of the ancient Near East.[5] The laws found in the Book of Deuteronomy reflected the importance of virginity in the sixth and seventh centuries B.C.E.[6] A description of the penalty for sexual crimes within marriage is found in Deuteronomy 22:13-28. If a man claimed that his newlywed was not a virgin when they married, it was up to the woman's parents (and in their financial interest) to prove her innocence by showing the authorities the bed sheets from the wedding night that, theoretically, would be blood-stained upon the rupture of the hymen.[7] A false accusation of nonvirginity on the part of the husband resulted in a flogging and a fine of 100 silver shekels (or twice the price paid for the bride) and a life sentence of marriage with no possibility of divorce.[8] If the accusation proved correct, the bride was stoned to death in front of her father's house and the bridal price returned to the groom. For women, the severe penalty for a violation of virginity was equal to that of the punishment for adultery.[9] Sexual purity was a gendered social norm for which much greater responsibility was placed upon women than men.

The female virginity norms recounted in biblical communities appear to have their origins in nonreligious considerations. L. William Countryman argues that the scriptural approbations against violating virginity were based purely upon economics. Women were not just second-class citizens, they were considered men's property. Women either belonged to their fathers or to their husbands. Sexual offenses against women were violations of a man's property in the same category as serious vandalism or burglary. The ownership of women was extended to the man's family as well.[10] Familial heritage, particularly the production of legitimate heirs, was extremely important in biblical society.[11] Virgin brides insured the purity of family lineage. A married woman with offspring—particularly male children—achieved the highest status accorded to females in this culture.[12] The corollary to the value placed upon unmarried women's virginity was a married woman's fidelity. Women could commit adultery by having sexual relations with any man, but men could only commit adultery by having intercourse with another man's wife. Slaves, prostitutes, concubines, and divorced or widowed women were all potential sexual partners for men, without legal retribution.[13] Current concepts of mutuality in relationships would have been foreign to biblical societies in which male property rights were the dominant consideration.

Violations of female virginity and marital fidelity were fundamentally crimes of economics and power rights. In a world in which the boundaries between religion and society were blurred, religious law served to enforce and maintain sexual mores, and therefore the social order. Women were the objects of law over which they themselves had no influence, and they often suffered because of circumstances over which they had no control.[14] Modern society has shed many, but not all, of the issues of property and power surrounding virginity and sexual chastity. Vestiges of the property tradition can be witnessed in the traditional wedding ceremony custom of a father handing his daughter over to the groom, or in the traditional terminology, "man and wife."

The biblical understanding of virginity did not have the lofty religious implications that later emerged with the Cult of Mary. Although it was part of religious law, virginity was only valued prior to marriage and therefore was not enshrined as the ultimate achievement of womanhood; it was not associated with salvation, achievement of special grace, or a higher position in heaven. This fundamental shift in understanding took place in the fourth century, when Mary's cultic virginity was popularized. Prior to that time, motherhood was women's highest achievement in Judaism as depicted in the Hebrew scriptures.[15] Sterility brought great disdain, such as in the biblical stories of Sarah and Hagar. The Cult of Mary maintained the valorization of motherhood but added her unique virginity in the tradition of goddess worship.

The Sources of Mary's Paradoxical Virginity

The Catholic doctrine of Mary's virginity takes on a unique complexity because it is not the type of virginity spoken of in common conversation. Mary was, of course, a mother. This fact would normally imply that she could have been a virgin until the conception of Jesus, but Catholicism takes the concept one step further and declares Mary a perpetual virgin: before, during, and after the birth of Jesus (*virginitas ante partum, in partum,* and *post partum*).[16] Mary is a "triple virgin." To support the Catholic belief that Mary was sexually untouchable, no imagery was too extreme. Sacred art depicts such wild formulations as semen emanating from the mouth of God and traveling through a long tube that led under Mary's skirt; a dove transporting God's semen to Mary; and Gabriel transmitting the semen from his mouth to Mary's ear.[17]

Five significant sources originated, or at least perpetuated, the idea that Mary was forever virgin: *The Gospel of Matthew, The Gospel of Luke, The Infancy Gospel of James,* Gnosticism, and the writings of St. Jerome.[18] In the following sections, the traditional apologetics for Mary's virginity will be presented in conjunction with their theological critiques. This background is essential to the feminist deconstruction of the concept of Mary's tradition of virginity. In addition, the evolution of moral theology with regard to Mary's virginity provides perspective for modern Church teaching.

The Gospel of Matthew

The primary verification of Mary's virginity is found in the infancy narratives of Matthew and Luke.[19] Continuity and fulfillment of the Hebrew scriptures was believed to be found in Mary's compliance with the messianic prophecy of Isaiah.

> The birth of Jesus the Anointed took place as follows: While his mother Mary was engaged to Joseph, but before they slept together,[20] she was found to be pregnant by the Holy Spirit. Since Joseph her husband was a good man and did not wish to expose her publicly, he planned to break off their engagement quietly.
>
> While he was thinking about these things, a messenger of the Lord surprised him in a dream with these words: "Joseph, descendant of David, don't hesitate to take Mary as your wife, since the Holy Spirit is responsible for her pregnancy. She will give birth to a son and you will name him Jesus. This means he will save his people from their sins." All of this has happened so the prediction of the Lord given by the prophet would come true:
>
> > Behold, a virgin will conceive a child
> > and she will give birth to a son,
> > and they will name him Emmanuel (which means "God with us").

Joseph got up and did what the messenger of the Lord told him: he took (Mary as) his wife. He did not sleep with her until she had given birth to a son. Joseph named him Jesus. (Matthew 1:18–24)[21]

The gospel of Matthew, by virtue of including an infancy narrative not found in Mark, is believed to be the first gospel (canonical or noncanonical) to indicate that Mary was a virgin.[22] Matthew is the only gospel account that found the virginal conception of Jesus foreshadowed in the Hebrew scriptures.[23] However, the use of the term "virgin" in Matthew's version of Isaiah 7:14 appears to be an incorrect translation of the original Hebrew. Biblical scholars generally agree that Isaiah used the term *alma,* which in its nine other uses in the Hebrew Scriptures refers to a "young girl" who had reached the age of puberty and was ready for marriage. The term does not necessarily indicate virginity. However, the Greek word *parthenos* used in Matthew does indicate virginity, but not necessarily perpetual virginity.[24] Even if *parthenos* was the correct translation, the presumption would be that a virgin would bear a child in the usual manner, and the mother would subsequently have ongoing sexual relations with her spouse. There is no indication that the "virgin" would conceive and give birth in a supernatural way. The prophecy of Jesus' birth to a virgin, under either interpretation, is hardly remarkable given that many babies are conceived by virgin women.[25] Nevertheless, there is little to support that such a prediction, made 700 years prior, was directed at the birth of Jesus to Mary. The use of this passage appears to be an act of "proof texting" by Matthew's author, and it is taken out of context in its virginal implications for Mary. Even if the author of Matthew intended to indicate Mary was a virgin, the concept of Mary's post-partum virginity was beyond his ultimate purpose: to demonstrate Jesus' Davidic sonship through Joseph.[26]

A more explicit prediction of the virgin birth than the reference to Isaiah is the passage that indicates Mary conceived by the Holy Spirit. Because of Joseph's sexual abstinence, the author of Matthew created an exceptional birth story to accompany the miraculous conception. Miraculous birth stories were a type of literary norm that coincided with the greatness of the individual. Moses, Isaac, Samson, Samuel, and John the Baptist were all credited with births that were out of the ordinary. This was true of non-Christian heroes as well, including Heracles, Pythagorus, Plato, Alexander, Augustus, and Buddha.[27] However, the remarkable conception and birth story does not substantiate a perpetually virgin Mary.

The Gospel of Luke

The Lucan account of the conception and birth of Jesus is much longer and quite different from the Matthean account in detail and tone:

> In the sixth month the heavenly messenger Gabriel was sent from God to a city in Galilee called Nazareth, to a virgin engaged to a man named Joseph, of the house of David. The virgin's name was Mary. He entered and said to her, "Greetings, favored one. The Lord is with you!"
>
> But she was deeply disturbed by the words, and wondered what its greeting could mean.
>
> The heavenly messenger said to her, "Don't be afraid, Mary, for you have found favor with God. Listen to me: you will conceive in your womb and give birth to a son, and you will name him Jesus. He will be great, and will be called son of the Most High. And the Lord God will give him the throne of David, his father. He will rule over the house of Jacob forever; and his dominion will have no end."
>
> And Mary said to the messenger, "How can this be, since I am not involved with a man?"
>
> The messenger replied, "The Holy Spirit will come over you, and the power of the Most High will cast its shadow on you. This is why the child to be born will be holy, and be called son of God. Further, your relative Elizabeth has also conceived a son in her old age. She who was said to be infertile is already six months along, since neither is impossible with God."
>
> And Mary said, "Here I am, the Lord's slave. May everything you have said come true" Then the heavenly messenger left her. (Luke 1:26–38)

The Gospel of Luke recounts a happy birth scenario which found the shepherds singing with joy (2:14). Matthew's version is more ominous because it includes the tale of Herod's mass killing of the infants (2:16). The points of real agreement between the two infancy narratives are the Davidic descent of Joseph, the role of the Holy Spirit, the virginal conception, and the birth of Jesus in Bethlehem. With regard to almost every other feature of the stories, one would not recognize them as describing the same event. While not including an allusion to the Hebrew scriptures, Luke does make use of the term *parthenos* twice in 1:27, with the inherent difficulty of this translation already mentioned.

The Gospel of Luke, like Matthew, describes Jesus as being conceived by the Holy Spirit. However, there have been instances in the scriptures in which the Holy Spirit worked through humans in the conception process (such as the case of Isaac in Gal. 4:29). This involvement of the

Holy Spirit would not preclude the idea of an earthly father. However, the Gospel appears to make Joseph's surrogate role clear in the genealogy of 3:23 when describing Jesus as "supposedly the son of Joseph."[28]

The author of Luke includes a curious scene in his infancy narrative that depicts the presentation of Jesus to God at the temple (2:22–39). Not only is there no such ritual presentation known in Jewish tradition,[29] but at this ceremony Jesus was declared holy according to the ancient passage, "Every male that opens the womb is to be considered holy to the Lord" (2:23). This "opening of the womb" is a theologically problematic statement given that, according to Catholic tradition, Mary was to remain virginally intact.[30]

Many biblical scholars reconstruct the chronological authorship of the Christian gospels in the reverse order of the life of Jesus.[31] Because Jesus' public ministry took place during the last three years of his life, the earliest accounts were mostly concerned with these events. As the popularity of Christianity spread, an oral tradition, and subsequent written tradition, met the demand of public interest. The infancy narratives found in Luke and Matthew are evidence of this development. In addition, later texts that were not accepted into the canon, such as the *Infancy Gospel of James*, also described the birth of Jesus.

The Infancy Gospel of James

The *Infancy Gospel of James*, or the Protevangelium of James, as it is sometimes referred to, was one of the most popular and influential of the noncanonical texts.[32] That popularity may have a connection to pre-Christian goddess worship. Stephen Benko finds the character and treatment of Mary in this text indicative of non-Christian religions.[33] Despite its title, the real focus of *The Infancy Gospel of James* is Mary. The author attempts to establish Mary's virginity before and during the birth of Jesus, as well as imply Mary's post-partum virginity. In a common practice of the era, credibility for the historical accuracy of the account was sought by attributing authorship to the apostle James. The text claims to have been written at the time of Herod's death, which would place it at about the year four B.C.E. Both the claim of authorship and origination date are not accepted by biblical scholars who date the text in the middle of the second century because of the extensive use of Matthean and Lucan material, amongst other reasons.[34] James died in 62 C.E., rendering the true author unknown.[35]

The claim of the apostle James as author is significant because of its implication for Mary's virginity. In other biblical texts James is identified as the brother of Jesus (for example, in the letters of Paul). However, the *Infancy Gospel of James* describes Joseph as an old man who had children by a previous marriage (9:8). The *Infancy Gospel of James* transformed Joseph into an elderly caretaker figure for Mary (9:7), implying that James was an older step-brother of Jesus and not a "blood" brother. This idea of Joseph's advanced age is not found in the canonical infancy narratives.

The first eight chapters of the gospel describe Mary's birth and childhood, with an emphasis on her purity. The second set of eight chapters deals with the relationship of Mary and Joseph and the social difficulties of legitimizing her miraculous pregnancy. The final eight chapters recount the birth of Jesus, and Mary's perpetual virginity. The text so explicitly supports Mary's virginity that it asserts she was actually tested for physical intactness.

> Then the midwife shouted: "What a great day this is for me because I have seen this new miracle!"
>
> And the midwife left the cave[36] and met Salome and said to her, "Salome, Salome, I have a new marvel to tell: a virgin has given birth, something physically impossible for a virgin!"
>
> And Salome replied, "As the Lord my God lives, unless I insert my finger and examine her, I will never believe that a virgin has given birth."
>
> The midwife entered and said, "Mary, position yourself for an examination. You are facing a serious test."
>
> And so Mary, when she heard these instructions, positioned herself, and Salome inserted her finger into Mary. And then Salome cried aloud and said, "I am damned because of my transgression and my disbelief, since I have put the living God on trial. Look! I am losing my hand! It is being eaten by the flames!" (19:18–20:4)

By implication, just as Salome's doubt led to her punishment, so too could those who doubted Mary's virginity be punished.

While the authors of the infancy narratives in Matthew and Luke intended, at most, to support Mary's ante-partum virginity, the *Infancy Gospel of James* provided evidence of Mary's virginity during the delivery of Jesus. The author was obtuse in his intention to verify Mary's virginity. He created two witnesses, two clear proclamations of Mary's virginity, and the explicit physical test. The story parallels the tale of the apostle Thomas, who doubted Jesus' resurrection (John 20:24–25). In adding the idea of Jesus passing through Mary's hymen, the author also foreshadowed a post-resurrection idea that Jesus passed through the locked doors (John 20:19-20).[37] In addition, *The Infancy Gospel of James* implied Mary's ongoing virginity by describing Joseph's advanced age and Mary's lifelong commitment to purity.

There is little doubt of the nonhistorical nature of the *Infancy Gospel of James*.[38] The text may have found its origin in an earlier myth concerning the birth of the superhuman figure Melchizedek.[39] Nevertheless, this story caught the imagination of Christians and helped spread the legendary virginity of Mary. Eventually the Church also adopted the ideas found in *The Infancy Gospel of James*, despite its noncanonical status. At the Lateran Council of 469, Mary's perpetual virginity was officially declared a part of Church teaching.[40]

Gnosticism

Another important force in the evolution of Marian virginity was the influence of Gnosticism. Much has been revealed about early Christianity since the discovery of the thirteen codices at Nag Hammadi, Egypt in 1945. One significant new discovery concerns the level of diversity among Christian communities during the first two centuries.[41] The Gnostic movement (Gnosis meaning knowledge or insight) would later be considered a great heresy, but during these early centuries it was just another type of Christian community. Defining Gnosticism presents a number of challenges, including the pluralism within these communities. For example, while most Gnostic groups apparently had an ascetic approach to sex, other communities embraced sexual norms beyond the social convention.[42]

Gnostics believed in a dynamic relationship between God and humans. Truly knowing oneself was to know God.[43] Salvation was dependent upon a personal awakening. Creation was considered a result of disobedience to God, which rendered the material world evil. However, in the process of creation, metaphoric sparks of divinity were trapped in human bodies. Jesus was the redeemer who released the sparks from their human captivity and gave believers special knowledge of the world and its beginning.[44]

Most Gnostic communities attempted to restore a feminine divinity that was missing in the Christian mythological system. This feminine divinity took the form of a creator figure or sometimes a member of a triune godhead (Father, Mother, Son).[45] Reflecting their gender balanced theology, many Gnostic sects also gave prominent roles to women.[46]

According to many Gnostic texts, Mary, the mother of Jesus, and Mary Magdalene held positions of leadership among Jesus' disciples.[47] In many of the texts, Mary Magdalene represents the Gnostic authority of women struggling against Peter's patriarchal authority.[48] Although much of Gnostic Christianity affirmed women's spiritual equality, it simultaneously devalued nature and bodily experience.[49] Numerous Gnostic groups reflected the sexual misogyny of their society.[50]

Gnosticism served to perpetuate Mary's virginity on two important fronts. To counter the Gnostic heresy that Jesus was primarily a spiritual being, Church fathers such as Origen and Tertullian forcefully argued that Mary was physically the means of bringing Jesus into the world. In the Gnostic *Gospel of Philip*, the author claimed that virginal conception by the Holy Spirit was only symbolic, given that the Holy Spirit was understood to be female and two women could not conceive. When the author wrote about a virgin birth, the virgin referred to was the Holy Spirit and not Mary.[51] This type of approach was unacceptable to Church fathers, who insisted on Jesus being both human and divine. Mary's conception, pregnancy, and delivery were the necessary human elements to insure that Jesus was not pure spirit. However, a balance had to be struck because Jesus could not be depicted as purely human. The Church fathers were backed into a theological corner that forced them to adamantly support both supernatural intervention and authentic human experience. A virginal conception and birth fit the theological requirements.

Because of their general embracing of asceticism and disregard for the human body, Mary's lifelong virginity was a tradition that Gnostics generally accepted and perpetuated. Gnosticism hailed the virgin as the true Christian. The plurality of beliefs of the time meant Christian and Gnostic orthodoxy were not as distinct as they appear from a modern perspective. Many of the Gnostic beliefs were assimilated into mainstream Christianity as it became more dominant. This assimilation included the spirit/body separation that is central to Mariology.[52]

The Writings of St. Jerome

A key figure in the early Church's development of an understanding of Marian virginity was St. Jerome. In *Against Helvidius on the Perpetual Virginity of Mary* written in 383 C.E. Jerome established the essential argument concerning Mary's sexuality that has been adopted by the Catholic Church through the present day. Self denial, virginity, and isolation were Jerome's principal messages to women, and Mary was his principal torch-bearer. For Jerome, virginity was the state of nature, and therefore authentically normative. Jerome's biblical exegesis espouses virginity on every page.[53] Had there not been a Fall, everyone would have been a virgin.[54]

Reflecting the growing acceptance of Christianity in the Empire, Jerome had come to Rome in 382 in the role of spiritual director to a group of wealthy women. Under his guidance, Roman noblewomen began to enter the ascetic life for the first time. One woman, Paula, became his prize student and ultimately his intimate companion (but not in a physical sense). In Jerome's perverse understanding of men and women, Paula was an exemplary woman because she made herself repulsive to men.[55] She practiced self-denial and self-mutilation to render herself completely unattractive, and her zeal to reject beauty made her companionship desirable to Jerome.[56] In 383 one of Paula's daughters died, and accusations circulated that her death had to do with Jerome's guidance through excessive ascetic fasting. Paula and Jerome later traveled to Bethlehem, where they established men's and women's monasteries.

It was during his brief stay in Rome that Jerome disagreed with Helvidius concerning Mary's perpetual virginity, and thus wrote his influential apologetic. In 393, Jerome wrote two books to counter the arguments of Jovinian and Helvidius, who doubted Mary's virginity during childbirth and who also did not believe that virginity was more holy than marriage. Jerome is credited with authoring the Catholic belief that Mary was a perpetual virgin: "a fountain sealed."[57] Jerome not only extolled the superior virtues of virginity, he demonstrated utter contempt for any opposition to this view. In responding to Helvidius, Jerome stated,

> You must be ignorant of men. By disregarding the whole field of scripture you have brought disgrace upon the virgin with your madness.[58]

History of religions scholar Peter Brown describes Jerome's fixation on virginity as sealing the gender differences between men and women for all time.[59] Virginity was a sign of bodily integrity that was part of the natural order. For Jerome, the distinctive behavior of men and women was divinely intended. What radicalizes Jerome's position was his extreme language to express his valorization of virginity.[60] For example, Jerome found the singular good that came from marriage to be the possibility of new virgins. Jerome's obsession with female virginity led him to make a singular exception to the sinfulness of suicide: A woman could take her life to avoid sexual violation.[61]

Prior to any distinctively feminist critique of Mary's sexuality, the previous review of the sources of Mary's virgin tradition leaves the claim of her virginity in doubt, particularly the claim of her perpetual virginity. The gospels only substantiate *ante partum* virginity, and even this is problematic. The *Infancy Gospel of James*, while traditionally popular, appears to have little historical value in terms of providing factual data on the life of Mary. Gnostic influences on Marian virginity merely reflect the movement's extreme dualism. Jerome's writings were more apologetic than historical. His work appears to reflect his own sexual perversions rather than authentic insight into what was known about the life of Mary at the time. Mary's virginity was a function of her constructed nature, created to meet the social, political, and theological needs of those (males) who contributed to it.

Sexuality, Sinfulness, and Autonomy

A number of theologians, not all of whom are feminists, have been critical of Catholic sexual morality. For feminist theologians, sexual ethics are a central issue and a paradigm for the relationship of men and women in the Catholic/Christian community. The feminist theological critique of Marian sexuality takes two fundamental directions. The first critique is from a historical standpoint and stems from biblical analysis. The historicity of Mary's unique virginity is brought into question. As already reviewed, Mary's perpetual virginity is considered problematic by modern biblical scholarship. Given modern understandings of the bible's formation, feminist theologians and scholars offer alternative histories to those found in popular tradition. As Elisabeth Schussler Fiorenza points out, a feminist reconstruction of history cannot take for granted the accuracy of existing accounts. Biblical texts are not history books. The bible does not, "tell us how it actually was, but how its religious significance was understood."[62] Therefore, historical criticism reveals that a modern reinterpretation of biblical events is consistent with the Christian tradition of religious interpretation or hermeneutics. While historical criticism is widely accepted in most disciplines, religion is slow to come to grips with this approach because it often challenges fundamental concepts of traditional theology. Within Catholicism, the heresy of "modernism," a pejorative label often given to scientific methods, has not yet been completely vindicated.

The second feminist critique of Marian sexuality is of greater significance. The reality of Mary's virginity is of less consequence than the perpetuation of the virginal myth as model of womanhood. Mary, the icon for Catholic sexual morality, is of paramount concern to feminist theologians because of the ethical message in her virginity. Catholic sexual standards and gender based hierarchies are on a collision course with women's liberation. In the following sections, each of these critiques is addressed.

Feminist Historical Criticism

The forces aiding in the development of Mary's virginity tradition were not independent but historically and socially interwoven. They established a momentum that made her virginity increasingly real (a "reification" in Berger's terminology) as well as increasingly important to Christianity. This momentum may have originated with the "push" of theology as it logically argued against heresy, or with the "pull" of the faithful who felt a need to project metahuman, extraordinary qualities onto Mary. Regardless of origin, the result was substantial support for Mary's virginity within Christianity by the end of the fourth century.

As with the Gnostic communities, there was not always a monolithic response to Mary's virginity among "orthodox" Christian communities. In the turbulent beginnings of the Church, alternative traditions thrived, only to be eventually squelched or assumed into the dominant tradition. Recently, feminist theologians and historians have begun to uncover the precursors of the dominant sex-gender system reflected in historical religious reification. Once a scientifically critical review is made of a social construction, the evidence can give support for plausible alternative histories of understanding to the traditional one.

Rosemary Radford Ruether uses an analysis of familial terms in the gospels to dispel the myth of Mary's post-partum virginity.[63] The critical texts include Mark 6:3, 3:31–35, Matthew 12:46–50, 13:44, John 7:3, Acts 1:13–14 and I Corinthians 15:5–7. Each of these cases specifically alludes to Jesus' brothers (and sometimes sisters). The traditional Catholic apologetic, which dates back to Jerome, has been to declare these passages as colloquialisms that refer to "spiritual brothers" or extended family, particularly referring to "cousins."[64] Protestants generally reject this rationale and accept that Mary had offspring after Jesus. Ruether finds the two Catholic approaches contextually and textually problematic, as well as unconfirmed by outside sources.

The belief that the individuals referred to were spiritual brothers appears discounted by the fact that these close relatives did not believe in Jesus. Mark 3:31–35 and its corollary Matthew 12:46–50 find Jesus reacting harshly to his family's appearance outside of his teaching space. The indication is that they are opposed to, or embarrassed about, his public ministry.[65] In John 7:3, the narrator specifically states that Jesus' brothers did not believe him. This behavior is hardly representative of spiritual fraternity. Another indication of authentic familial ties is that Mary, explicitly declared as Jesus' mother, is repeatedly listed adjacent to the names of the brothers of Jesus. The grouping seems to point to kinship. Finally, the Greek term for brother used in these texts is *adelphos*. That translates to "blood brother," and requires qualification to translate to "cousin."[66] The term *adelphos* is used 343 times in the Christian scriptures with a consistent literal meaning of "brother."[67] Furthermore, Mark 3:31 adds the term "sister" that was never used in any other context for extended family members such as cousins.[68]

Ruether also found sources outside the Christian scriptures failing to corroborate Mary's post-partum virginity. The historian Tertullian not only wrote of Jesus' brothers and sisters, but he countered Gnostic ideas of Jesus being purely divine by asserting the existence of his natural family, which included siblings. There exists a fragment of the work of Hegesippus, a second century Church historian and genealogist, that mentions Jesus' family and differentiates between cousins and brothers. This explicit distinction appears to counter the concept of the general term "brother" as used for extended family. [69]

There is also a noticeable absence of gospel support for Mary's perpetual virginity. The authors of Mark and John, as well as the letters of Paul, make no mention of virginity. Biblical-source theory indicates that Mark and Paul predate Matthew and Luke, which contain the infancy narratives and their allusions to Mary's virginity but not to perpetual virginity.[70] In fact, the author of Luke refers to Jesus as Mary's "first born" without any indication that he was her only son (2:7).[71] The specific mention of the virgin birth is made more problematic by its inclusion in the infancy narratives in Luke and Matthew which modern biblical scholarship regards as having questionable historical accuracy.[72]

Ruether concludes that, for the gospel authors, the theological significance of Mary's involvement in the birth of Jesus is far more important than proving that she was not perpetually virgin. The gospel writers made a statement about divine intervention in human history, and Mary was not the center of attention in their theology. It was only later interpretation and the writings of Church Fathers, like Jerome, that seemingly shifted the focus from Jesus' virgin birth to Mary's virginity. The gospels attempt to demonstrate the significance of Jesus' entrance into the world. The original exegetical efforts were Christological, and Mary was a minor player.

German theologian Uta Ranke-Heinemann recognizes the significance of *Sitz im Leben* for the basis of the virgin-birth myth, or "stork theology," as she calls it. The lack of biological understanding during this era results in male semen being thought of as a self-sufficient progenitor. The lack of a human partner gave God complete creative responsibility. Modern biological understanding of reproduction developed in the mid-1800s challenges this virgin-birth theology. It is now understood that men and women share in the creative process; thus, the myth of the virgin birth reduces God's role to that of a divine sperm donor. Ranke-Heinemann's argument is that the virgin birth myth grew out of androcentric world views imposed upon the Jesus story. The infancy narratives were a contrived ("fairy tale") addition to the gospels drawn from numerous sources to make a theological point.[73]

In *The Illegitimacy of Jesus: A Feminist Theological Interpretation of the Infancy Narratives*, Jane Schaberg examines accusations of Jesus being an illegitimate child. Despite the dominant Christian story of the virgin birth of Jesus in western culture, claims of Mary being raped or committing adultery are as old as Christianity itself. Origen reports that the pagan Celsus believed that Ben Panthera (Son of Panthera), a Roman soldier, was the father of Jesus.[74] A tradition of Jesus' illegitimacy is attested to in noncanonical sources such as the *Acts of Pilate*. In this Christian apologetic that was probably authored in the second or third century, Pilate is portrayed as a witness to Jesus' death and resurrection.[75] During the trial of Jesus before Pontius Pilate, witnesses claim that he was "born of fornication." Then the issue is dropped rather quickly and does not become a central theme of the gospel.[76] Although this illegitimacy tradition has circulated for ages, Schaberg is the first to develop the theory into a significant alternative tradition.

Besides the noncanonical sources, Schaberg finds an underlying illegitimacy tradition in the Gospel of Matthew. Numerous indicators of Jesus' illegitimate birth have been previously dismissed or explained away by biblical scholarship. Many biblical scholars are associated with mainstream Christian religions and therefore can not identify with an alternative perspective on history. A feminist perspective provides a different reading with no less scholarly rigor. Matthew began his infancy narrative with a genealogy (1:1–1:11), a practice consistent with a Jewish concern for lineage. The genealogy demonstrated Jesus' Davidic (and thus anointed kingship) origins. What is unusual about this genealogy is that it included four women—Tamar, Ruth, Rahab, and Bathsheba, none of whom fit traditional patriarchal roles for women. Tamar and Ruth were childless widows. Rahab was a prostitute and Bathsheba was an adulteress who bore her lover's child. Each woman was involved or accused of involvement in illicit sexual activity that caused them to suffer. However, each was eventually vindicated and exalted for accepting patriarchal values. Schaberg argues that the inclusion of these particular women creates a suspicious literary trajectory of expectation for Mary. The pattern is described as follows:

> a woman who becomes a social misfit in some way; is wronged or thwarted; who is party to a sexual act that places her in great danger; and whose story has an outcome that repairs the social fabric and ensures the birth of a child who is legitimate or legitimated.[77]

Schaberg disagrees with the traditional interpretations of Matthew and finds no intention of the author to describe a virginal conception. There is no parallel in the writings of antiquity to the type of conception story found in Matthew. While there were many miraculous birthing stories, the divine conception myths in the Christian tradition usually involved normal sexual intercourse or male penetration of some kind.[78] The lack of a parallel myth story, combined with no explicit mention of virginal conception, lends greater support to an underlying illegitimacy tradition. The theme of God's ability to bring greatness out of inferior social status in Matthew's gospel is harmonious with such a tradition. The Matthean messiahship of Jesus was the result of divine will, and no matter how ignominious his beginning, Jesus will still prevail.[79] For Matthew, this would be true even if he were the bastard son of a Roman soldier.

Luke also portrayed the illegitimacy tradition, but did so in a more obscure way.[80] The author of Luke made less of the potential scandal of Jesus' conception.[81] However, according to Schaberg, what prevents the concept of illegitimacy from coming through in Luke is a predisposition to read the gospels with the virginal conception presumed. The stories and traditions surrounding Mary's virgin motherhood are too pervasive not to have an effect on those reading the accounts. A truly unbiased reading can make no such conclusion. In Luke 1:46–55 (Mary's Magnificat or the Canticle of Mary), Mary expresses excitement to her relative Elizabeth over the impending birth of Jesus. This passage is only found in Luke. The first sentence has Mary proclaiming, "My soul extols the Lord and my spirit rejoices in God my Savior, for he has shown consideration for my lowly status" (Luke 1:46–48).[82] Schaberg finds no evidence in Luke to indicate that Mary's status was low in comparison to other women.[83] Elizabeth's previous statements concerning her prior barrenness and current pregnancy reveal that the conversation had a quasi-biological/sexual tone to it. Traditional interpretations find Mary's lowliness attributed to her humble Nazareth hometown, although the author of Luke made no such criticism of the city.[84] There was no reason for a betrothed virgin of Mary's station to express such humiliation. The context and the tenor of Mary's speech creates the possibility of her alluding to an illegitimate pregnancy through rape or adultery. Further, the Gospel of Luke's theme of exalting the outcasts of society—sinners, women, widows, Samaritans—gives this hypothesis even greater plausibility.[85]

What Schaberg has accomplished is a rereading of the gospels with an eye to the social violence historically perpetrated against women. She has brought to the surface a significant theme that has been hidden from view. The implication of her thesis includes a lowering of a purity-based high-Christology and a reduction of the alienation that women experience in comparison to the "Blessed Virgin Mary." According to this alternative history, the mother of Jesus was victimized as so many other women have been victimized. However, there is justice in the Christian drama because Mary is "redeemed" like no one else could ever be through giving birth to Jesus.

When Schaberg's analysis of Jesus' paternity and Ruether's work on Jesus' siblings, are overlayed upon the available historical data, the weight of evidence is that Mary's perpetual virginity is a mythic, albeit powerful, fiction. The only plausible portion of the myth is Mary's virginity *before* conceiving by the Holy Spirit. However, Schaberg's research recasts the father of Jesus as probably very human, although probably not the biblical Joseph. In the past, some Catholic theologians anticipated criticism from the lack of historical data. This was true even though they did not face the antivirgin evidence available today. They described Mary's virginity as *theologoumenon,* or religious truth, that cannot be supported with factual evidence.[86] A theologoumenon is a religious defense of last resort that essentially renders the topic a divine mystery, and therefore subject to no further debate.

The symbolism of Mary's virginity, regardless of its historical accuracy, is theologically potent. Through Mary, Christianity transformed a concept of virginity that was valued for economic "pure breeding" of women into a concept of ultimate religious significance. Mary's virginity revealed God's intervention into human history and the natural world, and began the process of salvation that was to end with the resurrection of Jesus. It also elevated the role of women by placing Mary at the center of Jesus' creation. The virgin conception, which was intended to focus upon Jesus, became focused on Mary. With the exception of Cybele, few Roman goddess precursors of Mary were characterized by virginity.[87] Mary was the unique virgin-mother creation of Christianity.

While Ruether and Schaberg provide examples of feminist alternative biblical exegesis, feminist historical criticism also debates the impact of ascetic virginity—as modeled by the Virgin Mary—upon women. From its beginning, Christianity embraced the ideal of virginity.[88] This connection between Christianity and asceticism went without formidable challenge for sixteen hundred years, until the Protestant reformation.[89] Early Christians linked purity, chastity, and virginity. Jesus and Paul are recorded as remaining unmarried for their entire lives and therefore they became the model of priestly celibacy.[90] In the belief that the second coming of Christ was at hand, Paul advocated celibacy but allowed marriage to temper the passions of the faithful (1 Corinthians 7:9). In philosophy and literature, the first centuries of Christianity found an increasing valorization of the virtue of *sophrosyne,* or self-control of the tongue, belly, and "the things below the belly."[91] For men, the institution of celibacy for the clerics of the church, and for women in both institutional and domestic virginity, provided an interesting continuity with what can be called quasi-masochism within the Christian tradition. As mentioned earlier, Michael Carroll provides one current theory surrounding the source of such asceticism. Using psychoanalysis, he finds "father-ineffective families" creating in some a strong, but strongly repressed, desire for mothers in sons. The need for self-punishment creates masochistic behavior. While this theory explains the behavior of men, it does not explain the masochistic behavior of women unless, in applying social construction theory, the male psyche had such a dominant control of the society that male guilt was imposed upon women. Alternatively, the fear of women because of their power to give birth may have led to a desire to control this danger by having priests and nuns avoid sex altogether.

Up to 313 C.E., as the Church was sometimes persecuted in the Roman Empire, Christians endeavored to achieve religious perfection by becoming martyrs. Approximately one hundred thousand Christians were martyred between 64 and 313.[92] Dying for one's beliefs emulated Christ's martyrdom. However, as the Christian religion became accepted and ultimately declared the state religion, Christians turned from being the receivers of sadistic torture and death to inflicting the torture upon themselves. The rise of asceticism in the fourth century allowed for a transfer of masochistic tendencies from martyrdom to sexual self-sacrifice. Subsequent centuries would find an increased number of crucifixions depicted in art and a parallel rise in the Cult of Mary.[93]

Self-denial and physical suffering were means for the faithful to right the wrongs of nature, or at least develop moral fiber by enduring a personal "cross." For women, virginity and self-inflicted hardships had the power to correct the faults of female nature (see Chapter Five). Nearly all the female martyrs were virgins, and the reason for their death was often so their chastity would be defended.[94]

Because woman's nature was considered flawed, one of the concepts in the early Christian valorization of female virginity was that virgins somehow became male.[95] Maleness was equated with the spiritual world and femaleness was identified with the material world and desire. Female virgins were described as "virile" and "manly." Furthermore, the implication of such a dualism was that when resurrected, the female body would take on its more perfect spiritual form—a male body.[96] The male body was normative and the female body, and her sexuality, a corruption. The conclusion of the *Gospel of Thomas* demonstrates this theme:

> Simon Peter said to them, "Make Mary leave us, for females don't deserve life."
>
> Jesus said, "Look, I will guide her to make her male, so that she too may become a living spirit resembling you males. For every female who makes herself male will enter the domain of Heaven."(114:1–3)[97]

Although scholars disagree as to which Mary is referred to here (Mary Magdalene; Mary Salome; Mary, the Mother of Jesus; or some other Mary), the concept of gender hierarchy is clear.[98]

St. Jerome and others viewed virginity as a step toward the glory of manhood:

> As long as a woman is for birth and children, she is different from man as body is from soul. But when she wishes to serve Christ more than the world, then she will cease to be a woman, and will be called a man. [99]

Church fathers, Clement of Alexandria, and Origen use the "becoming male" metaphor, particularly in reference to Ephesians 4:13. This passage, in discussing the diversity of gifts in the Church, describes the eventual attainment of the "perfect manhood" of all believers.[100] While virginity allowed women to gain social status, the drive for nonsexuality became a perverse effort to hide "femaleness." Besides virginity, women would also fast to the point of eliminating menstrual periods (amenorrhea)[101] and dress to diminish feminine attractiveness.[102]

In the *Odes to Solomon*, a first- or second-century collection of Christian hymns, male attribution is applied to Mary's delivery of Jesus: "She brought forth like a strong man with desire. . . ."[103] While the definitive interpretation of this passage is debatable, what is clear is that Mary is worthy of very high praise in being likened to a "strong man."

The collective literature that perpetuated the concept of female virginity as a means of becoming more like the superior male sex, fueled the growth of religious asceticism. In the fourth century, Athanasius and Ambrose portray the Virgin Mary as the model for women who consecrate themselves to virginity. She is described as modest, discrete, unacquainted with public places—a perfect example of the hidden life.[104]

Historian Elizabeth Clark and Rosemary Radford Ruether argue that, with Mary as the model, asceticism for women of the fourth century provided an empowering separatist lifestyle as an alternative to marriage.[105] While the ascetic lifestyle was quasi-masochistic in nature, it also provided an opportunity for the empowerment of women. Ascetic women who joined communities held a level of autonomy and authority that women in married life (and certainly the single life) did not hold. Education, travel, and political power were the positive aspects of monastic asceticism. Perhaps more important, these women were free from the health risks and pain of frequent childbearing that was the norm, for within marriage women could not deny their bodies to their husbands. Although contraception and abortion were practiced, they were unreliable and dangerous.[106] Virginity provided a level of personal freedom that married women did not enjoy.

Feminist scholars are not in agreement over the virtues of the ascetic lifestyle. Elizabeth Castelli questions the glamorization of fourth-century ascetic communities.[107] She produces evidence that the ideology of virginity was as stifling to women as marriage. Ascetic women who were religious were essentially asked to exchange their sexuality as a sign of worldly renunciation. Castelli finds this exchange concept in two significant phenomena. One is the widely used description of virgins as the "brides of Christ." This title belies the fact that virginity represented the same kind of exchange of goods that existed in nuptial agreements. Instead of having a woman's virginity, which represented a clean, untouched product, transferred from father to husband, the virginity was given over to Christ. This relationship went so far as to have women in religious communities who lost their virginities described as adulteresses. The second significant example presented by Castelli is the historical issue of virgins committing suicide prior to being raped. Church fathers Ambrose and John Chrysostom argued that these suicides did not constitute a sin because of the value of what these women tried to protect—virginity was a valued commodity.[108] Mary was the virgin *par excellence* who provided the ultimate religious legitimation for Christian women accepting the ascetic life.

Moral Considerations

There are three interrelated feminist concerns about Mary's sexuality within the context of Catholic moral theology: the perpetuation of compulsory heterosexuality, the valorization of virginity, and the denigration of female sexuality. Why has the momentum for the myth of her perpetual virginity been such an enduring part of Catholicism? The presupposition of such a question is that Mary's sexuality was socially constructed, which the historical evidence makes abundantly clear. Sexuality is an area of the human condition that lends itself exceedingly well to social interpretation. Feminist scholars have adopted the work of Michel Foucault and others to counter psychological claims that sex is a personal or natural force that must break through repression.[109] Sexuality is a social phenomenon whose organization and meanings differ by culture and era. What Christianity accomplished was to lock in a particular sexual value system that emerged from the early centuries of the Church. Out of plurality, a singular perspective on sex became sanctified and reified. This perspective reflected biological misunderstandings, misogyny, and the fear of the female. The popularity and influence of Christianity, combined with the Church's intolerance for change, allowed that particular view of sex to dominate Western civilization until the present. Religion was the significant impetus for this sexual understanding because it could call upon a court of ultimate authority—an all-powerful God. Mary, particularly for women, was the torch-bearer for Christian sexuality. Feminist Theologian Catharina Halkes reiterates the central position of Mary in Catholic sexual morality:

> I would venture the hypothesis that by the figure of Mary more than any other it is possible to demonstrate how *ambivalent* the church and its theologians have been about human sexuality, and especially about the *sexuality of women* [emphasis hers].[110]

Mary was blessed amongst all women. She was the means for God's intervention in human history. Mary was the vessel for salvation, so of course her way of life, including her virgin-motherhood, was the model for all women.

The Cult of Mary is not only indicative of Catholic negation and mistrust of sexuality,[111] but it is also exemplary of a form of social control sometimes referred to as "compulsory heterosexuality." Mary's virginity and motherhood (and therefore heterosexuality) are consistently linked in descriptive texts. Although virginity is presented as the superior lifestyle, women are reduced to having just two options: marriage or virginity. A woman's life is therefore morally licit only if one becomes like a male (virginity) or submits to a man through marriage. The underlying message is that maleness is so desirable that women either wish to emulate it or be at one with it through sex. John Paul II explicitly made this connection in what he described as the "spousal order."

> In the teaching of Christ, *motherhood is connected with virginity*, but also *distinct from it*. . . . *Mary* is the first person in whom this *new awareness* is manifested. . . . On the basis of the Gospel, the meaning of virginity was developed and better understood as a vocation for women too, one in which their dignity, like that of the Virgin of Nazareth, finds confirmation . . . In this wider context, *virginity* has to be considered *also as a path for women,* a path on which they realize their womanhood in a way different from marriage. . . . By freely choosing virginity, women confirm themselves as persons. . . . *One cannot correctly understand virginity*—a women's consecration in virginity—*without referring to spousal love* . . . The naturally spousal predisposition of the feminine personality finds a response in virginity understood in this way. . . . This is the evangelical ideal of virginity, in which both the dignity and the vocation of women are realized in a special way. . . . This cannot be compared to remaining simply unmarried or single, because virginity is not restricted to a mere "no," but contains a profound "yes" in the spousal order: the gift of self love in a total and undivided manner. [emphasis his][112]

The Pope used the language of "distinctive feminine nature" to justify two truly holy choices for women: marriage and virginity.[113] However, both options are "spousal" because virginity is a type of marriage to the

Church (and/or Jesus). Mary's virgin-motherhood makes her unique, but she can be "normalized and sanctified as wife."[114] The Christian god is now clearly identified as the god of heterosexuality and Mary as his bride. Heterosexuality is normative, even for those who abstain from sex. The pontiff has assimilated Mary's virginal life into a symbol of natural heterosexuality.

The Catholic tradition of natural law makes possible this theological interpretation of sexuality. According to this tradition, heterosexuality is, of course, normative because the ultimate purpose of the sexual organs is reproduction. Any other type of sexual activity is illicit because it violates the natural order. The natural-law argument is used to ascribe essential natures to women. "The natural spousal disposition of women" is a phrase in a long tradition of attributing certain characteristics to women. According to feminists, these attributes have ultimately served to oppress.[115] In this context, women are characterized by the need for a consecrated relationship with a man. Mary Hunt describes a prevailing moral acceptability of women in a hierarchy of heterosexual contexts:

> The Virgin Mary is the paragon of virtue. After her, all women fall in the following descending order:
>> A married woman sleeps with a man.
>> A widow did until her husband died.
>> A separated woman might again.
>> A divorced woman used to sleep with a man.
>> A single woman wants to do so.
>> A prostitute does it for a man's money.
>> A lesbian does not sleep with a man.
>> A nun can't talk about it.[116]

In each of the above cases the woman is defined by her relationship, or lack of relationship, with a man. The language of exclusive heterosexuality negates the possibility of viewing a woman's choice of virginity as an independent act demonstrating self-reliance. Mary is not just a virgin, she is a virgin-mother. A nonsexual and nonrelational lifestyle, virginity becomes part of the reification of heterosexuality.

Feminists criticize the imposition of heterosexuality upon Mary's virginity as divisive. Schussler Fiorenza describes Mary's virginal motherhood as having two detrimental effects upon women. One effect is the perpetuation of the body-soul dualism that serves to undermine the equality of the sexes. By fixating on motherhood as the essence of women the body becomes the sphere of women, while the mind and reason are the sphere of men. Therefore, a sexual stratification becomes entrenched in the Christian consciousness. The essentialism that gener-alizes a biological difference into a gendered ontological dualism has been a long-standing means of excluding women from theological, political, and intellectual endeavors (witness the dearth of recognized women theologians and philosophers prior to the modern era).[117]

The second detrimental effect of Mary's virgin-motherhood described by Schussler Fiorenza is the stratification of women within the Catholic tradition. The valorization of religious virginity over motherhood divides Catholic women. According to Schussler Fiorenza, any feminist revision of Catholicism must work to eliminate the sexual stratification that divides women from women and women from men.[118]

Historically, sexual stratification has translated into patriarchal subju-gation of women. Adrienne Rich describes heterosexuality as the historic means of insuring male domination over women.[119] In this understand-ing, heterosexuality is a sexual orientation for members of the opposite sex and symbolic of an orientation for the primacy of males. Rich's underlying psychology finds both males and females initially attracted to their mothers because of their mother's role as primary caretakers. Love, tenderness, and care have been historically associated with women. According to Rich, despite the original attachment to the mother, at some point women are re-oriented to be attracted to men. Because such a reorientation is not "natural," men must use coercion in the form of social taboos, rape, and religious sanction to maintain the preeminence of heterosexuality and in turn maintain male dominance. Rich concludes that through exclusionary heterosexuality, men maintain their political, economic, and sexual control.

Denise Lardner Carmody finds a pattern of patriarchal control through sexual control throughout religious mythology, which resurfaces in the concept of Mary's virginity. Carmody attributes the need for control to men's deep-seated psychological fears.

> If women were to control sexual relations, anything might happen. Male desire, already so difficult to control, might break out in a dozen fearsome directions. Sexed into submission, men might never regain their dominant position, and without their dominant posi-tion, they would not know who they were. Faced with the prospect of a dominant other sex, or even a simply equal other sex, they could well crack up, fall into psychic crisis.[120]

Because men hold dominant positions in society, their fears could be institutionalized in areas such as religion. Mary became a projection of male sexual neurosis. She had nothing to do with sexual desires as a virgin mother and was therefore above what men feared most about themselves. The Cult of Mary is a veritable Trojan horse for women's sexual expression. Women can identify with her because of shared gender, and they can feel empowered because Mary is elevated to quasi-divine status. However, she ultimately panders to male domination, particularly in her sexuality.

Many women have argued that authentic woman's liberation will only come when women can truly make free lifestyle choices. The control of birthing through contraception has evolved to a point at which women can make career/family decisions. However, the choice of mate gender (as well as the choice to live outside of a relationship) is still socially restricted and made more difficult by religious norms. Mary fuels homophobia by becoming the icon of male-dominated sexuality. The myth of the virgin birth of Jesus reflects the victory of spirit over matter, or male nature over female nature. Mary Daly describes the virginal conception as a retelling of ancient stories of the rape of the Goddess. Mary is "the Total Rape Victim," having conceived in a manner beyond physical invasion. Daly describes Mary as utterly compliant because her male-projected construction removes any possibility for violation. "Physical rape is not necessary when the mind/will/spirit has already been invaded." [121] God is not the perpetrator of this rape. In the process of Mary's sexual construction, it is the myth-makers who are the true rapists.

One of the arguments for a woman's right to a legal abortion is the right of autonomy or control over the body.[122] The tradition of Mary's conception and birth of Jesus depicts Mary as having little control over her body. She does not engage in sexual activity to conceive. The tradition of Mary's lack of pain in childbirth contains little imagery of her involvement in the contractions or spasms of the birthing process. In fact, the most common theological language to describe Mary's involvement in childbirth is as "vessel of the Christ." Mary's passive existence is in direct contrast to the values of the modern feminist movement that stress women's experience, passion, activism, and embodiment.

Uta Ranke-Heinemann, who claims to have lost her academic chair in New Testament and Ancient Church History at the University of Essen, West Germany, because she taught that the virgin birth of Jesus was a theological rather than a biological phenomenon, declares that the concept of a virgin birth robs Mary of her motherhood. Mary is completely divorced from the experience of women in the pain and joy of birth.[123] While this separates her from all other women—'Alone of all her sex'—she is not left as an anomaly of humanity but is elevated in Catholic dogma as a model of womanhood.[124] It is this very integration of that which is fantastic and that which is exemplary that creates the impossible for women. It is the combination of the nonhuman with the superhuman while attempting to label the combination as a model of behavior. Ranke-Heinemann finds the sexual distortion of Mary as part of a self-perpetuating cycle of oppression. An insecure clergy zealously promotes a Marian cult of true womanhood that helps legitimize virginity and therefore its own celibacy.

Ruether takes this analysis one step further and makes the connection between the virginal Mary and the Catholic understanding of the kingdom of heaven.

> Male eschatology is built on negation of the mother . . . antisexual asceticism is itself based on the fantasy that, by escaping the female realm of sexuality and procreation, one can also free oneself from finitude and mortality. . . . The doctrine of the Assumption of Mary symbolizes the Church triumphant, ascended to Heaven and seated at the right hand of Christ. . . . Mariology becomes a tool of ecclesiastical triumphalism.[125]

In Ruether's perspective, patriarchal concepts of sex and death are linked, and Mary, as the Virgin who ascended uncorrupted into heaven, has overcome both of these aspects of life. Therefore, faith in Mary takes on an immortalizing quality. In Ruether's perspective, the male hierarchy of the Church symbolically sacrifices women through Mariology to obtain immortality.

Implications of the "Virgin" Mary

Marian imagery reflects the pattern and direction of Catholic sexual morality particularly as it effects women. Because Mary's tradition is so uniquely Catholic, critiques of Mary can be closely identified with critiques of official Catholic teaching. The Catholic hierarchy's espoused defense and devotion to Mary creates the tension discussed in Chapter Two that finds the Church declaring equality of the sexes while continuing patterns of discrimination. The Church hierarchy's isolation from women heightens misunderstanding and facilitates a very narrow concept of what the feminine should be. However, the misunderstanding is not between equals, and the hierarchy determines official legitimations of sexuality. Ethicist Beverly Harrison finds a critical connection between the treatment of women and the Church's sexual morality,

> Nothing is more critical at the present moment than for the domi-
> nant traditions in Christianity to recognize and begin making the
> connections between the dehumanizing and patriarchal attitudes
> toward women and our present ideological entrapment toward
> human sexuality.[126]

Harrison, like many feminist scholars, finds the Church's narrow definition of sexual legitimacy to be complicit in the oppression of women. For
example, Harrison speculates that the Church's perspective on women
and homosexuality are linked in a cycle of repression. Compulsory
heterosexuality, she argues, forces many homosexual clergy to hide their
sexuality and redirect their anxiety, and the church's oppression, against
women. As Harrison observes, secrecy and hypocrisy are the only options
for homosexual clergy, creating moral dilemmas that are divisive and hurt-
ful. Catholicism, like other Christian denominations, fails to view homophobia as a serious social problem. Although sensitivity is growing, the
underlying message of religious language, such as is found in the Cult of
Mary, perpetuates exclusive heterosexuality.

Daly, Ruether, and others are critical of the fact that the Catholic hierarchy has used Mary as a tool in an effort to vilify human sexuality.
Women's liberation from traditional sex/gender systems has allowed for
the rediscovery of sexuality as a source of strength. Audre Lorde describes
the erotic as power. She characterizes the inversion that has historically
taken place as women were taught to suppress their sexuality and place it
in the service of men, or, in the case of Catholicism, place their sexuality
in the service of reproduction. Women should not know "carnal" pleasures, since the greatest woman of all time did not know such pleasures.
This is an inversion, according to Lorde, because the erotic is actually
powerful. Men have traditionally distorted the erotic and associated it with
pornography. However, the erotic resides at the depth of women's experience as a "replenishing and provocative force to the woman who does not
fear its revelation, nor succumb to the belief that sensation is enough."[127]
Theologian Carter Heyward not only describes the erotic as power, but as
the power and love of God.[128] She specifically wishes to bridge the dualism that exists in Western Christianity between sexuality and the divine.[129]
Heyward recognizes that the acceptance of her proposition would involve
"institutional transformation."[130] Although Heyward's project is not

directed at Mariology specifically, it is clear that she is part of a feminist movement to legitimize and celebrate sexuality in broader terms than found in the Catholic tradition. The language and direction of this recognition of sexuality as power is anathema to Marian imagery. The Cult of Mary has no resource to tap into sexual power.

Michael Carroll finds Mary's nonsexuality essential to the popular perception of her cult. He argues that it is necessary for Mary to be a sexless historical reality, not just a symbol, so that men may project their confused, psychologically developed maternal emotions upon her.[131] Men desire a real maternal goddess, but because they do not want to overstep oedipal barriers this goddess must be sexless. The psychological under-pinnings of the Cult of Mary only clarify why the struggle to control her is intensifying as women extend their power and influence in the world. A celibate male member of the church hierarchy who ostensibly has only had intimate relationships with his mother may perpetuate a historically virgin Mary as a safe object of desire. When Mary is elevated to the model of womanhood, it is damaging to all women. A Christian feminism strug-gling for reproductive rights, feminist spirituality, sexual legitimacy, and freedom collides with the trajectory of the Cult of the Virgin Mary.

Mary's unique heterosexual, perpetual virginity supports the Church's present position on sexual morality, which is abundantly clear and consis-tent through numerous pronouncements on the subject:

> *Sex outside of marriage is a sin.* ". . . every genital act must be within the framework of marriage."[132]

> *Sex that is not both physically and psychologically unifying for the couple, as well as open to the possibility of procreation, is a sin.* Thus masturba-tion and oral sex are a sin. ". . . masturbation constitutes a grave moral disorder. . . ."[133]

> *Artificial contraception is wrong.* "The Church is coherent with herself when she considers recourse to the infecund periods to be licit while at the same time considering as being always illicit, the use of means directly contrary to fecundation, even if such use is inspired by reasons which appear honest and serious."[134]

> *Only celibate males may participate in the hierarchy of the church.* "Through virginity or celibacy observed for the sake of the king-dom of heaven, priests are consecrated to Christ in a new and distin-guished way."[135]

> *Homosexual acts are wrong.* ". . . homosexual acts are intrinsically disordered and can in no case be approved of."[136]

This litany of approbations is a well-known aspect of Catholicism because the Church so vehemently defends its position in public. John Philips detects an underlying fear in the Church's defensiveness against feminist calls for greater sexual autonomy.

> It is fascinating to note that the notion of virgin motherhood remains as the mythical backdrop for modern moral battles of feminists. The Roman Catholic belief is that if women have control over their own bodies and are therefore free to abort potential offspring, they have reversed the triumph of the Virgin Mary over the ancient goddesses; sexual freedom is a threat to life.[137]

Mary is the Catholic icon of entrenched sexual morality. The events surrounding the Second Vatican Council, and the subsequent papal pronouncement of the encyclical *Humanae Vitae,* indicate how intransigent the Church has been on sexual matters.[138] Today, theologians who argue that sexual issues are not at the "core" of the Catholic faith, and thus subject to informed debate, become the subject of "creeping infallibility" and are often punished if they are within ecclesial authority.

The Catholic formulation of doctrine allowed the Church to develop and maintain a belief in Mary's perpetual virginity that would not have been possible (or desired) in Protestantism. Because Catholicism holds that God's revelation can have multiple sources—the bible, tradition, and experience—nonbiblical phenomena can be legitimated as divine revelation. A 1973 Pastoral Letter by the U.S. National Conference of Catholic Bishops declares:

> This teaching about Mary's lifelong virginity is an example of the Church's growth in understanding of Christian doctrine. In its ordinary teaching, reflected in catechesis and liturgy, as well as in more formal pronouncements, the Church has here recognized as an aspect of "public revelation" a belief not clearly demonstrable from the Scriptures.[139]

The primacy of scripture in Protestant concepts of revelation negates the role of tradition. In a sense, the role of tradition in theology gave the Catholic Church a license to socially construct reality. Such a dual source for revelation might give the appearance that the Church could be flexible in its theology. Not strictly tied to scripture, Catholics could find other sources of truth that are not historically culture-bound and are thus more responsive to social development. In some cases this has been true—for example, in Catholic development of doctrines on war, racism, and economics, which are foreign to the biblical revelation except by implication. However, regarding sexuality, the Church is even more restrictive than the gospels would suggest (for example, in extolling the virtues of virginity.)[140] Protestantism has not been as involved in interpreting tradition, and therefore has been less uniform in its sexual restrictions. Most mainstream Protestant denominations did not valorize virginity. Methodologically, Mary's virginity and the Church's sexual morality are uniquely possible because of the way Catholic tradition has constructed religious reality.

In analyzing the factions of the Church described in the second chapter as they relate to matters of sexual morality, the difference in consciousness becomes apparent. For example, Catholics in the United States do not differ significantly from the general population in their use of artificial contraception. Nevertheless, the hierarchy remains entrenched against this. Among theologians, all but the very conservative have argued that the Church's position should be revised.

Social views on sexuality have developed a great deal since the days of the early Church. One reason for the change is the reduction of influence that religion holds in the modern world. Nevertheless, it would be naive to claim that religion does not continue to influence popular understanding of sex. Mary's influence on sexual morality within Catholicism varies depending upon which segment is considered.

While many Catholics would like to believe that the Church teachings on Mary and the valorization of virginity have changed, official Church documents and statements demonstrate an enduring dedication to the nonsexual life over and above married life. In a paragraph from *The Dogmatic Constitution of The Church,* directed toward individuals who are not members of religious orders, the Bishops extol the spiritual dedication of a chaste lifestyle:

> The holiness of the Church is also fostered in a special way by the observance of the manifold counsels proposed in the gospel by our Lord to His disciples. Outstanding among them is that precious gift of divine grace which the Father gives to some men so that by virginity, or celibacy, they can more easily devote their entire selves to God alone with undivided heart. This total continence embraced on behalf of the kingdom of heaven has always been held in particular honor by the Church a being a sign of charity and stimulus towards it, as well as a unique fountain of spiritual fertility in the world.[141]

This passage is found in Chapter Four, titled "The Call of the Whole

Church to Holiness." While this chapter has a paragraph dedicated to married couples, there is no parallel indicating "particular honor" associated with marriage. Even when the Church is attempting to be egalitarian in its description of the lives of grace, the underlying bias is clear: Virginity is superior to any sexual activity, even within marriage.

Pope John Paul II has been even more explicit than the Bishops of the Second Vatican Council in upholding the value of virginity over and above marital sex:

> Virginity or celibacy, by liberating the human heart in a unique way, "so as to make it burn with greater love for God and all humanity," bears witness that the Kingdom of God and his justice is that pearl of great price which is preferred to every other value no matter how great, and hence must be sought as the only definitive value. It is for this reason that the Church, throughout her history, has always defended the superiority of this charism to that of marriage, by reason of the wholly singular link which it has with the kingdom of God.[142]

Ironically, this statement was made in a document on family life! Recall that this highly exclusive statement emanates from a pontiff who is radically dedicated to Mary. Orthodox Mariology only confirms the Catholic hierarchy's negative view of sex. In Church documents, Mary is continually referred to as ever-virgin and a model for all believers.

In words and actions, there appears to be a defensiveness associated with celibacy among the leadership of the Church. It is the line of demarcation for the faithful that does not indicate difference between equals, but rather a closer proximity to salvation, divinity, and its associated earthly power. This gendered sexual hierarchy, for which Mary is invoked, is the primary recipient of feminist critique. Ruether illustrates this criticism:

> Celibate males are the primary powerholders of the Church. They represent the "male feminine" in the hands of antiprocreative males. Female virgins are marginalized as humble servants of the male celibate control over the "spiritual feminine." After all, they are still female and potentially sexual. Married couples become a lower case in the Church. Within the "laity" women are at the bottom of the ladder. They are lower than slaves (whose subjugation is merely historical not cosmological) and tend toward the demonic. So it is not contradictory, but understandable, that a male celibate culture that exalted the symbol of the "spiritual feminine," as Mary and Mater Ecclesia, almost to the status of the divine vilified and demonized the sexual and maternal roles of real women.[143]

A more sophisticated laity makes rigid sexual morality difficult for Church officials to impose. For Catholics, Mary's virginity is a form of indirect advertising. The language of Mary's perpetual virginity is present at liturgies and the myths and stories Catholics grow up with as they learn about their religion. The message that exists as a constant whisper is that virgins are good and sex is bad.[144] No priest's homily would make such a bald statement, but the underlying tone is clear.

For Catholics, the sexual standards lead to alienation or rationalization. Many Catholics simply disregard tradition and teaching (e.g. by using contraception) but refuse to give up their Church. Other Catholics either leave the Church or form alternative communities (such as Dignity, an organization for homosexual Catholics). In either case, lay Catholics are forced to disengage themselves to some extent from their tradition.

Modern Catholics suffer dearly because of the Church's position on sexuality. Members of the faith community are often faced with the dilemma of choosing between following their Church's teaching and sexual activity. Mary is a constant reminder—on the dashboard, in Grandma's garden grotto, as Church statuary—of Catholic sexual morality. As serious as the implications of these dilemmas are for family economics, relationships, and psychological well-being, the Church's narrow view of sex has social implications as well.

As demonstrated at the 1994 United Nations conference on population in Cairo, the Catholic Church will not achieve credibility as a moral force for ecological consciousness until it alters its stance on contraception. Overpopulation affects the health of world ecology. The calls for the Church to change its position on the artificial/natural distinction of birth control are growing more numerous.[145] Increasingly, poverty and overpopulation in predominantly Catholic third world countries are blamed, in part, on the Church's influence.[146] Superficially, Mary's virginity appears to be a potential model for population control. However, the deep seated support for Catholic sexual orthodoxy negates this possibility. Mary is nonsexual but not nonprocreative.

The priesthood, which is the laity's primary contact with ecclesial authority and the key source of pastoral ministry, is undergoing a tremendous loss of credibility because of dysfunctional sexuality.[147] The number of cases of reported sex crimes committed by priests is on the rise in the United States. This crisis has caused a great deal of discussion within the Church. One constant source of debate is the necessity of a single sexual lifestyle for priestly positions in the Catholic Church. The relationship of a celibate priesthood and sexually dysfunctional behavior is unclear. However, the priesthood does not reflect a cross-section of lifestyles found in the general population, and therefore must come under scrutiny. While the hierarchy of the Catholic Church considers alternative lifestyles for priests a moot point, the consciousness of modern Catholics has risen to the point of opening debate. While Mary cannot be considered the reason for the sex offenses of priests, she is the primary symbol of the extreme celibate lifestyle and "the model of the faith."

Perhaps a new theology of Marian sexuality should begin with an expansion of the meaning of virginity beyond its purely physical sense. Feminism has effectively explored and recovered the meaning of words in the process of naming sexism in society, and the Catholic concept of virginity appears in need of such reconstruction. The etymology of the word "virgin" demonstrates how Mariology altered the ancient meaning of this world. John Phillips explains:

> Certainly at one time the word connoted strength and self-sufficiency, which suggested unlimited sexual activity. The idea was that having a harem of male divinities as consorts, virgin goddesses who so frequently incurred the wrath of the Old Testament prophets engaged in their sexual activity in ritual emulation of their divine patronesses. To be virgin was to be thus religiously dedicated, and therefore a cult prostitute. Such—ironically—is the history of the word.[148]

Recovering the original meaning of the word "virgin" may be an empowering exercise for women who wish to reclaim the Virgin Mary as Model.[149] Catharina Halkes undertakes this reclamation of virginity by associating it with "integrity."

> *Virginity*, as an attitude of being open and available to the divine mystery, to the voice and power of the spirit in us; from this we learn to live from our own centre, our own roots, in independence, and not in a one-sided and alienating dependence. Thus in my view virginity denotes more a human attitude than compulsory abstinence. Virginity in the sense of "integrity," of the inviolability of one's own body, can be a powerful influence for women to offer resistance to sexual excess and male marginalization and violation.[150]

Mary Daly finds it ironic that Mary's virginity, a state of non-relationality, is interpreted by theologians in a purely relational manner.[151] Mary's virginity only gains theological significance because it makes a statement about Jesus. Daly sees new meaning in the virgin birth if the overwhelming filter of Christocentrism can be removed. She finds the idea of a virgin mother has much to say about female autonomy. Mary can be seen as a model for relational and sexual independence in a parthenogenic fashion. No man was needed for Mary to bring divine intervention into the world—or to create life.

Feminist analysis, such as Daly's, has presented serious challenges to the dogma of Mary's virginity and its position at the zenith of human sexuality. However, deconstructing Mary's virginity only leaves a void that requires imagery to recapture religious imagination in the present social setting. A number of themes have emerged in feminist writings that would be significant in revitalized Marian imagery.

1. Greater sexual inclusiveness.
2. The valorization of female friendships.
3. The move from rigid biological definitions to empowering symbolism.
4. An emphasizes on the goodness of sexuality.

While there is no consensus for what constitutes a Christian feminist sexual ethic, these themes appear to elicit support. The traditional imagery of Mary runs counter to each of these themes. Mary perpetuates the exclusive value of heterosexuality even while denigrating sexuality altogether. Her imagery focuses on motherhood, not friendships. Her virginity is meticulously biological in its definition. The Virgin Mary demonstrates the evil of sexuality.

Mary's nonsexual imagery remains the ultimate model of alienation for Catholic women. According to the tradition, Mary is almost vaporous in her nonsexuality and nonsensuality. She is portrayed as not enjoying sexual pleasure in the conception of Jesus nor feeling the pain of childbirth. She does not have sexual intimacy with her husband in their married life. Through the doctrine of the Assumption, Mary does not even experience bodily corruption after death. The pronoun "she" hardly seems appropriate for Mary, because Catholic tradition creates a Mary who is nonhuman and nonfemale. Nevertheless, proclaimed as the zenith of womanhood, the "plastic" Mary is used to derogate the ordinary lives of women who experience pain, feel pleasure, and love passionately.

4

Mary, the Mediatrix and Asymmetrical Gender Power

> This power [of Mary in human imagination] has been operative despite all
> the efforts to tame and domesticate it—despite the simpering plaster
> statues, the saccharine prayers, sermons, poems, and hymns, and the sexist
> theology that has "explained" it.
>
> —Mary Daly[1]

> Mary is on the side of the poor and dispossessed. She can get people
> whom God has assigned to Hell into Heaven. She alone can force God to
> do what she wants; she can as it were, twist his arm because of her holiness
> and specially privileged position.
>
> —Karen Armstrong[2]

Mary's role as the great intercessor or mediatrix[3] in Catholic theology
demonstrates the ambiguity that exists in the Church regarding the ontological stature attributed to women. Is Mary the "Queen of Heaven" or
the humble "handmaiden of the Lord"? The answer is that she is both—
and neither. Mary's religious power is typical of the contradiction associated with this virgin-mother. In a parallel manner, Christian women also
find themselves at the center of the contradiction. Church authorities
state that women possess human dignity equal to that of men, yet they
are given no ecclesial power. Although Paul declares that there is "neither
male nor female" (Gal. 3:38) in the body of Christ, almost two thousand
years later, women still are not ordained to the priesthood and therefore
do not participate in Church governance. Women, and their divine
reflection, Mary, hold ambiguous, and thus confusing, stature within the
Roman Catholic Church. This chapter explores the relative nature of
Mary's power. Initially, the historical basis for Mary's role as mediatrix will
be presented. Derivative issues of Marian imagery that relate to power,

such as Christian goddess worship, women's ordination and Christian parenting relationships, will be explored.

The revelation of God is usually not a direct personal experience, so the principle of mediation is fundamental to the Catholic Church. Because God is infinite and humans are finite, the experience of God's self-disclosure must be mediated. In the spiritual life of most Catholics, the Church, and specifically the parish priest, is the primary mediator of God's revelation. The principle of communion is significant and related to mediation.[4] The Church is broadly defined as a communion of saints, both living and deceased, through which the Holy Spirit and grace flow. God's revelation is mediated by the Church and experienced communally. Therefore, within Catholicism, prayers directed to someone other than God are not considered polytheistic because they seek communal support and mediation to the one true God. Because of the trinitarian nature of Catholic theology, prayers directed to Jesus equate to prayers directed to God. Jesus is God. Therefore, Jesus is considered the perfect mediator in light of his divine and human nature. Despite this theological logic as to Jesus' role as the perfect mediator, Mary has historically been the primary recipient of intercessory prayers and devotion. Mary became known as "Queen of the Underworld" in her capacity to save the souls of the dead.[5] The significance of Mary's role in mediation, and its ethical implications for women, will be the focus of this chapter.

The distinction between *mediation* and *intercession* elucidates the spectrum of super-human power associated with Mary. As mentioned, mediation is a fundamental principle of Catholicism as well as Protestantism. However, it is more broadly understood in Catholicism as a cascading flow of divine power. Mary as a "mediator" of God's revelation in the world is actually understood to hold a relatively passive role. She is a vessel of God's will. Any praise for this role reflects praise for God's intervention in humanity and perhaps for Mary's assent to participate in God's incarnation. Historically the title, "mediator" has been more easily bestowed on Mary by Church theologians when it was understood in the perspective of this passive participation.[6] Although intercession is related to mediation, intercession represents a more active process. It is Mary's intercession that blurs the distinction between her divinity and humanity. Even though she has not officially been declared a goddess, it is part of popular belief that Mary can intercede or act on behalf of those who ask. Intercession, in the form of answering the prayers of the faithful, is a much more personal concept, while mediation, in the form of intervening between God and humanity, is a more theological concept.

The historical evolution of Mary's mediation reveals that theologians originated a discussion of Mary as Mediatrix in the context of Christological incarnation, while the faithful called for a personal intercessor to whom to plead their case. The two concepts become mingled as part of Mary's complex character. The result is a powerful popular intercessor with suspicious and inconsistent support from the hierarchy.

The Historical Construction of Mary as Mediatrix

Three sources have perpetuated the concept of Mary's mediatory powers. The first is a biblical apologetic for Marian mediation, although it is a tenuous defense. The second source is the religious construction of tradition characteristic of Catholicism. Finally, there is the ongoing phenomenon of apparitions. Each of these sources will be briefly considered to demonstrate the dynamics that support modern belief in Marian religious power.

Biblical Sources

It is difficult to find an extensive biblical basis for Mary's role as mediator. Traditionally, the story of the wedding feast at Cana found in John 2:1–11 has been interpreted to imply Mary's influence over Jesus.

> Three days later there was a wedding at Cana in Galilee. Jesus' mother was there. Jesus was also invited to the wedding along with his disciples. When the wine had run out, Jesus' mother says to him, "they're out of wine."
>
> Jesus replies to her, "Woman, what is it with you and me? It's not my time yet."
>
> His mother says to the servants, "Whatever he tells you, do it."
>
> Six stone water-jars were standing there—for use in the Jewish rite of purification—and each could hold twenty or thirty gallons.
>
> "Fill the jars with water," Jesus tells them.
>
> So they filled them to the brim.
>
> Then he tells them, "Now dip some out and take it to the caterer."
>
> And they did so. When the caterer tasted the water, now changed into wine—he had no idea where it had come from, even though the servants who had taken the water out knew—he calls the groom aside and says to him, "everyone serves the best wine first and only later, when people are drunk, the cheaper wine. But you've held back the good wine till now."
>
> Jesus performed this miracle, the first, at Cana in Galilee; it displayed his majesty, and his disciples believed in him.

This passage, found only in John, is the single recorded conversation in the bible between Jesus and Mary. The conversation is rather impersonal, consisting mostly of a series of commands.

Raymond Brown reveals some of the historical difficulties with this pericope. First, the miracle appears geographically and socially out of context. It is performed by Jesus in his homeland among friends and family. These characteristics run counter to the synoptic tradition of Jesus' ministry, in which his miracles are performed in foreign territories and among strangers. Second, the miracle is the only one in the Christian scriptures that Jesus performs on a nonperson and for the sake of convenience. Third, there is the difficult dialogue between Jesus and Mary. Jesus appears to rebuke Mary, although he performs the miracle.[7] For Brown, these difficulties raise a concern over the historical nature of the entire Cana passage. Regardless of the factual content, the intent of the author appears to have been Christological rather than Mariological. The theme of the "hour" of Jesus and the metaphor of Jesus' ministry as new wine are significant to his ministry and message.[8] Despite the passage's Christological focus, the author specifically names Mary as an important character in this scene.

Many theologians and popes have used the Cana story as a biblical foundation for Mary's mediation.[9] As a mother, she had power over her son, even when he did not wish to comply. Mary made Jesus perform his first miracle against his better judgment, and she could therefore persuade Jesus to judge sinners kindly. Modern biblical scholars, such as Brown and Pheme Perkins, reject this interpretation.[10] Perkins concludes that in the Cana story, Mary is considered one of the disciples rather than a maternal figure.[11] Nevertheless, Mary has often been viewed as the protagonist in this passage. A few modern examples will demonstrate this perspective. In 1947, Pope Leo XIII stated,

> The grace of Christ comes to us through the Mother of Christ. She in fact "Sumens illud Ave Gabrielis ore," who greeted her as full of grace, became at the same time Mother of Christ and Mother of divine grace. The maternal office of "Mediatress" really began at the very moment of her consent to the Incarnation; it was manifested for the first time by the first sign of Christ's grace, at Cana in Galilee; from that moment it rapidly spread down through the ages with the growth of the Church.[12]

Popular television evangelist Archbishop Fulton J. Sheen represented the Church's position in the 1950's and 1960's, when he interpreted the wedding feast of Cana as a sign that Mary's motherhood was the essence of her ability to influence Jesus.

> It was not a personal request; she was already a mediatrix for all who were seeking the fullness of joy. She has never been just a spectator, but a full participant willingly involving herself in the needs of others. The mother used the special power which she had as a mother over her Son, a power generated by mutual love.[13]

Interpreting the story of the feast of Cana, Pope John Paul II in his encyclical *The Mother of the Redeemer* attempted to balance Mariology and Christology. He proclaimed that Mary did indeed intercede at Cana, but the Pope placed this intercession in the context of Jesus' mission.

> At Cana in Galilee there is shown only one concrete aspect of human need, apparently a small one and of little importance ("They have no wine"). But it has symbolic value: this coming to the aid of human needs means, at the same time, bringing those needs within the radius of Christ's messianic power. Thus there is mediation. . . . At Cana, thanks to the intercession of Mary and the obedience of the servants, Jesus begins "his hour."[14]

Recent application of historical critical methods to biblical passages (including the previously mentioned analysis of Raymond Brown) has diminished the interpretation of the Cana story as the paradigm for Marian mediation in Catholicism.

The Mediatrix in Tradition

Outside of biblical sources, the belief in Mary's mediation takes on a life of its own in the history of the Church. Within the Catholic tradition, the origin of Mary's role as mediator is more ambiguous than that of her characteristic virginity. The lack of canonical and non-canonical testimony, in addition to the dichotomy between the practices and beliefs of common believers and the pronouncements of religious leaders, likely played a role in this ambiguity. The title "Mary, the Mediatrix" developed in the Eastern Church, which had more zealously embraced Mary in literature and preaching. The Western Church was more concerned with Mary's perpetual virginity.[15] Mary's mediation was originally associated with her role as the Mother of Jesus, the incarnation of God.[16] Because Jesus was the source of human salvation and Mary was his mother, she brought forth, or mediated, the Christian salvific force in the world.

In the fourth century, St. Ephraem of Syria foreshadows widespread belief in Marian mediation in his hymn devoted to her: "I call upon you, Mediatrix of the World; I invoke your prompt attention to my necessities."[17] At the Council of Ephesus (431 C.E.), St. Cyril of Alexandria professed the religious formulation that through her motherhood, Mary was forever linked with the saving of humanity.[18] Cyril was a dominant force at this council, and his legacy was extensive documentation. Mary became the center of much of the discussion at the council (recall that she received the title *Theotokos* at Ephesus). Cyril delivered a significant sermon on behalf of Marian intercession:

> Through thee, the trinity is glorified; through thee, the Cross is venerated in the whole world ... through thee, angels and archangels rejoice, though thee, demons are chased ... through thee, the fallen creature is raised to heaven ... through thee, the churches are founded in the whole world, through thee the peoples are led to conversion.[19]

The preaching of Germanus of Constantinople in the early eighth century represented a shift in theological perspective on Mary's mediation. Previously, Mary's mediatrix title was a reflection of her role in the incarnation, but she was now imbued with greater power. Specifically, she had an all-powerful influence over God.[20] Mary could not be denied any request. This shift probably reflected the practices of the faithful in devotion to Mary. It became popularly understood that through her mercy, Mary could reverse just condemnation or alter the judgment rendered upon sinners. Germanus, who referred to himself as, "Our Lady's Slave"[21] glorifies Mary as Mediatress in an often-quoted passage,

> No one is saved save through you, most holy one; no one is delivered from misfortune save through you, most pure one; there is no one to whom a gift is given save through you, most chaste one; there is none to whom in mercy the gift of grace is granted save through you, who are most venerable. Who in return would not bless you; Who would not exalt you, if not as you really deserve, at least with his whole heart, you who have been glorified, beatified, who have been the object of great things from your Son and God. This is why all generations will proclaim you blessed ... you have the words of eternal life. These words are the prayers by which you intervene on our behalf before God. In fact you never cease to work wonders for us, holy is your name; it is blessed by angels and men, for all generations.[22]

Note the devotional tone that moves beyond the passage from Cyril. The divine nature of Mary's power is evident. One could substitute the name of "Jesus" for that of "Mary" in the Germanus quotation and it would be a fitting devotional statement for a Christian. In terms of power, Mary had become a type of Christ in the transition from the late patristic to the early middle ages.

A genre of medieval apocalyptic literature emerged, primarily in the Eastern church, fueling the popular belief in Mary's intercessory powers. The title of this literature was the "Apocalypses of the Virgin," with several extant versions dated as early as the ninth century. While the details varied, the stories were fundamentally the same. Mary descends into the depths of hell, where she is aghast by the tortures (often vividly detailed) inflicted upon sinners.[23] She begs Jesus for mercy and he grants the damned some period of reprieve. In addition, Mary secures an agreement from Jesus that he will always heed her prayers on behalf of sinners. A covenant of mercy is established. Although these stories circulated widely in the East, the Western church developed a similar understanding of Mary's power over sin and eternal judgment.

The legend of Theophilus, which circulated in the Eastern and Western church in the eighth century (although written as early as the seventh century), was an influential myth regarding Mary's intercessory powers.[24] Theophilus held a significant administrative post within the church in Asia Minor. The death of the bishop brought a successor who dismissed Theophilus from his duties. With the help of an intermediary, Theophilus made a pact with the devil to reclaim his position. However, he was guilt ridden by his arrangement and desired to renege. The devil did not release Theophilus, who fell into deep despair. He turned his prayers to the Virgin Mary. She intervened on his behalf by entering hell and taking the contract from the devil. Theophilus made a public confession and subsequently died a peaceful death.[25] The anonymous author of this legend claimed to have witnessed the events culminating in the death of Theophilus in 538 C.E.[26]

The Story of Theophilus is but one of many legends that demonstrate Mary's power. Marina Warner describes many popular myths of the Middle Ages in which Mary cheats the devil, circumvents God's judgment, and even resurrects the dead. According to Warner,

> The more raffish the Virgin's suppliant, the better she likes him. The miracles' heroes are liars, thieves, adulterers, and fornicators, footloose students, pregnant nuns, unruly and lazy clerics, and eloping monks. On the single condition that they sing her praises, usually by reciting the *Ave Maria*, and show due respect for the miracle of the Incarnation wrought in her, they can do no wrong. Her justice is loyalty to her own [believers]. . . .[27]

The key to gaining Mary's intercession was repentance and faith in her power. The burgeoning claims of Mary's power in the middle ages were completely removed from a biblical foundation. Unlike the self-effacing woman of the bible, Mary was the principal actor on behalf of humanity in the religious consciousness of the time.

It is difficult to overstate the extent of Mary's power and influence in Europe of the Middle Ages. In Maastricht, Holland, there is a chapel dedicated to the "Star of the Sea" (one of the many titles given to Mary in this era). She is the patroness of sailors. The following prayer is posted in the chapel:

> O dearest Mother, I come to you now with greatest trust. The mani-
> fold wonders that have come to pass here by your intercession fill
> me, miserable sinner, with the sweetest hope that you, Mother of
> Mercy, will hear my Prayer also. Yes, I supplicate and pray to you, O
> sweetest Mother, O most merciful Star of the Sea, let me not go
> away from here without being heard. You can help me, you are the
> most powerful one only after God; you will help me because you are
> so full of love for all your children. Remember, O most merciful
> Virgin, that it has never been heard that anyone who came to you
> full of trust to take refuge in you has been forsaken by you; should
> I, then, be the first unlucky one to go away unheard by you? No, no,
> O good Mother, at this holy place may you be, through your
> omnipotent intercession, my help in my distress and comfort in my
> suffering.[28]

Note the statement, "omnipotent intercession." In popular belief, the significance of Mary "the most powerful one after God" superseded that of Christ (who is not mentioned by name in the above prayer).

St. Bernard of Clairvaux, an influential medieval theologian of the first half of the twelfth century, perpetuated a child-like faith in Mary. He coined an analogy of Mary as the "aqueduct" of divine grace because God willed everything through her.[29] Bernard added psycho-logical analysis to his Marian insights. He believed that because Christ was the judge of humanity, and the one true mediator, human nature required that there be a mother mediator. Mary was the mediator's mediator.[30] Mary's maternal characteristics made her more approachable, and therefore the mediator role was perfect for her. Bernard's character-ization of Mary was more representative of gender relations of the peri-od than demonstrative of explicit evidence of Mary's personality. Mary's character was and is unknown, but of course she was more approachable. She was a mother.

Medieval Christian thinking divided the kingdom of God into the realm of Justice and the realm of Mercy, Jesus being the King of Justice and Mary the Queen of Mercy. In this configuration, mercy was considered superior to justice—therefore, Mary had the better position. This construction facilitated her becoming a type of Christ.[31] The work of St. Thomas Aquinas marked a challenge to the popular and theological momentum for divinizing Mary.[32] The thirteenth century's preeminent theologian did not use the term "mediatrix" in his writing.[33] The theology of Aquinas returned the mediating role of Mary to that of the birth of the one true mediator.[34] In concert with the patristic theologians, Aquinas viewed Mary as an instrument of God's intervention in human salvation and did not give her an ongoing role in that salvation. Aquinas, a Dominican, disagreed with his contemporary St. Bonaventure, a Franciscan, over the issue of Mary's mediatory powers. Bonaventure drew upon St. Bernard extensively in supporting Mary's ongoing, active role in human salvation.[35] Ultimately, even the work of a theologian as significant as Aquinas could not halt the popular tide of the Cult of Mary.

With the Protestant Reformation of the early sixteenth century, Mary's religious prominence came under attack. While the reformers were not centrally concerned with Mariology, the level of idolatry and excess that surrounded her did subject Marian images and cathedrals to zealous reformist removal and defacement.[36] A new theological perspective, nominalism, which rejected all mediation between God and humanity, arose. Martin Luther had an evolving view of Mary. Initially, he seemed favorable to invoking Mary's intercession. However, later in his life, Martin Luther became more entrenched in the concept of *Christus Solus*.[37] Of all of the reformers, Lutherans were the most favorable toward Mary. John Calvin and Ulrich Zwingli were absolute in their rejection of Marian mediation. While the Catholic Church initially rejected and then slowly adapted many of the reforms, Mary remained relatively unscathed. The attack upon her only entrenched many of her devotees. For example, Counter-reformation theologians such as Peter Casius, Francis Suarez, and Robert Bellarmine defended Mary's prominent role in human salvation in a number of popular books.

Despite the attacks of Marian minimalists, popular devotion in the post-reformation period grew based on a genre of devotional literature such as Louis Griguid de Montfort's *True Devotion to the Blessed Virgin* and *The Glories of Mary* by Alphonsus Liguori. These works promoted the popular belief that Mary served to assist in the dispensation of Christ's grace, and she could mediate the well-being of sinners before Christ, the judge of humanity.[38] Elizabeth Johnson notes that during this era Mary displaced the Holy Spirit in Catholic piety. She was portrayed as a spiritual guide and the path to Christ. These were traditional roles of the Holy Spirit that Mary usurped.[39]

The golden age of Mary, a century bracketed by the Dogma of the Immaculate Conception (1854) and the Dogma of the Assumption (1950), was also a period of great fervor for Marian mediation. Mary's role as Mediatrix of humanity almost achieved official dogmatic status during this period. In 1921, at the initiation of Cardinal Joseph Mercier of Belgium, a special mass for Mary, the Mediatress of all graces, was granted for his diocese. He urged other bishops to follow suit, and 450 of them did so.[40] This spurred a worldwide petition to the Vatican for a definition of Mary as Mediatrix. Commissions were established to examine the idea of a Marian Dogma of Mediation. The 1950 International Mariological Congress sent the following resolution to Pope Pius XII:

> Since the principal, personal attributes of the Blessed Virgin Mary have already been defined, it is the wish of the faithful that it should also be dogmatically defined that the Blessed Virgin Mary was intimately associated with Christ the Savior in effecting human salvation, and accordingly, she is a true collaborator in the work of redemption, spiritual Mother of all men, intercessor and dispenser of graces, in a word, universal Mediatress of God and men.[41]

Despite the ecclesial momentum for an official Marian statement on mediation, the Pope felt that the timing for such a declaration was not right. In a few years (1959), the Second Vatican Council was announced. This meeting of the world's bishops would represent another opportunity for those who advocated a Dogma on mediation to get an official declaration.

Much like the other issues concerning Mary, the subject of mediation was a point of controversy for the bishops of the Second Vatican Council. The notion of mediation centers upon power. How much salvific power could be vested in Mary? In this period just after Mary's golden age, there was still much momentum for defining her role in human salvation, and a faction of the bishops represented this perspective. However, other significant theological movements found themselves in conflict with the promotion of Mary's role. There had been advances in ecumenism, which helped shape many of the conciliar documents. The promotion of Mary's role in redemption alienated other Christian denominations. In addition, biblical scholarship, as well as historic and scientific methods were becoming prevalent in Catholic theological studies. The nonbiblical and mythological development of intercessory powers was of great concern to many bishops.

The issue of how to address Mary's mediation was secondary to determining what place Mary should be given in conciliar documents. Once it was decided to retain Mary in the schema of the Dogmatic Constitution on the Church (rather than a separate document), the tone was set for the articulation of her role in salvation. Five successive drafts on Mary's mediation would be reviewed. The first draft reflected the wishes of those requesting a clear definition of Mary's part in salvation.

> Therefore, when this humble "Handmaid of the Lord" for whom "He who is might has done great things" (Lk 1:49) is formally named Mediatrix of all graces, because she was associated with Christ in acquiring them; and when too, remaining an associate with Christ now glorious in heaven, she is invoked by the Church as our Mediatrix and our Advocate, because she intercedes for all through Christ in such a way that the maternal charity of the Blessed Virgin is present in the conferring of all graces to human beings; then in no way is the unique mediation of our Mediator, in the absolute sense spoken of by the Apostle who said: "For there is one God and one Mediator between God and human beings, the human being Jesus Christ" (1 Tim 2:5), obscured or lessened; on the contrary, this mediation of Christ is enhanced and honored. For Mary is Mediatrix in Christ, and her mediation arises not from any necessity but from divine good pleasure and the superabundance and excellence of the merits of Jesus.[42]

In a single statement, the Bishops attempted to affirm Mary as Mediatrix but declared that this did not diminish the ultimate mediation of Christ. This draft never made it to the floor of the council for discussion because it was sent back to committee for rewriting in light of the agreed-upon schema for the Dogmatic Constitution on the Church. It was not until the third session of the Vatican Council that a compromised version was submitted. However, the retention of the term "Mediatrix" brought spirited speeches of opposition. The draft was withdrawn for further revision, whereupon hundreds of bishops submitted observations to influence the next draft: 191 bishops requested that the title be kept, 196 bishops desired the title be removed, and 34 argued the title could be kept if it were mitigated by other titles or notations. Successive drafts relativized

Mary's mediation and incorporated greater use of biblical and papal texts. The final draft won overwhelming approval, but it was a compromise meant to appease both factions. The final text is ambiguous enough not to threaten those devoted to Mary, although it does position Mary's role as ecclesiatypical—a type of the Church and not as a type of Christ. "This sacred Synod intends to describe with diligence the role of the Blessed Virgin in the mystery of the Incarnate Word and the Mystical Body."[43] The final version does not directly refer to Mary as Mediatrix, but does state that this is one of the many titles historically attributed to Mary. Elizabeth Johnson notes that the effect of the Second Vatican Council on Mary's role as Mediatrix was quieting upon Mariology, particularly in the United States.[44] Until recently, post-conciliar theological discussion of Mary's mediation has been practically nonexistent.

Apparitions

Nothing has fueled popular devotion to Mary as much as her apparitions.[45] These visions also perpetuate the idea of Mary's power, and specifically, her ability to intervene on behalf of the faithful.[46] While reports of apparitions have been recorded since the origins of Christianity, Mary and not Jesus has been the predominant subject of this phenomenon, particularly since the 11th century. It is this medieval piety, with its themes of Mary's exceptional power and loyalty toward those who entrust themselves to her, that appears to run throughout the history of apparitions.[47] However, these apparitions have a political nature. Orthodoxy appears to rule their messages. Bruce Malina observes that the traditional function of apparitions has always been to defend the Church against its enemies.[48] Nevertheless, popular piety drives the power of Marian apparitions. Whether or not an apparition is officially recognized as legitimate by the Roman Catholic Church, hundreds of these sightings have resulted in the establishment of shrines. These shrines become a local center of devotion and often result in pilgrimages of believers from all over the world. These shrines also become icons of Mary's power in modern human affairs. Zimdars-Swartz describes a pattern to the apparitions that give rise to shrines:

1. Mary appears in a community that is suffering and whose very existence may be threatened.
2. Mary explains the underlying reason for the suffering or threat.

3. The problem is usually a pervasive sin linked to religious ritual (lack of prayer, poor liturgical attendance, eucharistic desecration).
4. The solution centers on religious reparation by the establishment of a shrine or a devotional practice.[49]

Michael Carroll argues that the significant similarity among apparitions may be a sort of self-fulfilling prophecy. International publicity may contribute to apparition patterns at a conscious or subconscious level.[49]

The hierarchy of the Catholic Church finds apparitions to have both positive and negative aspects. The apparitions bring many converts to Catholicism and strengthen the faith of some Catholics. Apparitions also bring the Church a great deal of publicity, since an appearance of Mary makes for the kind of sensationalist material adored by the media. Because many of the apparitions appear in poor rural areas, the pilgrimages assist the local economy. Church sponsored tourist/devotional trips to these areas have become a profitable enterprise. More importantly, the apparitions are a significant part of popular Catholicism. There is something of an underground following of apparitions. The enormous amount of literature distributed by the "Blue Army" and other such organizations indicates apparitions' popular appeal. Furthermore, the conservative nature of messages in these apparitions appeals to those in the Catholic hierarchy who find modernism anathema.[51] Defending apparitions is a method of demonstrating that modern science cannot explain everything, as the Church increasingly feels threatened by the ability of science to elucidate the world.[52] Nevertheless, many in the Church hierarchy wish to keep the apparitions at arm's length to avoid a mitigation of Christology. Serious theologians tend to avoid the topic (other than for sociological interest) and church officials seem to "wink" at the phenomenon.

Mary, Mediation, and Women-Power

Mary's mediation and intercession in Catholic theology represents a model of a powerful woman operating within severe patriarchal restraints that render her power far from absolute. This poses a great dilemma for modern feminist theologians. To deny Mary's role as the great mediator would be to deny an existing religious power base. To accept Mary's position would be to assent to her imposed limitations. There exists a Marian power continuum with Mary as "Handmaiden of the Lord" at one end and "Mary, the Christian Goddess" at the other end. Christian feminists disagree as to where to place Mary along this continuum.

In this section, the "goddess" portion of the power spectrum will be explored as the logical extension of Mary's mediatory powers. Can Mary move beyond mediating the divine and actually become divine? The discussion of Mary's divinity will be viewed in the context of women's struggle for official power in ordination to the priesthood. The two issues are intimately linked, with a breakthrough on either side potentially giving rise to the end of the domination of men's experience in official Catholic spirituality.

Two significant and related themes demonstrate the importance of Mary for the exercise of women's spirituality in the Catholic Church. The issues of Mary as a Christian goddess and the ordination of women are modern discussions that struggle with the issue of gender equality. The first is the question of the extent to which Mary is a Christian goddess. The second question is whether women should serve as priests within the Catholic Church. Both are also issues of mediation. The issue of human understanding of the divine can and often does have a gendered approach. Feminist theologians question the perception of the gender of God. Should there be a corollary of God known as the Goddess? Is Mary that Goddess? Does God consist of both genders or neither gender? Can Jesus be represented by both men and women as priests, or is gender essential for that representation?

The Goddess Question

The previous review of Mary as Mediatrix in Church history revealed that Mary was invested with power not easily categorized or contained. Throughout the ages ecclesial authorities have attempted to place various degrees of limits on piety, although the Catholic faithful have been less than acquiescent. Church officials have never argued for the designation of Mary as a goddess. However, the assumption of pre-Christian goddess worship into the Cult of Mary is well documented.[53] Mary's popular power could not always be kept in check by Church officials. According to Mary Daly, "Mary malfunctioned as an archetype: the situation was intolerable to the mind molders."[54] Mary appeared to have an "independent" power that manifested itself in apparitions, popular devotions, intercessory prayers, etc. Catharina Halkes describes a historical schizophrenia:

> Gradually two Marys began to emerge. The first of these is the Mary of the Church's teaching, in which great care has always been taken to ensure that her person remains subordinate to that of Christ so that her luster will not outshine that of Christ and in which Mary owes

her excellence entirely to God's grace and the birth of Christ. The second Mary is the figure at the center of increasing and sometimes excessive piety, usually of a popular kind, but also including that of such male theologians as St. Bernard. That piety, has a radiating effect and acts evocatively. It is the result of deep-seated need on man's part for what will give, nourish and sustain life. As long as that situation of the "two Mary's" continues, the confusion will also persist. . . .[55]

Beginning in the 1970s, Catholic feminist theologians began to discuss the idea of Mary as a goddess. Interest in goddess worship burgeoned in the 1980s. This phenomenon has gained such interest that the best seller *Megatrends for Women* devoted a chapter to "The Goddess Reawakening," and a discussion of Mariology plays a central role in this text.

> Considering the social, political and economic power women wield today, the emergence of Goddess worship might be considered as a form of spiritual catch-up reflecting new sociological realities that have unfolded over the past 25 years.[56]

Part of the motivation for feminist theologians in seeking the goddess, and perhaps Mary, is to rework unsatisfactory beliefs about divinity that exist in Christian language and symbols for God.

> As women and men search today for life-giving symbols, Mary embodies the feminine so obviously missing from the current Christian belief system.[57]

The terms "king," "lord," "master," and "father" reflect the almost exclusive male imagery found in expressions of divinity. Feminist theology attempts to raise consciousness of the impact of gendered language upon religious imagination.

> [Feminist theology] challenges a pervasive idolatry that has crept into Christian thought and practice and at the same time provides new awareness, for women and for the whole Church, of God as the fully transcendent mystery who encompasses all of creation, all of our lives in universal presence.[58]

The feminist concern for language represents a consistent objective: the equal valorization of women's experience. This gender equality must extend to concepts of God.

Feminism has been keenly attuned to ways in which language influences perception and behavior. The concern for inclusive language is an outgrowth of this respect for the power of words. A presupposition of

Elizabeth Johnson's book, *She Who Is: The Mystery of God in Feminist Theological Discourse,* is that speech about God shapes the life behavior of the faithful. Johnson finds that how people speak about God has great significance.

> Christian feminist emancipatory discourse aims at empowering women in their struggle to make their own humanity as *imago Dei* historically tangible, and thereby to secure a foothold for the glory of god in history. Given the interlocking of oppressions in the world, that is, the connivance of sexism with racism, classism, militarism, humanocentrism, and other forms of prejudice, this effort at renewed speech about God is vitally significant for the church and the world in all of their constitutive dimensions.[59]

A decade earlier, Rosemary Radford Ruether concurred with Johnson on the issue of god language or "god-talk" when she warned that the issue of how God is "imaged" would arouse tremendous passions. She described God as a representation of a transcendent male ego. To change god language is to challenge that male ego.[60]

While feminist theologians agree upon a general objective of ending gender-based oppression, many scholars disagree on how this is accomplished. A separate entity or Goddess is one approach. Another approach is to view God as neither male nor female—or both. Each approach represents a new way of speaking about God. Carol Christ defends the need for a goddess on the following four grounds:

1. The goddess legitimizes female power as autonomous and beneficial. Historically women have been either powerless or depicted as participants in evil (see next chapter).

2. The goddess, because of female personification in imagery and iconography, would legitimize women's bodily experience, which has historically been derogated.

3. The goddess symbol would valorize female will.

4. The goddess would place greater emphasis on women in relationships, a subject given little attention in the Western tradition.[61]

Christ, who does not endorse Mary for this role, correctly points out that a complete feminist theology of Mary has yet to be written.[62] Marian imagery would require quite a transformation to provide the four areas of empowerment Christ has described for the goddess.

Elisabeth Schussler Fiorenza finds that Mary has given Catholic women the opportunity to experience divine reality. While the Church is dominated by the reification of male experience as transmitted by male symbols and language, "The Cult of Mary in the Catholic Church provides . . . a tradition of theological language which speaks of the divine reality in female terms and symbols."[63] Stephen Benko corroborates Schussler Fiorenza's view in the conclusion of his study of the non-Christian sources of Mariology. He finds the Cult of Mary to be a corrective to the Christian deficiency in female deity imagery. According to Benko, this deficiency did not exist in pre-Christian religions.[64]

The lack of female deity imagery is not lost upon the religious imagination of popular Catholicism. Schussler Fiorenza separates Church teaching about Mary from the lived experience of Catholic women.

> Even though any Catholic school child can explain on an intellectual-theological level the difference between the worship of God and Christ and the veneration of Mary, on an emotional, imaginative, experiential level the Catholic child experiences the love of God in the figure of a woman.[65]

Schussler Fiorenza is cautious not to absolutize this concept of the Goddess because she wishes to avoid a simple dualism in which the divine is portrayed exclusively as female. In addition, Schussler Fiorenza recognizes that the image of Mary has integrated a great deal of patriarchal teaching, and to dissect the positive aspects from the negative aspects in such a religious icon is nearly impossible. The early writings of Mary Daly were also concerned with the patriarchal baggage that Mary carries. While Daly does not reject the idea of pursuing a female divine (the "Archimage"), she nevertheless finds Mary to be a mere vestige of the ancient goddess because of ecclesial intervention, "dogmatically draining this symbol of her residual vibrancy. . . ."[66]

E. Ann Matter directly explores divinity in the article "The Virgin Mary: A Goddess?" Similar to Schussler Fiorenza's observation, Matter finds Mary achieving the stature of a goddess in popular piety. However, Matter concludes that Mary is perhaps more indicative of the female aspect of God.[67] There appears to be greater theological agreement in viewing Mary as the "feminine face of God" rather than a separate figure of divinity. Nevertheless, the distinction between the two approaches is lost in the popular potency of Marian images.

Andrew Greeley has compiled significant sociological data on the implication of the power of imagery for modern Catholics in the United States, and he finds that modern popular perception of Mary does not conflict with feminist efforts for equality. He distinguishes between propositional Mariology and imaginative Mariology.[68] Propositional Mariology is indicative of the dogmas associated with Mary, a view widely rejected or ignored by the faithful. Imaginative Mariology, which links Mary with divine motherhood and expressions of mother love, is the more pervasive view. Greeley argues that it is this "analogical imagination," or the ability to imagine God as present in the world, that distinguishes Catholics from Protestants.[69] *The single most significant Catholic religious image is Mary. Her imagery is more powerful than the image of Jesus or God.*[70] Greeley's statistical findings, based on national surveys, hold true even for young Catholics, who were educated under post-conciliar religious minimalism.[71] Greeley is not optimistic that the Church hierarchy will alter its stance on Mary or women (he favors women's ordination), and he believes the Catholic Church is missing a great opportunity to capitalize on its most powerful female figure: Mary.

Author Rose Romano reflects Greeley's findings in her description of the piety of her Italian Catholic family: "Even on Good Friday, more attention is paid to Mary than to Jesus. Jesus may have died on that day, but Mary was a woman alone who lost her son."[72] This is another example of popular faith transforming the focus of religious ritual from Jesus to Mary. The theme lurking below the surface in Catholicism is that Mary is very much Godlike.

Rosemary Radford Ruether rejects the concept of the goddess whether it is associated with Mary or not. Ruether is concerned that gendered concepts of the divine will further reify ideas of sex-typed characteristics such as woman = nature.[73] Ruether also rejects the notion of a "feminine side of God." This divine androgyny maintains a gendered split of masculine and feminine that is ripe for asymmetrical treatment, and ultimately, subordination of the female aspect. Ruether adopts an ecclesiatypical approach to Mary, describing her as a great symbol of the Church. The symbolic ecclesiology of Mary is not in the tradition of the hierarchy of the Church. It is a liberating symbol. Ruether coins the phrase "liberation Mariology" to reinvent Mary in an empowering manner consistent with liberation theology.[74] Within liberation Mariology, sexism is clearly defined as sin, and men and women are freed from the gendered dualism that religion and society have constructed. Mary is the model of liberation in her freedom and autonomy in bringing salvation into this world. Ruether uses the Lucan infancy narrative as the paradigm for the new relationship created in

Christianity.[75] Mary does not consult Joseph in assenting to the angel. She makes a free choice.

> To do this, to follow the dictates of this voice [the angel in Luke], Mary would have to risk antagonizing all the powerful men in her life—men on whom she depended for food and clothing, shelter and status. To do what she was asked to do she would have to set aside the hallowed traditions of the Jewish people concerning marriage. She would have to disobey the laws laid down by her Jewish priests concerning the sexual conduct of women. She would have to ignore the legitimate claims and expectations of the man she had promised to marry. The voice asked that she treat the claims of all these men—her people, her priests, and her partner—as of secondary importance, that she relativize these and that she give priority is heed to that mysterious urging voice. It asked that she agree to a course of action which in the eyes of all these men and indeed even in her own eyes, would seem to be immoral and wrong.[76]

In addition to a new interpretation of Mary's fiat, liberation Mariology also gives rise to a new perspective on Mary's virginity. Mary's virginity was not a model for the valorization of sexual abstinence. It was a symbol of her radical independence. Mary was not under the control of any man—she was an autonomous, powerful woman.[77] Dorothy Solle offers a modern version of Mary's Magnificat that captures the spirit of liberation Mariology:

> My soul sees the land of freedom and
> my spirit will deliver itself from fear.
> The empty faces of women
> will be filled with life and
> we will become human beings—
> awaited by generations before us
> who were sacrificed.[78]

The choice between Mary as a goddess and Mary as the feminine side of God is inadequate despite the popular piety demonstrative of this association with divinity. Neither choice addresses the religious liberation that Christian feminists seek. Mary as goddess, while giving voice to a much-needed identification with the divine, creates the possibility of competing images of deity. While such a dualism is perhaps better than the singularity of a male God, it traps women into a type of separatism that is merely oppositional. A competing cosmology is not a lofty enough goal for feminism. Integration of feminist consciousness is sought over an equilibrium of two opposed forces. Creating a new myth of the Goddess will repeat the process of patriarchal religion.[79] Mary is particularly inadequate in this role because reinventing her image would be a major undertaking. The biblical arguments for her autonomy are as sparse as the evidence for her mediation. Mary's primary qualification as a Christian goddess is her popular support, including the concept of her intercessory abilities. Patching Mary onto God to represent a female aspect is also inadequate for meeting feminist objectives. Such an approach does not critique religious patriarchy and may, in fact, sanction it under the guise of balanced or competing imagery.[80]

The Ordination Question

Traditionally, women have been kept from the priesthood based on explicit arguments of their inferiority and evil nature. Ethicist Beverly Harrison describes the defense of male priesthood as reactionary.

> First we need to recognize that the hierarchicalization and centralization of the Catholic tradition of Christianity, including the solidification of power in priestly orders and in a centralized hierarchy was the result of an active attack on the growing role of women in early Christianity.[81]

Harrison describes the Catholic hierarchy as based on "male bonding" that developed an apologetic that systematically oppressed women through alienating images, such as those found in Mariology. The modern defense of the male priesthood has taken a more subtle approach in defining the special nature and vocation of women. This "special nature" is primarily supported by tradition, and therefore is something of a circular argument.[82] Proof of women's nature is found in historic behavior; however, since historic behaviors were limited and socially controlled, the proof is vaporous.

The women's movement not only raised consciousness of the reflection of male experience in the symbols and language used to express divinity, it also challenged prevailing concepts of pastoral leadership. Mary's symbolic challenge to a male God is paralleled by the effort of women to obtain leadership in Church hierarchy or through ordination. The issue of power is central to both issues, as is the figure of Mary. Richard McBrien delineates five primary arguments against the ordination of women, used by the hierarchy of the Catholic Church:[83]

1. The tradition of Roman Catholicism has consistently opposed women's ordination.
2. Jesus did not call women, *not even his mother*, to the priesthood.[84]
3. An ordained priest must act in the name of Christ, and therefore must be a physical as well as a spiritual representation.
4. No one has a right to ordination.
5. Women who were called deaconesses in the New Testament may not have been ordained.[85]

Mary is invoked by the hierarchy to segregate women from the priesthood; she is the model and zenith of womanhood. Because she was not a priest, other women should not seek this role. This issue of ordination is about power: the power to control resources, to influence the church, and to minister to the faithful on equal footing with men.

Catholic feminist theologians such as Anne E. Carr, Margaret Farley, and Rosemary Radford Ruether address the five points presented with a number of rebuttals.[86] According to Carr, the first statement with regard to the maintenance of tradition assumes a static Catholicism that is not borne out by history.[87] Carr utilizes historical critical methods in revealing that Mary's tradition of nonpriesthood status rests on the assumption of women as an inferior class by those performing traditional biblical interpretation. Social and religious understandings of women have evolved, and so has the Church. For example, the Church had long-standing traditions: masses spoken in Latin, appointing Italian Popes, and opposition to usury—all of which changed over time.[88]

There is also a growing body of evidence that women were ordained priests in the Church's formative years. For example, the recent discovery of a tombstone in Italy with the inscription "Leta the Priest" is considered strong evidence of fifth-century women's ordination. Mary Ann Rossi comments upon and translates the work of Giorgio Otranto, an Italian scholar of classical and Christian studies who finds the fifth-century *Epistle of Pope Gelasius*, which mentions ordained women, to be solid evidence for the historical vocation of women in the priesthood.

> We may infer from an analysis of Gelasisus's epistle that at the end of the fifth century, some women, having been ordained by bishops, were exercising a true and proper ministerial priesthood in a vast area of southern Italy, as well as perhaps in other unnamed regions of Italy.[89]

Antiquity scholar Karen Jo Torjesen presents a barrage of evidence that whether women were ordained or not, they played key leadership roles in the early church. Prior to the fourth century, when Christianity was an underground institution, it existed in the private spheres of society—the homes of believers. Householders, both men and women, provided a place for gathering and resources for the communal meal. These private associations were often run by women, as corroborated by numerous extant sources. Only after Christianity became part of the public sphere as an accepted state religion were women relegated to lesser roles. Torjeson's concludes that modern, tradition-based arguments for maintaining a male religious hierarchy cannot rest upon early Church history.[90]

Precedent exists for devotion to Mary as a Priest. During the "Golden Age of Mary" (circa 1850–1950), a short-lived offshoot of the Cult of Mary in France worshipped Mary as the "Virgin Priest." This belief emanated from a turn-of-the-century writing that claimed Mary was called a "Virgin Priest" by the fathers of the Church. After briefly endorsing the cult, the Vatican became wary of heresy and condemned such devotion.[91]

Biblical scholarship renders moot the argument that Jesus did not call Mary, or any woman, to the priesthood. Raymond Brown notes that there is no biblical evidence Jesus thought of any of his followers as priests. Furthermore, there is no biblical evidence that Jesus had any concept of a new religion or structured Church.[92] If one wishes to simply analogize "discipleship" as "priesthood" (a distinction that theologians would not obfuscate), then the second argument revolves around an exclusive male discipleship of Jesus. However, biblical scholarship also challenges this presupposition.

> That Jesus' mother was thought to belong, not only to the kinship, but also the discipleship category is attested in different ways in Luke-Acts, John and some extra canonical writings.[93]

Evidence is mounting that Mary and other women did play a prominent role amongst Jesus' disciples. Susan Brooks Thistlethwaite notes that not only is it reasonable to assume Jesus counted many women among his inner circle, a reader of the bible changes his or her perception of the message if women are perceived to have received Jesus' intimate instructions and teachings. Power and authority are given to those who hear "the word," and if previous assumptions are set aside, women can claim a tradition of participation as well.[94] Robert Kress argues that in the early Church, priesthood did not hold the exclusive holiness status that it does today. Many people served the Church in leadership roles without being ordained. Kress proposes an ironic solution: If Mary, who is considered the holiest of Christians and "first Christian," was not ordained, perhaps no one should be ordained.[95]

Catholic feminists critique the mandatory maleness of priests as an inconsistent construction of theological logic. Why is gender the determining characteristic for representing Christ? Why not race, height, or shoe size?[96] Gender exclusion is a form of male idol-worship because a particular aspect of humanity is established as sacred over other aspects. This position maintains the connection between maleness and divinity that has been an undercurrent of Church history.[97] Ruether sees the implication of this connection as challenging what the Christian message of redemption has to say to women.

> The 1976 Vatican declaration against women's ordination expressed in crude and graphic terms women's inability to "represent Christ." As long as the theology of this document stands as normative, women's second-class status in redemption remains basic to Catholic views of women, whether or not a woman might actually aspire to the priesthood. Such a view of the essential maleness of Christ and women's inability to represent Christ is incompatible with the doctrine that the incarnation of God into human nature is an inclusive representation of female as well as male humanity. The logical response to such a document is to conclude that if women can't represent Christ, then Christ does not represent women. Women are not included in salvation in Christ at all.[98]

This critique does not question the maleness of the historical figure of Jesus, but Jesus' maleness should not be "theologically determinative of his identity as Christ nor normative for the identity of the Christian community."[99] The primacy of Jesus' maleness is part of what Ruether refers to as the Catholic hierarchy's creation of myths and statements contributing to women's inferior status by divine imperative.[100] In Berger's social-construction terminology, this is a reification. According to Ruether, the espoused gender difference represents a moral injustice created by human sinfulness and manifested in the Catholic hierarchy's perspective. Margaret Farley views women's ordination as a religious moral imperative because all persons are supposedly created in the image of God. Without female representation, the priesthood can only reflect a *de facto* male god.[101]

The third argument addresses ordination rights. While no one has a right to ordination, the arbitrary exclusion of a substantial portion of the Catholic population is an injustice that appears to violate fundamental concepts of fairness. The issue becomes one similar to that of the discrimination against a minority group by the majority. What is ironic is that women are not a minority in the Catholic faith.[102] Farley finds the Church perpetuating a male leader/female follower relationship through its gender-exclusionary priesthood. She speculates that were men not allowed to lead, they might not participate in the life of the Church at all.[103] Generally, women participate in greater numbers than men in Church activities. She also notes that the gendered division of labor in society that often finds men in powerful positions and women in support roles is mirrored in the Church. Farley views these dynamics as part of the Church's requirement of an all-male priesthood, and concludes that it is a moral imperative that there be greater collaboration between men and women in Church leadership. In this respect Farley does claim that women have a "right" to ordination.

The last objection regarding the ordination of deaconesses is also a moot point based upon Raymond Brown's comment that Jesus did not ordain anyone. Albeit somewhat rhetorically, McBrien asks perhaps the most significant question about women's ordination. Reversing the burden of proof, McBrien questions why Jesus would have denied women the priesthood. The implication is that the teachings of Jesus are not consistent with a notion of gender exclusion.[104]

Despite the hierarchy of the Church declaring the equality of gender, its own system of governance and ministry does not reflect this value.[105] This hypocrisy is reflected in the U.S. Bishops' failed attempt to write a pastoral letter on women despite ten years of work (1982–1992) and several circulated drafts. The initial draft contained a statement condemning sexism as a social evil, although this statement was removed in subsequent drafts due to political pressure.[106] One of the forces behind the pastoral letter's failure was the lack of adequate rationale for the exclusivity of male priesthood, given the fundamental Christian moral value of equal human dignity.[107] Mary's name was invoked in the letter once again as a model for women. The bishops did mention that she took on nontraditional roles, but this was in addition to wife, mother, and widow.

Ruether extends the Church's logic of male priesthood to expose its underlying religious anthropology. She asks,

> If women cannot represent Christ, how does Christ represent women? Or to put it another way, if women cannot be ordained, they cannot be baptized either.[108]

Ruether and others contend that what lurks behind the Church's defense of an all-male hierarchy is the Aristotelian contention that women are defective and inferior to men. This asymmetrical anthropology was adopted by Aquinas in his claim that only men can represent Christ as priests.[109] The inconsistent and lukewarm response of the Church to growing worldwide moral consciousness regarding gender equality is causing the Church to lose ethical credibility.

The late Conservative Catholic theologian Hans Urs von Balthasar made explicit the Catholic orthodox view of the connection between the Cult of Mary and women's ordination. In a brief article titled, "The Marian Principle,"[110] Balthasar finds an underlying "Supratemporal feminine principle" that is derived from Mary and resonates throughout the Catholic Church. He goes so far as to state that, "without Mariology, Christianity threatens imperceptibly to become inhuman."[111] He develops a clear understanding that Mariology is a servant theology to Christology. Balthasar's language assumes knowledge of Mary's desire: "Mary the mother wanted to be the pure 'handmaid of the Lord,'"[112] Although the article is only a few pages long, the author covers the topic of women's ordination and ecclesial leadership. Efforts to ordain women run counter to the Marian principle and the "permanent sexual order." von Balthasar's message is that women should emulate Mary, remain in the domestic sphere, and not seek power. Such an effort will alter the balance of nature.

> The marian element holds sway in the Church in a hidden manner, just as a woman does in a household . . . the spirit of the handmaid, of service, of inconspicuousness, the spirit which lives only for others. No one demands personal "privileges" less then the mother of Christ. . . .[113]

Balthasar perpetuates a theme of female self-denial and "other-directedness" that has been a source of great disempowerment for women. Mary is the vehicle of this message.

Mary's divinity and women's ordination are linked. The elevation of the power of either Mary or women would require the other to follow. It is difficult to imagine women being ordained and functioning in ministry for very long before Mary, or a feminine Christian concept of the divine, became pastorally and theologically necessary. Women priests would not be able to disregard their experiences as women, and eventually this would give voice to new dimensions of spirituality and its divine expression.

Schussler Fiorenza makes an inverse prediction to what is proposed above. She states that were women ordained in the Catholic Church, Jesus' maleness would become insignificant.[114] Ultimately, Schussler Fiorenza's vision is compatible with what is suggested about Mary's relation to women's ordination. Whether Mary becomes more prominent as a divine woman, or Jesus becomes less prominent as a divine man, the result is the mitigation of sexual stratification.

As women reach a critical mass in any group or institution, their influence over the demeanor and direction of that group becomes significant. This is perhaps the reason that the ordination of women represents such a fundamental threat to Catholicism. Women do not seek token ecclesial involvement.

> The "woman question" facing the Church is not just a question of ordination but that it requires an intellectual paradigm shift from an androcentric worldview and theology to a feminist conceptualization of the world, human life, and Christian religion.[115]

Schussler Fiorenza expresses concern that a token ordination of women who are perhaps already members of religious orders and express dependence upon ecclesial authority may lead to the further alienation of women.[116]

Pope John Paul II is not oblivious to the challenge that Catholic feminism raises to the religious institution. The pope recognizes and expresses public concern over the end of traditional Catholicism that can come with the ordination of women.

> It is not simply that some people claim a right for women to be admitted to the ordained priesthood. In its extreme form, it is the Christian faith itself which is in danger of being undermined.[117]

The liberation of Mary as the embodiment of how female divinity is experienced will be a part of the paradigm shift threatening conventional Catholicism.

It is equally difficult to imagine Mary being given a new understanding as the mediation of the female experience of the divine in Catholicism without that having an effect on women in the Church. An official admission that Mary may be of equal importance to Jesus in the role of human salvation will only add greater fuel to the movement for women to have equal roles in pastoral leadership. The fates of Mary and Catholic female ontology are interconnected.

Implications of Mary as the Mediatrix

The socially constructed role of Mary as mediator on behalf of the faithful demonstrates a relational ethic. This relational ethic appears to be a part of the truth of human experience that was missing in Christian cosmology and moral theology and was reintroduced by Mariology. Carol Gilligan's model of a gendered ethic of care and an ethic of justice will be applied to mediation to analyze the ethical perspective created by Mary's role in salvation.

What is the resultant ethic of Mary's intercession, or at least the desired ethic of those who pray to her? One desired outcome of Mary's intervention is a contextualized justice. Historic myths about Mary's mediations depict her as the hero of sinners. Serious sin may have been perpetrated and therefore deserving of righteous punishment, but the individual is usually penitent to Mary and she takes pity. Mary looks beyond the punishable act and takes into account the individual's character. She provides a responsive or passive ethic. Except perhaps in apparitions, she is not depicted as actively seeking the faithful who are deserving of clemency and appropriately adjudicating. The remorseful sinner seeks Mary and she responds. The righteous indignation of God is much more active and certain than is the intervention of Mary that must be initiated by the prayerful. Mary's response is future-oriented and therefore nurturing, while divine justice is historically determined by the sin. In a sense, Mary is hopeful or optimistic about future good coming from mercy, while God's justice is concerned with the historic act. As a corollary to nurturance, there is something maternal about Mary's intercession that runs parallel to the traditional familial roles in asymmetrical parenting, in which the father is the exacter of punishment and the mother listens and pleads the case of her children.

Does the dualism of ethical approaches that the intercession implies truly reflect the justice found in Christian ethics? Certainly the justice this intimates appears more indicative of the warrior God found in selections of the Hebrew Scriptures than that found in the God or the Father that Jesus speaks of in the gospel accounts. However, Mary has virtually no direct salvific role in scripture other than being the mother of Jesus. It is much later that the myths evolve. Therefore, the Christian ethic with which the mercy must be compared is the one operant from the eighth century through the middle ages, when mediation rose in popularity.

The key influence upon Christian moral theology in the eighth century was a theologian who lived almost 400 years before—St. Augustine of

Hippo. Augustine remains significant in Catholic theology today through his writings in areas of sexual morality and just-war theory. Augustine's moral theology was permeated by his pessimistic anthropology. He formulated a great dualism between the sinfulness of humanity and the grace of God, derived from the fall of Adam, or original sin, upon which Augustine would spend his life dwelling.[118] Original sin represented the pollution of all of humanity. Translating this position into an ethic, one finds a vigorous zeal for personal condemnation, with the presumption being the weakness of humanity.

Perhaps just as significant a characteristic of eighth-century Christianity as its passion for personal condemnation was its legalistic morality. The sacrament of penance became widespread during the sixth century, resulting in a concern for determining the nature of sin. Appropriate penances had to be determined for individual sins, so penitential books were developed to assist an uneducated clergy in performing their sacramental duties. The absolution of particular sins became more important than the concept of a virtuous life.[119] Individual acts were judged out of the context of the morality of the whole person's life. These judgments were often out of proportion to the sin.[120]

The addition of St. Thomas Aquinas' work in moral theology in the thirteenth century perpetuated an extremely rational system of justice within Catholicism. Aquinas's *Summa Theologica* epitomizes a comprehensive moral theology with a reasoned, hierarchical approach to ethics. The cascading system of law—eternal law, divine law, natural law, and human law—reflects Aquinas' Aristotelian organization of virtues and indicates the rationality of Catholic moral theology.

Carol Gilligan describes a justice ethic as the moral orientation dominant in North American society that is exhibited predominantly by men.[121] This orientation is distinguished by moral reasoning that is hierarchical, rational, rights-oriented, and conclusive. Traditional Catholic moral theology, particularly as it has been practiced, fits a justice moral orientation. As sociologist Peter Berger observes,

> To be sure, Latin Catholicism absorbed a highly rational legalism inherited from Rome, but its pervasive sacramental system provided innumerable "escape hatches" from the sort of total rationalization of life demanded by Old Testament prophecy or, indeed, by rabbinical Judaism.[122]

Mary is one of those "escape hatches." The Church is hierarchical in its development of sources of moral authority and in dogmatic application, which includes a system of rights.[123] Through principles of natural law, human reason is explicitly a partner in Catholic moral theology. However, Mary as Mediatrix is given the freedom to transcend strict moral rationalism.

Political theorist Seyla Benhabib contrasts the description of the ethic of justice with an ethic of care by referring to a justice ethic as "substitutionist."[124] The justice tradition attempts to universalize a generalized case that can be substituted into any situation to help adjudicate the morality of that case. Benhabib refers to this application as the "generalized other." The substitutionist approach allows for the privatization of justice to the exclusion of all the relationships and forces involved in individual acts, and ultimately denies a plurality of perspectives. An ethic of care resists such a substitution in favor of learning the particulars of the case, including relationships and dynamics, before making a moral evaluation. Neither Gilligan nor Benhabib attempts to argue that one method of moral orientation is superior to the other.

Benhabib's analysis serves as a strong critique for the case study method so important for the traditional justice ethic and jurisprudence that parallels the development of casuistry in the Catholic Church for the adjudication of sins. Gilligan had strong opinions against the case study method as well,

> Hypothetical dilemmas, in the abstraction of their presentation, divest moral actors from the history and psychology of their individual lives and separate the moral problem from the social contingencies of its possible occurrence. . . . Only when substance is given to the skeletal lives of hypothetical people is it possible to consider the social injustice that their moral problems may reflect and to imagine the individual suffering their occurrence may signify or their resolution engender.[125]

Gilligan posses a model of moral orientation in which justice and care, differ in essentially four ways. First, the ethic of care emphasizes relationships over formal and abstract rights. Second, the ethic of care is more consequentialist in determining the various outcomes, while the ethic of justice is focused more on principles. Third, an ethic of care is more forgiving and open to excuses, whereas an ethic of justice tends to judge behavior as morally inexcusable. Finally, the ethic of justice tends to try to universalize moral choice, while the ethic of care tends to consider historical circumstance.[126]

Mary's intercession appears to fit Gilligan's model for an ethic of moral care orientation. God as strict judge is ready to punish individual acts while Mary attempts to intervene (and always succeeds) because of mitigating factors. One mitigating factor is simply the person's level of repentance as shown in their spiritual sensitivity in pleading their case to Mary. The developing Catholic Church needed the influence of a care orientation as a corrective to an overwhelmingly justice-oriented, legalistic morality. The sacrament of penance and the writings of moral theologians were among the forces behind the building of a powerful justice orientation, and it was the power of popular belief that created the alternative in Mary. Popular devotion to Mary preceded dogmatic legitimation. Because there is so little historical knowledge about Mary, the phenomenon of her ongoing cult raises questions about how it serves a sociological function.[127] Mary is truly a social construction, but to what end? Perhaps Gilligan's model can provide some of the explanation in that Mary helps legitimate an alternative moral perspective of mercy and care that was so powerful, not even the hierarchy of the Catholic Church could suppress it.

Gilligan makes a distinction between care as a moral perspective and care that is compelled to operate within a justice framework. To exemplify this distinction, Gilligan relates the story of two medical students faced with the dilemma of reporting a colleague who broke school rules regarding abstention from alcoholic beverages.[128] One student argues that the violator deserves forgiveness because of contrition and because the rule might not be just anyway. The other student believes that turning in the colleague will not help the colleague's drinking problem, nor will it have a positive effect upon their relationship. The former decision making process represents care subsumed in a justice framework. Gilligan elaborates:

> Within a justice construction, care becomes the mercy that tempers justice; or connotes the special obligations or supererogatory duties that arise in personal relationships; or signifies altruism freely chosen—a decision to modulate the strict demands of justice by considering equity or showing forgiveness; or characterizes a choice to sacrifice the claims of the self.[129]

In this process the justice system remains intact. None of the justice assumptions are undermined. Being "sorry" for breaking the rules does not question the system of justice. Critiquing the justice of the particular rule does not reform the basic moral orientation (exceptions to the rule could be made; other rules could perhaps replace this one). The second student demonstrates a different moral orientation. Rules are not central to the thought process; rather, what is best for the individual and ongoing relationships are the prime consideration. This example helps to clarify the moral significance of Mary's intercession.

The mercy of Mary is an ethic of care viewed through the lens of a justice framework. Mary does not question the system of justice. Mary is not subversive or even reticent. Her mercy legitimizes the existing ethical system. She merely wishes to plead for forgiveness. The court of final appeal is clear—God. Mary does not reflect an authentic ethic of care in an independent moral orientation that considers relationship before making a decision. Her role is one of throwing herself before the mercy of the great judge. Mary represents an ethic of care overwhelmed by an ethic of justice. Mary's mercy is underdeveloped as an alternative ethical model because of its deference to the constructed justice system of God.

The theology that stems from the tradition of Mary's mediation is one that entrenches the dominant role of men in society all the way down to the smallest political and economic unit: the family. The theological language of Catholicism makes the family metaphor evident. God is the omnipotent judge and father of the house. Mary is the approachable, nurturing mother who can hold back the father's wrath. Warner recapitulates,

> The theology of the Virgin's intercession assumes the state of affairs in heaven to resemble the conditions in, say, a Neapolitan artisan's family. And by doing so it reinforces society's belief in mothers' moderating and merciful influence, in the woman's role as the hen who really rules the roost but lets the cock think he does. The natural order for the female sex is ordained as motherhood and, through motherhood, domestic dominion. The idea that a woman might direct matters in her own right as an independent individual is not even entertained. In Catholic societies, such a state of affairs is general, and finds approval in the religion's chief female figure.[130]

Mary legitimizes asymmetrical familial relationships. Zimdars-Swartz's analysis of apparitions reinforces Mary's mediatory role in the cosmic Christian family. God is angry with the world because of the sins of humanity.[131] Mary's motherhood is emphasized because she desires to save her flock, the children of the earth. In fact, if one did not believe in Mary's motherhood, many apparitional messages indicated that such a person was beyond hope. Competing moral imagery is presented. Mary represents divine mercy while God/Jesus represents divine justice. Divine mercy often appears irrational because it can transcend just and righteous punishment. However, divine justice appears cold, exacting, and even mean-spirited in its attempt to punish sinners.

Pope John Paul II specifically associates Mary's mediation with her motherhood. Part II of his encyclical *The Mother of the Redeemer* is titled "Maternal Mediation." The implication for family dynamics in this theology of mediation is a specific hierarchy. Mary mediates the power of God to humanity. She is not all-powerful, but she does retain influence. The mother is not the equivalent of the father. Ironically, Mary is not even the perfect Mediator; this role is reserved for her son. In continuity with the temperance of Vatican II, any mention of Mary's mediation is cautioned with the note that Christ is the perfect mediator.[132] Mary is not only subordinate to the father but also to her male son. In the words of Simone de Beauvoir,

> For the first time in human history the mother kneels before her son: she freely accepts her inferiority. This is the supreme masculine victory, consummated in the cult of the Virgin—it is the rehabilitation of woman through the accomplishment of her defeat.[133]

The words of de Beauvoir describe an inversion of honor and power in the family in which both mother and father are respected as mutually responsible adults. A familial hierarchical reversal takes place based on the Catholic "holy family" model.

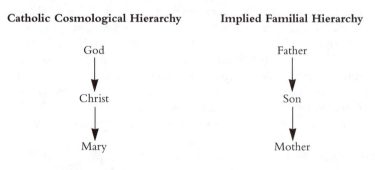

Catholic Cosmological Hierarchy **Implied Familial Hierarchy**

God → Christ → Mary

Father → Son → Mother

Figure 3: The Catholic Distortion of Familial Hierarchy

In the 1950s and 1960s, as post–World War II female consciousness of working roles was raised and a new wave of feminism began to emerge, a genre of literature promoted by the Catholic Church and Church-related groups attempted to reinforce the traditional position of male head of household.[134] Mary was consistently invoked as the symbol of the good wife and homemaker. To further legitimate the family hierarchy, the family structure was deemed "sacred," and any other configuration was profane. The following excerpt is an example of the literature circulated to support the male-dominated family.

> We have certainly underestimated Mary's role as home-maker. The Mother of God was the truest Lady of the House. . . . This, Mary's work, is part of every Christian mother. It is for the father to build the house and to be ever the master there. It is for mother to give it warmth of love that alone can make of a house a Christian home.[135]

The often-used analogy was that of father as "head" of the house and mother as "heart" of the house. In this configuration, men had the freedom to enter the public sphere. Any attempt by women to enter the public sphere was rebuffed by representations of the Church as a violation of the sacred order. To have women work outside the home, obtain birth control, smoke, engage in politics, and play sports was considered a modernist error.[136] The active nature of the male God, as contrasted with the passive nature of Mary, places women in what Elizabeth Johnson refers to as a hopelessly inferior position. God and Mary create a divine pattern that recreates and/or reinforces social relationships.

> The pattern is translated into normative social mores which shape relationships and structures on the premise that men are active, women passive; men take initiative, women respond; men are slated for the public sphere, women for the private; men exercise power, women are supportive of them.[137]

Mary became the model of domestic bliss, and the threat to the tradition of male dominance in the home brought her to the defense. In the words of Mary Gordon, "In my day, Mary was a stick to beat smart girls with. Her example was held up constantly: an example of silence, of subordination, of the pleasure of taking the back seat."[138]

Today, social consciousness has been raised to the point that representatives of the Church cannot make such overt statements against women. However, the Church hierarchy continues an attack on the equal roles for men and women, with Mary at the center of this offensive, as exemplified by the excerpted Papal comments. Many feminists argue that the Church has not abandoned the concept of asymmetrical parenting as normative. The issue of parenting is crucial to feminism. If a list of desired feminist social changes could be prepared, one of the key ideas would be "dual parenting," or an understanding that both individuals in a marriage must be equally responsible for the upbringing of children.[138]

In the words of Valerie Charlton, "The liberation of women is insepara-ble from, among other things, the development of different ways of caring for and relating to children."[140] Although nothing is known about Mary's parenting, she has been socially constructed over time to represent a tradi-tional model of domestic motherhood.

The morality of Mary's status in Catholic theology reflects the moral-ity of the liberation of oppressed peoples, whether it be women in fami-ly structures or third-world cultures in the broader global arena.

> Mary's presence in the midst of peoples who struggle today for their liberation, especially in Latin America, helps us break away from a limited version of her past, that is, a version in which she is submis-sive to her Son, an expression of the submission of women to the established order of the prevailing patriarchal system.[141]

Can Mary escape the patriarchically proscribed roles while retaining enough of her tradition to tap into the power of her worldwide follow-ing? Can women break from prescribed roles to assume greater public power? It is easy to slip into personalizing language and describe Mary in terms of a being that is involved in a great struggle. Mary's mythological tradition appears to be alive and well. The reality is that as a religious construction, Mary can only be invested with power by others. Historical-ly, the faithful gave Mary intercessory powers, and the social construction became reified and legitimized. The issue for living, breathing women is different. Enlightened Catholic women are demanding a share in the power structure of the Catholic Church. This demand includes a rethink-ing of theology, ecclesiology, and pastoral aspects of the Church. The onus of moral action is on the hierarchy of the Catholic Church as holder of the official power. It can choose to share that power and participate in the worldwide consensus and trajectory toward an understanding of the equal dignity of all humans, or it can choose to defend precepts into which the church was locked during its formative years under misogynist social conditions. However, women may take power anyway. Social relationships have evolved to improve women's power in other areas of life. Women can now choose to leave the Church and not fear negative repercussions. In a sense, the Church can either share power now or see its power crumble from beneath it. Catholic feminists such as Ruether are not so utopian as to believe that all oppression can be eliminated from any institution.[142] That is the nature of a human institution, or a "pilgrim church." However, the starting point must include an admission of fallibility.

Already many Catholic feminist theologians have challenged the boundaries of membership in the Catholic Church. Self proclaimed post-Christian Mary Daly has long disavowed the Catholic Church, but even "reformists" like Ruether and Schussler Fiorenza have written challenging works that do not resemble Catholic orthodoxy. The Second Vatican Council may have been the last time an all-male hierarchy in the Catholic Church will define the limits of Mary's power in a socially legitimized way. As the Bishops of the United States could not write a Pastoral Letter on women with any moral force, neither will future definition of Mary by the Catholic hierarchy have much ethical muster. The fate of Mary's power is now in the hands of women who will decide what role she should play, just as women are taking control of their own life choices.

5

Women and Evil / Mary and Eve

To be female is to be deviant by definition in the prevailing culture. To be
female and defiant is to be intolerably deviant.

—Mary Daly[1]

The story of Adam and Eve has been relegated to the background of
modern consciousness despite the efforts of certain Christian communities to revive the teaching of creationism. The fall of humanity is a familiar myth, but it isn't given a great deal of thought or discussion today.
However, precisely because it is so familiar, Mary Daly and others have
argued that it undergirds a dangerous misogynist mindset that tacitly
acknowledges that women are somehow associated with evil. A long-
standing teaching of the Church is that Mary is the abnegation of the evil
set loose by Eve. Much like her other images, this view of Mary as the
New Eve, without much depth of analysis or a feminist sensitivity, might
appear to be empowering. She is a "superheroine" whose goodness over-
comes evil for herself and her gender. However, the complex weaving of
history, politics, and theology that enmeshes Mary as the New Eve makes
this title a source of much feminist criticism. The Eve/Mary parallel
perpetuates good-woman/bad-woman characterizations used to ensnare
women in a false moral dichotomy.[2] Elizabeth Johnson describes the

juxtaposition of Mary and the lives of Catholic women as a great paradox because Mary's exaltation grew in direct proportion to disparaging rhetoric regarding woman's nature.[3] Mary has not been viewed by the Church as a representative of women—she has been hailed as the great exception among women.

This chapter discusses the sources of the theology of the "New Eve," as well as the origins of the Eve myth. The story of Eve in the context of the second story of creation and the fall of humanity found in Genesis (2:4–3:24) has often been identified as a mythic explanation of the association of women with Eve/evil. However, the Judao-Christian creation story is part of a religious tradition of creation myths that began with Goddess creators as an extension of human motherhood. Over time, the power of creation was usurped from the Goddess.[4] The creation story is the final blow to the ancient myths, as the Goddess is completely removed and her vestige, Eve, vilified as the source of sin, death, and destruction in the world. The convergence of the Mary and Eve myths creates a polar dualism in the construction of women that Christian feminists and secular feminist have opposed. Feminists have put forth varied approaches to deconstructing the Eve/Mary dualism. Finally, the moral significance of segmenting women into oppositional categories through the perpetuation of the good/evil dualism will be discussed. In each category, women are viewed as "other"—virgin or vamp—thus dehumanizing them and creating the subtle rationale for woman hating. An otherwise positive title for Mary is inverted into another mythical burden for women.

The Historical Development of Mary as the New Eve

Biblical Sources

Consistent with the images of Mary explored in the previous chapters, she is never explicitly declared to be the "New Eve" in the Christian scriptures. Nevertheless, certain biblical passages have been used to formulate the basis for this title in Catholic literature. Specifically, Genesis 3:1–7, Genesis 3:15, Luke 1:28–38 and Revelation 12: 1–6 will be discussed for their contribution to the creation of Mary's role as the New Eve. The development of the idea of "Eve" will also be explored in this section.

In the remonstration of the serpent by God in Genesis 3:15, the "woman" mentioned was traditionally believed to be Mary.

I will put enmity between you and the woman,
and between your offspring and hers;
He will strike at your head,
while you strike at his heel.

The Mariological exegesis is far from obvious. This passage only became associated with the Eve/Mary connection through the third-century interpretations of the fathers of the Church.[5] An error in the Vulgate bible (the last in a series of Latin translations of the bible made by St. Jerome[6]) found "he" read as "she" in God's condemnation of the serpent. Marina Warner notes that this is one of three critical errors in Jerome's translation of the Vulgate bible, which perpetuated Mariolatry. Besides the error in the curse of the serpent, there was the error discussed in Chapter Three regarding *almah* translated as "virgin," and there was the translation of Gabriel's greeting of Mary, "full of grace," to imply that she was without sin prior to the atonement that her son would provide some thirty years later.[7] These translation errors by Jerome are intriguing, considering he was instrumental in perpetuating the Cult of Mary in his theological reflections and apologetics.

Justin Martyr, and later Irenaeus, viewed the language of the dialogue between God and the serpent as symbolic of the struggle between the human race and the devil.[8] In this struggle, Christ becomes victorious, and so too Mary. This somewhat obscure Christological and Mariological interpretation is an example of eisegesis (an interpretation of scripture that reflects bias), which was not universally accepted by Christian theologians. Later, Protestant reformers would also thoroughly reject this view. Nevertheless, this interpretation remained as an extension of Mariological fervor. Modern exegetes do not believe the author of Genesis 3:15 had a Mariological intent.[9] In the *Jerome Biblical Commentary*, Richard Clifford and Roland Murphy refute the association of the snake with Satan.[10] Current exegesis is much more literal in this case. Modern translations reflect a simple condemnation of snakes, creatures to be forever regarded as enemies by the human descendants of Eve.

A second biblical source for the New Eve title of Mary is the antithetical parallel that has been observed in the dialogue between Eve and the Serpent and between Mary and the angel Gabriel, recounted:[11]

Genesis 3:1–7   **Luke 1:28-38**

1 Now the serpent was the most cunning of all the animals that the Lord God had made. The serpent asked the woman, "Did God really tell you not to eat from any of the trees in the garden?"

2 The woman answered the serpent: "We may eat of the fruit of the trees in the garden;

3 It is only about the fruit of the tree in the middle of the garden that God said, 'You shall not eat it or even touch it lest you die.'"

4 But the serpent said to the woman: "You certainly will not die!

5 No, God knows well that the moment you eat of it your eyes will be opened and you will be like gods who know what is good and what is bad."

6 The woman saw that the tree was good for food, pleasing to the eyes, and desirable for gaining wisdom. So she took some of its fruit and ate it; and she also gave some to her husband, who was with her, and he ate it.

7 Then the eyes of both of them were opened, and they realized that they were naked; so he sewed fig leaves together and made loincloths for themselves.

28 He [Gabriel] entered and said to her [Mary], "Greetings, favored one. The Lord is with you!"

29 But she was deeply disturbed by the words, and wondered what this greeting could mean.

30 The heavenly messenger said to her, "Don't be afraid, Mary, for you have found favor with God.

31 Listen to me: you will conceive in your womb and give birth to a son, and you will name him Jesus.

32 He will be great, and will be called son of the Most High. And the Lord God will give him the throne of David, his father.

33 He will rule over the house of Jacob forever; and his dominion will have no end."

34 And Mary said to the messenger, "How can this be, since I am not involved with a man?"

35 The messenger replied, "The Holy Spirit will come over you, and the power of the Most High will cast its shadow on you. This is why the child to be born will be holy, and be called son of God.

36 Further, your relative Elizabeth was also conceived a son in her old age. She who has said to be infertile is already six months along,

37 Since nothing is impossible with God."

38 And Mary said, "Here I am, the Lord's slave. May everything you have said come true." Then the Heavenly messenger left her.

Tertullian utilized the previous passages in characterizing the Eve/Mary parallel as one based on the relative beliefs of the protagonists in the respective stories. While Eve believes the word of the serpent, Mary believes the word of God's emissary, Gabriel. The latter belief emends the error of the former belief. A simple good/evil dualism exists in the work of exegetes of the early Church. Accordingly, the will of God was made clear to both Eve and Mary. Each woman listened to a supernatural being, and each made a free choice to obey or disobey God's will without the aid of their consort. Each woman was also a virgin. Mary obeyed God's will and Eve disobeyed.[12] The parallel is strong enough that Phillips suggests perhaps the author of Luke made use of the Fall in the development of the infancy narrative.[13]

Another biblical source traditionally used to support Mary as the New Eve is the passage found in Chapter 12 of the Book of Revelation. This pericope (Rev. 12:1-6) is commonly referred to as the "Woman and the Dragon" or the "Woman Clothed with the Sun."

> A great sign appeared in the sky, a woman clothed with the sun, with the moon under her feet, and on her head a crown of twelve stars. She was with child and wailed aloud in pain as she labored to give birth. Then another sign appeared in the sky; it was a huge red dragon, with seven heads and ten horns, and on its heads were seven diadems. Its tail swept away a third of the stars in the sky and hurled them down to the earth. Then the dragon stood before the woman about to give birth, to devour her child when she gave birth. She gave birth to a son, a male child, destined to rule all the nations with an iron rod. Her child was caught up to God and his throne. The woman herself fled into the desert where she had a place prepared by God, that there she might be taken care of for twelve hundred and sixty days.

The chapter goes on to describe the pursuit of the woman by the dragon. Subsequently, the dragon gives up on the woman and pursues her offspring.

The apocalyptic literature found in the Book of Revelation has been the source of varied interpretation. The use of symbolic language makes this text ripe for dispute and discussion. Beginning with Epiphanius of Salamis in the late third century, the Catholic tradition has been to interpret the "woman clothed in the sun" as Mary.[14] The apocalyptic battle with the dragon, viewed as evil, recreates the Eve/Mary theme by reinforcing Mary as the force for God and Eve as evil. The allusion to painful childbirth recalls Gen. 3:15 as the punishment given to Eve.

Modern biblical scholars reject the Eve/Mary connection in this text. Adela Yarbro Collins, for example, finds Chapter 12 of Revelations recasting a non-Christian mythic story of a dragon doing battle with a pregnant woman whose child threatens to depose him. The preferred modern interpretation is that of the woman symbolizing Israel, and the birth pangs are the events that precede the end times and the return of the Messiah. The dragon symbolizes the chaos surrounding Israel.[15] The claim that the woman in Revelation 12 is Mary is also complicated by the Catholic tradition that Mary did not experience pain in giving birth to Jesus. She was the exception to the curse of Eve placed upon all women.

The biblical origins for Mary as the female counterpart to Eve are tenuous at best.[16] The basis for these claims rests upon innuendo and symbolism that do not appear to stem from the intent of the authors. The lack of clear biblical declaration of Mary as the New Eve leaves a question for sociologists and cultural historians to answer: Why did the New Eve become such a prominent and enduring title for Mary? What purpose did this title possess?

The Eve Myth

While the historical existence of Mary is not questioned, the very existence of Eve is improbable. Nevertheless, her role in the Christian creation narratives makes her a prominent mythical character of paramount significance in soteriology (the study of salvation through Jesus) and concepts of ontological female evil. Much like Mary, the character of Eve was often molded to suit the patriarchal needs of the religious leadership. For example, Karen Armstrong, who analyzed Protestant literature on the family from the sixteenth to nineteenth centuries, found the evil aspect of Eve mitigated in favor of her weakness and inferiority. Women were told they were ontologically weak in comparison to males. That is why Eve brought about the Fall. Women were reinforced for subjugating themselves to men, lest they suffer the fate of Eve.[17]

Similar to what has been observed about the images of Mary, Eve's biblical origins do not match her mythic development. There are two creation stories in Genesis (1:1–2:4a and 2:4b–3:24). The first creation story is less anthropocentric (the animals are created first) and more egalitarian than the second.[18] The two stories appear in reverse order of their chronological authorship. The first story was written several hundred years after the second, although tradition and artistic representations have always favored the latter.[19] Eve is only mentioned in the second creation story, after which she is only named again in the Christian scriptures (1 Tim 2:13 and 2 Cor 11:2-3).[20]

Only the second creation story of Genesis has the Fall attached to it, and it is this tradition that Christianity adopted with its vilification of Eve and her gender.[21] The "Fall" is traditionally understood as the moment in time at which Adam and Eve, because of their disobedience, became separated from coexistence with God in paradise. The Fall also ensured that a similar fate was the destiny of all subsequent generations. The theological development of the Fall spawned the concept of original sin, with which all of humanity is born (except Mary) because of the first sin perpetrated by Adam and Eve.

For women, the Fall is also significant because it was traditionally associated with the curse of the female gender for all generations. Specifically, in verse 3:16 of Genesis, God realizes that Adam and Eve have been disobedient, and he speaks to Eve:

> To the woman he said:
> "I will intensify the pangs of your childbearing;
> in pain shall you bring forth children.
> Yet your urge shall be for your husband,
> and he shall be your master."

Again, the Fall does not appear in the first creation account, and the differences between the two creation myths have concerned theologians for ages.

Hebrew mythology attempted to explain the difference by creating the character of Lilith. According to legend, Lilith was Adam's first wife, and she was even more "evil" than Eve. The Lilith myth was an extension of a non-Jewish deity legend. God created Lilith as an equal to Adam (in the first creation story of Genesis), and she refused to be subordinated by Adam.[22] Lilith subsequently fled and was banished. She ultimately consorted with demons to produce many evil offspring. Attempts to bring her back and control her failed. Eve was created as the second wife because she was more compliant. However, she is still a source of great evil.[23] The gendered pattern of this story—deviant females as the source of the downfall of humanity—was repeated in a number of "Fall-like" stories in antiquity.[24]

Judith Plaskow, in a modern retelling of the myth of Lilith from a feminist perspective, demonstrates the significance of gendered experience in informing sacred stories. Plaskow's version of the myth transforms Lilith and Eve into a symbolic sisterhood that is viewed as mysterious and dangerous by the male God and Adam.[25]

In developing a theology of the Fall, Church fathers went beyond the passages found in Genesis. There is no explicit consideration of the concept of original sin in the Hebrew scriptures. Non-canonical sources such as *The*

Secrets of Enoch, The Apocalypse of Moses, and *The Books of Adam and Eve,* as well as the non-Christian story of Pandora, appear to have influenced the mythology and theology surrounding the shadowy figure of Eve.[26]

The story of the Fall in Genesis is part of a trajectory of Judeo-Christian stories that increasingly lay the blame for evil in the world upon women. While the early stories are less explicit, there is a trend toward making women culpable for the evil in humanity. For example, *The Book of Enoch* retells a popular story that describes how angels, called "Watchers," descended from heaven en masse to sleep with women and satisfy their lust. These angels revealed enchantments and powers to women. The women gave birth to a generation of evil offspring that infested the earth. The evils of war and how to wage it were brought into the world by these women, who were taught by the watchers.[27]

This watcher myth was retold in the *Book of Jubilees* and the *Testament of Reuben,* but in them the women become increasingly blameworthy. They were transformed into the seducers of the angels, and therefore were held more directly responsible for the subsequent evil.[28] The amount of imagination and zeal that the authors had in developing women as scapegoats in the watcher myths indicates the high level of sexism in the patriarchal societies in which they circulated. Over time, the story of Eve and the Fall replaced the Watcher Myth as the dominant creation story, although it retained the theme of women as the vehicle for human evil.[29]

According to Elizabeth Johnson, the zealous portrayal of the responsibility of women for evil in the world borders on flattery.[30] In a negative way, Eve, and therefore all women, are attributed with great power over men. Nevertheless, rather than creating a holistic approach to human morality, the Church fathers created a gendered moral dualism that vilified woman.

While Eve appears in the second chapter of the first book of the Hebrew scriptures, and Mary appears largely in the infancy narratives of the Christian gospels, it should not be presumed that the characterizations of these figures that have lingered to the present day—Eve as disobedient and sexual and Mary as obedient and virginal—had the same chronological development as their biblical texts.[31] As religious constructions, the biblical bases for these characterizations are weak. Ruether notes that Hebrew thought portrayed in scripture, as well as subsequent Rabbinical thought, did not take the story of the Fall very seriously. It is not referenced anywhere else in the Hebrew scriptures, as the source of evil.[32] The authors of the gospels do not mention the story of the Fall. It is Paul who provides the foundation for focusing upon Eve by describing Jesus as the New Adam (1 Cor. 15:22 and Rom. 5:17).

While some traditions supporting a negative portrayal of Eve existed, they were not truly solidified until the development of the Cult of Mary. Eve and Mary are complementary figures whose increased polarization through extreme characterizations of good and evil helped create each other.[33] They are significant characters in the Catholic story of redemption. Unfortunately, the polarization transforms the story into a tragedy, as the lives of real women were also splintered.

There is evidence that Church fathers did not have a unified understanding of virginity until the second century C.E.[34] However, the Cult of Mary was not a significant factor at that time. As Mariology gained momentum, the virginal definition became more and more precise, to the point of physical intactness of the hymen. As a parallel, Eve became increasingly viewed as a sexual siren. The development of the doctrine of Mary's virginity served to support the sexual interpretation of the Fall. Paradise became understood as a virginal state of grace. Losing virginity was a fall from grace. Eve's failure was her fall from virginity, while Mary's victory was her perpetual virginity.[35] There could be no "New Eve" without "Eve," since the Cult of Mary needed Eve to give it greater theological significance.[36] Mary's completion of the redemptive cycle became such a popular theological theme that some, such as St. Ambrose, praised the Fall because it gave Mary the opportunity to bring about salvation.[37] Eve became Mary's foil. In this respect, the triumph of Mary is sometimes viewed as the end of the Goddess because of Eve's identification with ancient Goddess worship.[38]

The Theological Basis

Second-century theologian Justin Martyr was probably the first to make the Eve/Mary parallel.[39] However, Justin did not develop the theme fully, although he maintained that the idea of women as the source of evil was normative. Justin Martyr was apparently aware of the Watcher myth and alluded to it in his *Apology*.

> [God] committed the care of men and all things under heaven to angels whom he appointed over them. But the angels transgressed this appointment, and were captivated by love of women, and begat children who are those that are called demons; and besides, they afterwards subdued the human race to themselves . . . and among men they sowed murders, wars, adulteries, intemperate deeds, and all wickedness.[40]

Ironically, given Eve's association with sexuality, Justin's basis for comparing Mary and Eve is their common virginal state and their subsequent conception of the forces of evil and good. Eve is not explicitly described as a virgin in the Genesis creation story, although Justin makes this assumption. Justin describes both Mary and Eve as receiving "the word." For Eve the word was rooted in evil, and for Mary it was rooted in salvation. He makes it clear that the difference between the response of the two women is one of obedience to God's command.

> [The Son of God] became man through the Virgin, that the disobedience caused by the serpent might be destroyed in the same way in which it had originated. For Eve, while a virgin incorrupt, conceived the word which proceeded from the serpent, and brought forth disobedience and death. But the Virgin Mary was filled with faith and joy when the Angel Gabriel told her the glad tidings that the Spirit of the Lord would come upon her . . . and she answered: "Be it done unto me according to thy word." And through her was He born . . . by whom God destroys both the serpent and the angels and men who have become like the serpent, and delivers from death those who repent of their wickedness and believe in Him.[41]

Disobedience is the definition of Eve's foible, and the ultimate difference between Eve and Mary.

It was Irenaeus who in the latter part of the second century integrated the Eve/Mary parallel into a more comprehensive theology of salvation.[42] Irenaeus extended the Pauline theme of Jesus as the New Adam to Mary as the New Eve, establishing a symmetrical atonement theology. According to his analysis, the evil that came to the human race through Adam and Eve was vanquished through the redemptive work of Jesus and Mary. For Irenaeus, Adam becomes a "type" of Christ and Eve a "type" of Mary.[43] Eve's disobedience and susceptibility to evil brought suffering into the world. Mary's obedience and steadfastness brought redemption and salvation. Mary and Eve were viewed as "accessories" to God's plan for human redemption. While Eve "cooperated" with Satan to bring about spiritual death for humanity, Mary's cooperation with God functioned to overcome the Fall.[44]

In Irenaeus's theology, the theme of the "New Eve" represented a shift in soteriology. The incarnation was not merely Jesus proclaiming a new kingdom; he also had to redeem a fallen world.[45] This theological theme is of great significance in Christianity. The belief that Jesus died for sins gave new depth of meaning to his life, death, and resurrection. The idea of the incarnation, or that God intervened in human history by becoming human, was brought to a higher level of purpose by constructing it as a sacrifice for human sinfulness. Atonement theology had not been a part of the very early theology of the Christian Church.[46] Giving Mary the title of the New Eve assisted in the closing of the redemptive loop. Adam and Eve began the tide of human sinfulness that Jesus and Mary would end. Declaring Mary the Second Eve was not the exclusive support for atonement theology, but it did help solidify its standing.

Tertullian in the third century would repeat the theme of Mary as the New Eve in an emphatic fashion:

> And do you [women] not know that you are an Eve? The sentence of God on the sex of your lives in this age; the guilt must of necessity live too. You are the devil's gateway . . . the first deserter of the divine law; you are she who persuaded him whom the devil was not valiant enough to attack. You destroyed so easily God's image, man. On account of your desert—that is, death, even the Son of God had to die.[47]

The theme of Mary as the New Eve has not undergone any serious development from Tertullian's time through the present day. The Eve/Mary parallel has endured in its third-century form. The Eve/Mary moral distinction has become an accepted presupposition of Catholic theology. St. Augustine made the gender dualism explicit when he declared, "Through a woman death, through a woman life."[48]

Zeno, the bishop of Verona in the latter part of the fourth century, provides a unique biological insight into the Eve/Mary parallel. He described Eve as being literally seduced "through the ear" by the devil's message of corruption. Christ, or "the Word," entered Mary through the ear to bring her salvation. It is the word spoken to women that brings the Fall and redemption of the human race. Zeno's contemporary, Ephraem of Syrian, would repeat the theme of the redemptive cycle of the word. Ephraem glorified the New Eve as intimately associated with all of Christ's saving work. [49]

The dogmas of the Immaculate Conception and Bodily Assumption of Mary are part of the internal Catholic logic that supports the Eve/Mary parallel. Stephen Benko describes Mary's immaculate state as a prerequisite for the *hieros gamos,* or impregnation, by the Holy Spirit. Mary is equivalent to Eve prior to Eve's "corruption." This is the critical prerequisite for salvation—an immaculate, sinless woman who can be in communion with God.[50]

Traditionally, some Catholic theologians associated the dogma of Mary's assumption into heaven as an extension of her title as New Eve. For example, the influential nineteenth-century theologian John Henry Newman believed that the Assumption was a logical procession from New Eve typology.[51] While Eve was thrown out of paradise because of her disobedience, Mary eternally resides in heaven because of her sinlessness and cooperation in human redemption.[52] Many of the same biblical resources used to defend the title of the New Eve are used as a basis for Mary's assumption (Luke 1:28 and Rev. 12).[53] In Pope Pius XII's declaration of Mary's bodily assumption into heaven, he explicitly makes the connection between the dogma and Mary's title of New Eve. As discussed in the first chapter, many Marian doctrines were shaped to fit larger theological requirements. The dogma of the assumption was believed necessary to support the victory of good over evil. In the words of theologian Avery Dulles, "If Mary's body had been given over to corruption, rather than being taken up into heavenly glory, Satan would have triumphed over her in some measure."[54]

The bishops of the Second Vatican Council reinforced the Eve/Mary parallel in the *Dogmatic Constitution on the Church,* in which they recalled the words of Irenaeus:

> Rightly therefore the holy Fathers see her [Mary] as used by God not merely in a passive way, but as cooperating in the work of human salvation through free faith and obedience. For, as St. Irenaeus says, she, "being obedient, became the cause of salvation for herself and for the whole human race." Hence in their preaching not a few of the early Fathers gladly assert with him: "The knot of Eve's disobedience was untied by Mary's obedience. What the virgin Eve bound through her unbelief, Mary loosened by her faith." Comparing Mary and Eve, they call her "the mother of the living," and still more often they say: "death through Eve, life through Mary."[55]

The bishops shed no new light on this Marian imagery, and in their statement they recall the patristic fathers in supporting the idea of Mary as New Eve. Again, what made Eve the source of evil was her disobedience.

In their 1973 pastoral letter on Mary, *Behold Your Mother Woman of Faith*, the United States bishops affirm Mary as the New Eve and make the often-cited connection between the Church and Mary. The appropriation allows for the praises heaped upon Mary to be shared by the Church.

The early comparisons were between the disobedient Eve and the obedient new Eve. Eve believed the word of deceit; the new Eve heeded Gabriel's message. A woman helped introduce death; Mary became the "cause of salvation" and "advocate of Eve." By St. Jerome's time it was common to hear: "death through Eve, Life through Mary." Even more anciently, the Church was regarded as the "new Eve." The Church is the bride of Christ, formed from His side in the sleep of death on the cross, as the first Eve was formed by God from the side of the sleeping Adam. As the first Eve was "mother of the living," the Church becomes the "new mother of the living." In time, some of the maternal characteristics of the Church were seen in Mary, and so St. Epiphanius calls Mary "the mother of the living."[56]

The themes presented are now familiar. There is no development of the theology, but simply a restatement of ancient understanding about Mary.

The enduring dichotomy of the characteristics of Eve and Mary in Catholic tradition leaves the following polar descriptions:

Eve	Mary
disobedience	obedience
sorrow	joy
woman cursed	woman blessed
darkness	light
sin	salvation
Fall	restoration
condemnation	praise
death	life
paradise lost	paradise gained
cooperation with the devil	cooperation with God
sexual	virginal

The history of the Marian imagery of the New Eve versus Mary's virginity and mediation imagery has been notably static. There were no special councils, heresies, controversial dogmas, or split votes. The Eve/Mary dualism has been taken for granted in Catholic theology. The Bishops of the Second Vatican Council did not hesitate to use the ancient title of New Eve for Mary, with little concern for the implication of this label for women. By contrast, Mary's virginity was the subject of a great deal of theological scrutiny. Mary's power of mediation has been an ongoing controversy. Mary as the female embodiment of good, as opposed to Eve as the female embodiment of evil, has been a relatively fixed belief since the third century. Only Christian feminism of the last several decades has argued that this religious construction may harm women.

Redefining Good and Evil.

Philosophers generally agree that evil involves pain, suffering, terror, and destruction.[57] Traditionally, evil is divided into the categories of natural evil (sometimes referred to as ontic evil) and moral evil. Natural evil is that occurring with no human intent, such as in natural disasters and accidents. Moral evil is a human phenomenon that requires intentional harm or disregard for others. The refinement of these categories is subject to debate, but the general conceptualization is agreed upon. When moral evil is defined in a religious context, it becomes sin. The problem with moral evil or sin is that at some point someone has to define it. Moral evils in a secular society are a function of the culture and historical setting. In Peter Berger's social construction terminology, a reification occurs. The definitions of sin, reified as the will of God, are presumably not subject to historical criticism.

Feminist scholars reexamine many of the religious notions of moral evil, finding that they reflect historical social norms and men's experience as the leaders in those settings. The myth of Adam and Eve is just such a religious reification, demonstrative of a pattern of evil projected onto women—particularly disobedient women. As Mary Daly points out, the male perspective becomes metamorphosed into God's perspective.[58] The association of Mary with Eve creates a moral contrast that forces women to be categorized with Eve because of Mary's unattainable "goodness."

Ultimately, feminist analysis of Mary as the New Eve is a critique of Catholic moral theology as it relates to the inherent morality of humanity. Two broad categories of critique can be found in the feminist literature addressing Mary's title of New Eve. One category concerns the deconstruction and/or reconstruction of the myth itself. This discussion will be the focus of the following sections. The second broad category of critique deals with the moral implications of the Eve/Mary dualism. This will be the subject of later sections in this chapter.

Feminist analyses of the Eve/Mary distinction contains two themes or lines of thought:

1. *Recovering the Entire Myth of Eve.* This position finds a truncated version of the Eve mythology incorporated into Judeo-Christian scriptures. The incorporated portion of the Eve myth is utilized

for patriarchal oppression and is not representative of the entire goddess story.

2. *Reinterpreting the Myth of Eve.* This approach finds more fault with the early interpretations of the Fall and the creation of the Eve/Mary polar opposition. This position corresponds to Carol Christ's type 1, or reformist category, of feminist analysis.[59]

Of course, there are Christian feminists who cross these artificial boundaries, but the themes provide a starting place for understanding the critique.

While researching her book *Reinventing Eve: Modern Woman in Search of Herself,* psychologist Kim Chernin came across an old Jewish folk saying that is an appropriate opening for this section: "Adam's last will and testament read:'Don't believe Eve's version.'"[60] The story of the Fall found in the second creation account of Genesis is a singular version of the myriad of myths surrounding Eve and her predecessor goddesses. However, it is this version, because of its inclusion in the Jewish and Christian canons, that is remembered and retold today. Other myths abounded in the biblical age, and feminist scholars are critical of the fact that this particularly misogynist story was chosen for canonization. The entry on "Eve" in Barbara Walker's *The Woman's Encyclopedia of Myths and Secrets* lists numerous stories about Eve.[61] "Eve" was one of the common Middle Eastern names for the superior feminine power. There were myths of the goddess Eve who had no spouse. The Gnostic gospels, which were generally egalitarian in their gender orientation, were much more enamored of the first creation story in Genesis.[62] Some traditions described Eve as creating Adam, as in the *Hypostasis of the Archons.*

> And the spirit-endowed Woman came to [Adam] and spoke with him, saying, "Arise, Adam." And when he saw her, he said, "It is you who have given me life; you shall be called "Mother of the Living"—for it is she who is my mother. It is she who is the Physician, and the Woman, and She Who Has Given Birth." . . . Then the Female Spiritual Principle came in the Snake, the Instructor, and it taught them, saying, ". . . you shall not die; for it was out of jealousy that he said this to you. Rather, your eyes shall open, and you shall become like gods, recognizing evil and good." . . . And the arrogant Ruler cursed the Woman . . . [and] . . . the Snake.[63]

Eve is portrayed as a powerful woman, not clearly associated with evil.

An exhaustive account of Eve myths will not be attempted here.[64] However, the existence of various Eve stories is significant enough to raise questions about why the particular account of Adam and Eve is included in the second creation myth of Genesis. Is the fact that this version was included in the canon sufficient to make it more authoritative than the other creation stories surrounding Eve? An understanding of the precarious method in which books of the bible were included in the canon clouds any such legitimation.[65] Current evidence reveals that no definitive closed canon came into use until after the second century C.E.[66] However, even the early Christians could make use of the variety of sources without necessarily violating a sacred canon. This discussion brings us back to the description in Chapter One of Mary as a social construction. It is highly probable that the brief story of Eve in Genesis was included in the canon as a reflection of the existent social norms, or at least the desired norms, when the canon was forming. Historical critical methods have given feminists the tools to question the existence of the Eve/Mary parallel by revealing that perhaps there was more to Eve than is found in Genesis.

Were the canonized version of creation, and the story of Eve, different, it is only speculation as to how Mary as the New Eve would have changed, or whether this title would have existed at all. As Barbara Walker explains,

> Had one of the other versions of the Eve myth prevailed over the canonical version, sexual behavior patterns in western civilization almost certainly would have evolved along very different lines. Christianity managed to project man's fear of death onto woman, not to respect her as Kali the Destroyer was respected but to hate her. The uncanonical scriptures were no more and no less creditable than the canonical ones.[67]

Perhaps Mary would have been viewed in continuity with a more powerful Eve. The notion of Eve as the gateway of the devil so undergirds the paradigm of Christian womanhood that imagining a different Eve and a different Mary requires a fundamental shift in theological reflection.

Because of the bible's cultural significance, and because the second creation story is prominently displayed in the opening book of the bible, many feminists have sought to address and reinterpret this text. Women who have reflected upon the impact and misogyny of this creation story include such pioneer feminists as Elizabeth Cady Stanton and Simone de Beauvoir.[68] One hundred years after Stanton's commentary in *The Woman's Bible*, feminists continue to focus on reinterpreting this key Judao-Christian myth.

In *The Myth of the Goddess*, Anne Baring and Jules Cashford point out that regardless of the variety of Eve myths that circulated, a literal reading of the second creation story in Genesis does not necessarily lead to the misogynist extrapolations that have been attributed to Eve.[69] For example, there is no explicit sexual intercourse in the pericope of the Fall. Nevertheless, symbolic interpretations have made Eve into a wanton sexual siren.[70] Mary Evans in her analysis of the Fall notes that Genesis 3:16 contains no explicit curse of women. What God said of women was merely a statement of what separation from God meant.[71] According to Evans, the intent does not appear to be to damn the female gender. Nevertheless, Eve, and therefore women, have been cursed through the ages, if not by God, then by Christian theologians. Feminist scholars have offered nonsexist alternative exegeses for the pericope the Fall.

Baring and Cashford use symbolic exegesis of the Fall to interpret it as the myth of the birth of consciousness.[72] In such an interpretation, the moral guilt of Adam and Eve, which was transformed by Catholicism into original sin, is viewed as a kind of tragic guilt. What occurred was necessary for humanity to become aware of good and evil; blame is not an issue. Eve's biting into the fruit of knowledge entails consciousness raising and the moral burdens of responsibility that go with it. The state of paradise is then viewed not so much as utopian, but as a state of being in harmonious existence with all living creatures. For humans to move beyond nonconscious, animal-like existence, the fruit of knowledge had to have been eaten. Eve was not the "gateway of the devil" but a participant in the origins of human consciousness raising and transcendence from mere biological life.

A number of feminist authors have developed the concept of Eve as the mother of consciousness or knowledge. In *Beyond God the Father*, Mary Daly describes the second coming of woman as the arrival of the anti-Christ in the form of a "surge of consciousness."[73] This provides a shift in perspective. If Eve was responsible for the awakening of human consciousness, then, extending Daly's idea, the "New Eve" should have been the anti-Christ that would arise to lift human consciousness against patriarchal religion. However, Mary became a false New Eve because her tradition did not rebel against Catholicism.

Kim Chernin transforms Eve into a heroine. Eve was a rebel, "the first woman to challenge the subjugation of woman in the patriarchal garden."[74] Chernin reinterprets the myth of the Fall as an empowering story for modern women. Ironically, given the pervasiveness of eating disorders among women, Eve disobeys a food taboo. She eats of the fruit of knowledge and therefore recreates herself in the image of the goddess. Recognizing the underlying cultural power of religious tradition, Chernin offers a personal exegesis of the creation story that transcends traditional patriarchal interpretation. In this process, Chernin affirms the potency of spiritual female imagery, and therefore wishes to address it directly through greater identification with Eve. Chernin wishes to vindicate Eve and women.

In a positivist interpretation, Gebara and Bingemer view Mary's title—the New Eve—as based not in a negation of Eve but in continuity with her creative work as a woman. "She [Mary] is Eve in the totality of her being—mother of the living, mother of life."[75] The good/evil dualism is eliminated in favor of cosmic creative sisterhood that represents a tangible experience of divinity. Gebara and Bingemer do not discuss obedience and disobedience but place Eve and Mary, as the New Eve, on a different plane of theological significance. Their perspective is not a competitive one for Eve and Mary; it is a developmental understanding.

Another alternative view of the Adam and Eve story requires a shift in creation valorization from primacy to recency. The traditional approach was established by Paul in 1 Tim. 2:11–15.

> A woman must receive instruction silently and under complete control. For Adam was formed first, then Eve. Further, Adam was not deceived, but the woman was deceived and transgressed. But she will be saved through motherhood, provided women persevere in faith and love and holiness, with self-control.

Paul emphasizes Adam's earlier creation as indicating the superiority of men. As part of a process she describes as "depatriarchalizing the bible," Phyllis Trible offers an alternative approach. Adam may have been created first, but God's masterpiece was the final product—Eve. In the first creation story of Genesis, humans were created last. There is nothing to indicate that the order of creation was intended to imply a hierarchy of beings.[76] This interpretation negates the implication that a secondary being somehow was more susceptible to the seductiveness of evil.

Yet another of Trible's insights is to view Eve in the episode of the Fall as the protagonist and not as the antagonist. Trible asks why the snake spoke to Eve over Adam. Trible's answer is that Eve was more intelligent. Eve fully contemplated her action and then ate the fruit of the tree without any spousal consultation (Gen 3:6). She acted independently. By contrast, Adam simply ate the fruit without comment or contemplation.[77] Eve appeared to be a leader, albeit a rebellious one. Trivka Frymer-Kensky concurs with Trible:

> Eve is portrayed as the spokesperson for the couple, and during her talk with the serpent she presents theological arguments. She is never portrayed as wanton, or as tempting or tempted sexually, nor does the biblical author single her out for greater blame than her partner.[78]

Trible interprets the judgment of God as a condemnation of subjugation of any kind. "Whereas in creation man and woman know harmony and equality, in sin they know alienation and discord."[79] For Trible, scripture contains no vilification of Eve, on which the dichotomy with Mary depends.[80] Vilifying Eve was a task for subsequent patriarchal theologians to pursue.

Trible's analysis is reminiscent of that made by a foremother of the modern feminist movement, Elizabeth Cady Stanton. Writing at the turn of the century, Stanton's *The Woman's Bible* recasts Eve as a positive representation of the female gender.

> Reading this narrative carefully, it is amazing that any set of men ever claimed that the dogma of the inferiority of woman is here set forth. The conduct of Eve from the beginning to the end is so superior to that of Adam. . . . The unprejudiced reader must be impressed with the courage, the dignity, and the lofty ambition of the woman. The temptor evidently had a profound knowledge of human nature, and saw at a glance the high character of the person he met by chance in his walks in the garden . . . compared with Adam she appears to great advantage through the entire drama.[81]

As one might expect, Stanton was roundly criticized for her pioneering effort. Ironically, the book was often condemned as "the work of women and the devil."[82] Her farsighted analysis reveals that religious social constructions are not absolute in their socialization, and subversive alternatives are possible. Stanton was a true pioneer in the face of a gender-oppressive society.

Each of the feminist reinterpretations of the Fall renders the Eve/Mary dualism unnecessary by reassessing Eve's moral culpability. Positive, empowering portrayals of Eve reduce the polar opposition of the Eve/Mary characterizations and in turn mitigate the rigid good/evil categories placed upon women.

Ethical Implications of the New Eve

The categorical opposites created by the Eve/Mary distinction are part of a tradition of characterizing women as either good or evil. Only recently has feminist scholarship begun to explore the full ramifications of this dualism. In *Women and Evil*, Nel Noddings argues that the good/evil label represents a means for controlling women by reinforcing their behavior when it is obedient, service oriented, nurturing, and compassionate.[83] To deviate from this definition of good is to be immoral or evil. For Catholics, Mary embodies the "good" behavior of women. Daly refers to this dichotomy as the punitive function of Mary. Mary's "goodness" is so absolute that no woman can achieve it. Thus, all women are relegated to being a type of Eve and are therefore inferior and, ultimately, a source of evil.[84] Noddings notes that it is feminist theologians like Daly and Ruether who are attempting to renegotiate the traditional definition of evil.

The traditional Eve/Mary dualism projects a cosmological battle of good and evil between the devil and God. The good/evil schizophrenia of Christianity led Daly to suggest that the symbols of Christianity deserve to die.[85] The creation of an all-good God required an antithesis in the creation of the devil. The result is an ongoing morality play/battle in which evil is persecuted and punished. This cosmology, however, is subjective and leaves it to the Church hierarchy to determine the evil to be punished. The Eve/Mary dichotomy helps define good/evil models for women. Those who emulate Mary are good women, and those who emulate Eve are bad women. However, since most women are incapable of being virgin-mothers, their lot is cast with Eve. This gendered dualistic ethical language continues to permeate Catholic official pronouncements.

The determination of what human behavior is good or evil is an ongoing subject of debate. However, the Eve/Mary dualism represents a moral "short cut" for the Catholic Church that allows discussion (and women) to be cut out of the deliberatory process. There is no parallel concept in men's experience. While Paul declared Jesus to be the New Adam, these titles have not taken on the ethical dimensions associated with Mary as the New Eve. Historically, Adam has been exonerated from much of his role in the Fall of humanity. While Jesus is viewed as the ultimate moral model for Christians, this model is generalized to both sexes and does not have the specific gender identification given to Mary as the New Eve. The Eve/Mary dualism is not directed at men as a moral lesson. Moral control through the "divide and conquer" approach of the Eve/Mary dichotomy is directed at women.

Men's fear of women may have motivated the development of the moral dualism found in the imagery of the New Eve. In a psychological examination, Maria Kassel found the Eve/Mary phenomenon to be an attempt by men to placate their fears of becoming "swallowed up" by the archetype of the Great Mother.[86] The primeval Great Mother, psychologically nurtured by the experience of birth and child raising, is to be feared because she can both create and destroy. Men feel particularly vulnerable because they cannot emulate the Great Mother. To protect itself, the male ego attempts to dominate women. It accomplishes this within the Christian myth by dissecting the Great Mother into Mary and Eve, and by imposing moral implications on this dissection. Mary is the good mother, and Eve is the bad or dark aspect of the Great Mother. The imposition of sexuality on Eve, and the generalization of her evil to all women, served to create a "safe" Mary that men felt comfortable would not destroy them. Naomi Goldenberg concurs that Mary's creation was, in large part, motivated by fear. "Mary has been castrated by popes, cardinals, priests, and theologians who fear the sexual and emotional power of natural womanhood."[87] According to Kassel, "'Mary' was defused by 'Eve,' and could thus fulfill the masculine longing for security in the feminine without giving rise to anxiety or fear."[88] In Kassel's analysis, there is psychological logic to the irony of simultaneous veneration of Mary and the derogation of women. Both are defensive conditions of a weak male ego which in turn suppresses the development of female egos, because women are subject to the Eve/Mary categories of self-understanding.

Noddings views the source of the problem of feminine evil as the religious construction of God that the theology of Jesus, Mary, and Eve must support. "When men posited a God [who was] supposed to be all powerful, all knowing, and all good, the "problem of evil" emerged."[89] To solve this problem of evil, a theodicy was created by Church theologians to reconcile the conflict. This theodicy is, in essence, a mystification of reality. The conflict of an all good and powerful God with the experience of pain and suffering in the world forced religious leaders to turn to the explanation of "mystery" to rationalize the contradiction. Humans cannot access aspects of "God's plan" because it is of divine origins and therefore remains a mystery. God is free to act without explanation. Elizabeth Johnson describes this mysterious freedom as a reflection of male behavior: "the affirmation of divine freedom produces language about God as the quintessential macho man, unmoved and unfeeling in the face of human suffering."[90] Divine mystery requires that the faithful place their trust in the authority of Church leadership. Mystery reinforces hierarchy and the alienation that comes with stratification.

Without attempting a comprehensive assessment, it is fair to assert that the concept of religious mystery has great potential for abuse. Political, social and economic interests can "help" shape the religious mysteries of a given era. The mystery of evil in the world has been supported by the cosmic battle between God and the devil. For Christian women, the Eve/Mary battle is not cosmological but personal. It takes shape in the moral characteristics attributed to women. Ethical assessment is transformed into control as religious hierarchy and tradition portend knowledge of the divine in designating good and bad female behavior.

While Eve represents the evil that has historically been attributed to women, Mary represents the equally damaging and companion challenge to women in a tradition of innate morality. Women have been portrayed, particularly in the Victorian "cult of true womanhood," as innately moral. This morality was characterized by piety, purity, submissiveness, and domesticity.[91] Essentially, women were described as angelic. However, men only ascribed these qualities as long as women maintained their proper spheres. Once a woman questioned the social order, and her role in it, the characterization shifted from Mary to Eve. There is no well-developed middle ground for women in the Christian tradition.

Noddings suggests a unique approach for reversing social connections of women with evil. She advocates teaching the biblical story of creation in secular public schools, including an analysis of the implication of the Fall for gender relations throughout history.[92] Rather than relegate religious mythology to private teaching, she believes it should be brought into public education so students can confront the reality of sexism in cultural history.

Mary, conceived as the New Eve, creates an impossible moral dichotomy for women. She is the model of moral perfection, and Eve's evil deviance is the cast for everyone else. This dualism has the effect of disempowering women by further alienating spiritual experiences of the divine. Identification with Mary is mandated in Catholic teaching, but it is impossible in the realm of women's experience. The very existence of Mary solidifies the identification of women with Eve, and therefore supports the theology of the Fall: Humanity is not inherently good and can only be redeemed by Christ.[93] The Eve/Mary dichotomy helps create a redemptive dependency that requires a savior.

The definition of good as nonsexual, other-directed submissiveness in

Mary, were it even possible to achieve, would not be empowering. Christian feminism strives to redefine good and evil in nondichotomous terms, grounded in human experience and with an emphasis on right relation. A religious morality without a concept of sexism or belief in any other kind of unjust human oppression as inherently evil, lacks credibility in feminist consciousness. The Catholic Church has failed to officially declare sexism sinful, and thus continues to perpetuate traditions such as the Eve/Mary dualism that distort concepts of good and evil.

Violence Against Women

The amount of violence perpetrated against women throughout history has been the subject of much feminist analysis.[94] Many authors, such as Elisabeth Schussler Fiorenza, believe that society's ambivalence toward violence committed against women is a means of social control in a patriarchal culture.[95] Catholic Christianity participates in the pattern of violence by dehumanizing women in the language of the Eve/Mary dualism. This imagery represents a subtle complicity with a pattern of violence that Margaret Miles describes as justified and perpetuated by "the small increments of sexism occurring constantly on a daily, intimate level."[96] Only by explaining the deep roots of misogyny in religious imagery and symbols can its modern form be recognized. An analysis of Marian imagery reveals this underlying rationale for violence against women.

In a provocative collection of essays edited by Joanne Carlson Brown and Carol Bohn and titled *Christianity, Patriarchy and Abuse: A Feminist Critique*, a number of feminist authors describe the abuse directed at women under the guise of Christianity.[97] The theme of the good/evil dichotomy imposed upon women through Christian doctrine is repeated throughout the essays. The Eve/Mary parallel reinforces a cycle of victimization and blame. In a unique way, women are once again objectified as the "other" and are therefore portrayed as less than fully human. In this instance, the otherness of women is a result of being evil. Women are the "bad guys" in Catholicism who can be punished because of their immorality. Demosthenes Savramis describes women as either being "satanized" or "tolerated" in Catholic theology.[98] The Cult of Mary helps the Church conceptualize women as mothers or whores. Savramis finds either construction as a means to an end: the service of men. According to Savramis, the irony is that despite this role of service projected onto women, men still despise women. As will be discussed further in this chapter, mothers are feared as too powerful and whores are simply evil.

The moral essentialism associated with gender mitigates the need to consider women and their lives as a whole. As in a war situation, if the opponent is labeled as something other than fully human, it is easier to commit violence against him or her. Labeling women as "weak" and "sinful" accomplishes this devaluation and lays the groundwork for a rationale for violence. Brown and Parker describe the devaluation of women:

> Our full personhood as well as our rights have been denied us. We have been labeled the sinful ones, the other; and even when we are let in, so to speak, we are constantly reminded of our inferior status through language, theological concepts of original sin, and perpetual virginity—all of which relate to sex, for which, of course, women are responsible.[99]

Returning to the theories of the social construction of reality, Mary as the holy Madonna, the virgin mother, is constructed as the ideal good woman. The other construct of woman is the whore, the Eve. There is no well-defined middle ground. Women are objectified at either extreme, although because Mary's pedestal is unattainable, women are largely associated with Eve. In her critique of American gynecology, Mary Daly reiterates the lack of authentically normative female status:

> there is actually no natural (wild) state of femaleness that is legitimated/allowed. . . . There are only two possibilities. First, there is a fallen state, formerly named sinful and symbolized by Eve, presently known as sick and typified in the powerless but sometimes difficult and problematic patient. Second, there is the restored/redeemed state of perfect femininity, formerly named saintly and symbolized by Mary, presently typified in the "normal" woman. . . .[100]

When the tension between ontological concepts of man and woman is considered, an authentic conception of female is unavailable for consideration. The constructed polar tensions are both male projections. The ideal woman (Mary) is portrayed as having a greater degree of passive dependence than that of a healthy "normal" adult; therefore, women who act like adults tend to be described as "unfeminine," and women who act as their male-constructed ideal are viewed as being child-like in their submissiveness. Thus, women are faced with an impossible double bind,[101] the worst aspect of which is that it can serve as an underlying rationale for male aggression against women.

Polly Young-Eisendrath and Demaris Wehr believe that the tolerance of terror and violence against women in modern society means there exists, at least at the subconscious level, a rationale making it possible for men to engage in this kind of violence.[102] Religion plays an important role in creating social beliefs about women that may provide cultural permission for the physical abuse of women by men. Minister and feminist theologian Susan Brooks Thistlethwaite notes that women with strong religious backgrounds have great difficulty believing violence against them is wrong. Resistance to the injustice of violence is "unbiblical and un-Christian" for these women.[103] Extending Young-Eisendrath and Wehr's analysis, the Catholic Church can be viewed as perpetuating the conditions for abuse through,

1. Perpetuating the Impossible Ideal in Mary.
2. Valorizing self-sacrifice and suffering.
3. Teaching gender moral essentialism.[104]

We have discussed at length the image of Mary that the Church perpetuates: domestic, docile, obedient, and nonsexual. Margaret Miles finds a consistent pattern of "obedience, submissiveness, and innocence" in traditional artistic representations of Mary. This view of Mary—the most significant female represented in Western civilization—models unequal power relationships between men and women as the difference between the strong and the weak. Many suggest that such unequal socializations may contribute to the presence of widespread violence perpetrated against women in today's society. For example, in a historical analysis of family violence in the United States, Linda Gordon found female socialization toward passivity as one contributing force in the complex issue of wife beating.[105]

The theme of the redemptive nature of suffering is also powerful in Catholic theology. However, suffering has often taken on a gendered perspective, as women are the suffering servants of Christ and their sacrifices are their glory.[106] According to Miles, men are also depicted as suffering, but they are not assigned the exclusive role of salvific suffering in Christianity. Religious imagery portrays men in many roles; however, for women, suffering is the primary image.[107] Historically, the portrayal of the martyrdom of women saints has bordered on what Miles describes as the "pornographic eroticization of violence."[108] In her view, the exclusion of women from various religious activities limited their social and spiritual acceptance and led to exaggerated and often self-imposed suffering. Such valorization of female suffering allows for a subliminal rationalization of violence against women. In commenting on the theology of women put forth by Christian ethicist Helmut Thielke, Brown and Parker find male aggression justified:

> In this twentieth-century formulation of Christian ethics, woman is cast as a Christ figure; she is imagined to be a victim who does not deserve the suffering that comes to her . . . the actual deaths or violence against women are part of the system just as necessary as the death of Jesus. . . .[109]

According to Rita Nakishima Brock, the valorization of innocence also serves to justify violence against women. The western ideal of "pure" women who are childlike in their innocence, as exemplified by Mary, breeds victimization. Brock advocates reversing this Christian value by placing greater emphasis upon wisdom rather than unquestioning trust.[110]

Elizabeth Johnson observes that the concept of a suffering God also steals a source of religious empowerment from women.[111] In the position of the oppressed, a selfless, suffering God does not provide the means for escaping subjugation. The cross of Christ only reinforces that women should accept their suffering as a mysterious part of God's divine plan. If there is to be retribution, it will come in heaven, so everyone should accept their lot. Preeminent Catholic theologian Edward Schillebeeckx, explicitly describes how Mary's character makes human suffering more palatable:

> the Catholic learns the meaning of generosity from the boundless and indeed almost wasteful goodness of Mary . . . She is who enables us to participate in Christ's sacrifice in a spirit of *gentle* submission.[112]

Mary lightens the burden of Christians not by seeking earthly justice, or ending subordination, but by eliminating psychic distress through submission. This moral perspective benefits the oppressor over the oppressed. There is no source of inspiration for earthly justice in the Cult of Mary.

The Church also teaches that there are fundamental, ontological differences between men and women. Unfortunately, as history has shown in the church, differences often became a euphemism for a hierarchy in gender relationships. Women were considered inferior in their creation, an idea related to Eve's fundamental moral weakness in the Fall.[113] Ruether finds that traditionally this belief in ontological difference and subordination to men has allowed for sanctioned violence against women. She finds a tacit acceptance of wife beating in this formulation of female inferiority.[114]

The medieval witch hunts exemplified organized violence against women. The number of victims is conservatively estimated at 100,000 to 200,000, with 80 percent of them female.[115] Many scholars have documented that marginalized women who violated the ideal type of behavior were subject to scrutiny and torture.[116] Adrienne Rich speculates that the practice of dissecting womanhood into "motherliness" (nurturing, self-sacrifice), "female sexual attractiveness," and "motherhood" (the power of procreation) made the brutal witch hunts of living women possible at the very same time that the Virgin Mary was being so highly venerated.[117] Psychoanalyst pioneer Karen Horney observes the irony of Mary's veneration simultaneous with medieval witch-burning, but also finds the phenomenon to have subtle continuity with modern behavior.

> The Cult of the Virgin side by side with the burning of witches; the adoration of "pure" motherliness, completely divested of sexuality, nest to the cruel destruction of the sexually seductive woman. Here again is the implication of underlying anxiety, for the witch is in communication with the devil. Nowadays, with our more humane forms of aggression, we burn women only figuratively, sometimes with undisguised hatred, sometimes with apparent friendliness.[118]

Horney hints at an underlying psychology, rooted in a dualistic ontology, that was used against medieval women, and which remains, with less overt manifestations, in today's society.

Feminist theologians have made the connection between structures such as the New Eve and preconscious conditioning. Modern violence against women shares the historic ontological rationale of patriarchy, but in a more subtle fashion. Ruether observes,

> Domestic violence against women—wife battering or beating—is rooted in and is the logical conclusion of basic patriarchal assumptions about women's subordinate status.[119]

A recent court case illustrates the lingering images of women used to justify violence. In *People v. Valorie Jean Day*, the defendant was sentenced to six years in prison for involuntary manslaughter for killing her boyfriend. The boyfriend had abused Day physically with repeated beatings, resulting in her permanent disfigurement. After one attack, Day defended herself with a knife, resulting in her boyfriend's death. However, in court, the prosecution was able to demonstrate that Day did not exemplify the "good" battered woman because she was not "docile, submissive, humble, ingratiating, nonassertive, dependent, quiet, conforming, and selfless."[120] These adjectives should have a familiar ring because they are the kind of praise used to describe Mary. Even liberation theologian Leonardo Boff projects feminine essentialism upon Mary in his praise, ". . . silently and unassumingly . . . Mary is a woman par excellence."[121] Had Jean Day been more like Mary, she would have qualified as a "good" battered woman and remained in her abusive relationship.

Another condition that psychologists describe as conducive to violence against women is involvement with a man who perceives he is in a love/hate relationship. According to Kathleen Barry, "Wife beaters exemplify men who contain the mandate to both love and hate women within one relationship."[122] The dualism of the Catholic characterization of women is exemplary of a love/hate relationship. Men desire women to be both Mary and Eve. This results in mixed messages to women and to men, who both love and hate their wives. Either women must be schizophrenic or they will be loved and hated in relationships with men. Elizabeth Johnson describes this situation as the "Madonna-Whore syndrome," which, ". . . enables men to love and respect their ideal of woman in Mary, but to ignore or dominate concrete real women with impunity and with immunity even from the searchings of their own conscience."[123]

The Sado-Ritual Syndrome

Perhaps no feminist theologian has so thoroughly examined religiously justified violence against women as Mary Daly. In her 1978 book *Gyn/Ecology*, Daly attempts to ". . . unmask the very real existential meaning of Goddess murder in the concrete lives of women."[124] She focuses on five rituals: Indian Suttee, Chinese footbinding, African female genital mutilation, European witch-hunting, and American gynecology. A pattern emerges that is common to each of these rituals and results in sanctioned violence perpetuated against women. Daly refers to this pattern as the Sado-Ritual Syndrome, which consists of seven elements:

1. An obsession with purity.
2. Total erasure of responsibility for atrocities because of religious justification.
3. Widespread appeal of the ritual.
4. Women become scapegoats and token torturers.
5. Fixation on orderliness, repetitiveness, and minute details that diverts from horror of rituals.

6. Behavior that otherwise and in other places is unacceptable becomes acceptable because of condition through repeated ritual atrocity.

7. Legitimation of rituals by "objective" scholarship despite appearance of disapproval by the profession.[125]

While Daly's insights are intended for rituals, violence against objectified women that is perpetrated because of the Eve/Mary (evil/good) dualism has much in common with the Sado-Ritual Syndrome. Sexually and morally pristine, Mary is certainly a figure invested with a compulsion of purity (1). The lengths that theologians have gone to demonstrate Mary's purity in dogma and doctrines of the Church reveal a zealous compulsion about this issue.

Mary's theological significance has allowed a number of atrocities to be performed in her name, while those perpetuating them have felt no particular moral responsibility (2). Whether it was witch burning or the invoking of male authority within the family, Mary is the model of female submissiveness that is contrasted with Eve's disobedience. To punish women who do not behave like Mary is simply to act in accord with the divine cosmology. However, Mary maintains widespread appeal with little public consciousness over the detrimental effects of her theology (3), and stories about Mary remain among the most beloved in Christianity.

As a model of womanhood, the internalization of Mary's character allows the Eve/Mary dualism to be passed on by and through women (4). Men do not have to "force" each generation of women to accept Mary. Catholic women who train their daughters in the faith perpetuate the tradition. For some Catholics the zest for the minute details of Mary's constructed life, such as her perpetually intact hymen, lack of birthing pains, or her nondecaying body, divert attention from her alienation from the existential lives of women (5).

Violence and abuse of women become more acceptable because a behavioral pattern that would otherwise be unacceptable is sanctioned by religious tradition (6). Labeling someone a Madonna or a whore makes it easier to mistreat the whore rather than view the whole humanity of the person.

Daly's last element of the Sado-Ritual Syndrome indicts alleged objective (male) scholarship that fails to recognize the connection of the Cult of Mary and the abuse of women (7). Mariology, as an internal Catholic pseudoscience, does not generally qualify as objective scholarship. However, sociology, while useful in its describing religious phenomenology, fails to condemn the negative repercussions for women.[126]

The resonance of Daly's Sado-Ritual Syndrome as it applies to Mary, and particularly the Eve/Mary dualism, demonstrates that Marian imagery is complicit in establishing a consciousness that legitimates the abuse of women. Daly's conception of Mary as the total mind/body rape victim reveals the moral message of her symbolism for women. Mary is rendered "unable to resist divine aggression/lust/rape."[127]

As previously discussed, Mary as the New Eve perpetuates a rationale for violence against women in two ways. The first is through her polarization of women in the Eve/Mary dualism that objectifies women in oppositional characterizations. This theme has been developed at length to this point in the moral implications of this Marian imagery. However, another avenue of Marian complicity with abuse of women is her very definition of "goodness." Recall that obedience is one of the distinguishing characteristics of Mary in comparison to Eve. The connection between the definition of goodness projected onto Mary and abuse can be traced in Marian apparitions.

Zimdars-Swartz documents a pattern of abuse in Marian apparitions.[128] In a number of cases, the apparition seer was physically abused by her parents. The subsequent visions of Mary do not represent rebellion or revenge by the seer. On the contrary, the New Eve exonerates the physical abuse by ascribing spiritual meaning to it. Suffering must take place to atone for humanity's sinful nature.

> The motif of suffering is pervasive in most modern Marian apparitions. Its manifestations range from the suffering of the mother who appears and voices her laments, sometimes with tears, to the suffering both before and after her appearances of those who bear her messages. . . . [129]

Mary finds herself in a mythical dysfunctional family in which she attempts to mitigate the violence that an abusive father God commits against his children. Mary is the New Eve because she is willing to stay in this relationship and therefore be declared "good" as the morally acceptable response of woman. Eve, and certainly her foresister, Lilith, would have left the abusive situation because they were a "disobedient" pair.

Zimdars-Swartz describes the apparition at Fatima, Portugal in 1917 to three shepherd children, as an apparition in which the theme of physical abuse is an important backdrop. Lucia dos Santos, who played the leading role in the six appearances of Mary to her and her two cousins, was told by an angel, "Above all, accept submissively the sacrifices the Lord will send you."[130] Lucia's mother beats her with a broom handle because she thought Lucia was lying about the apparitions. However, Lucia, through Mary's instruction, learned that her suffering was "for the love of God and the conversion of sinners."[131] She exonerated her mother as simply a participant in God's mysterious plan. This behavior and reaction to a Marian apparition was not atypical of other Marian appearances.

Mary did not protect Lucia against suffering, nor did she speak to the injustice of violence or physical abuse or admonish Lucia's mother to stop the beatings. Mary simply rationalized and therefore justified the violence. In her mediation, Mary does not question the wrath of God or Jesus, but merely mitigates the punishment. Mary is ultimately obedient to religious violence. As the New Eve, Mary's praiseworthiness is pure obedience to patriarchy.

Certainly, Mary is not the singular cause of domestic violence in societies where Catholicism is influential. However, she is a significant religious icon who still captures the modern religious imagination of the Catholic faithful. The transformation of the Eve/Mary dualism into a continuum or spectrum that does not dualistically define morality can be a step in breaking down the objectification of women, and therefore lessening the existing rationale for violence. There is hope for such a reversal. Almost every feminist author who explores the subject of violence ends with a message of hope, such as Ruether's comment, "Christianity has in it the seeds of an alternative theory, a theory of liberation, equality, and dignity for all persons."[132]

6

The Recasting of Marian Imagery

The reality of her [Mary's] myth is over; the moral code she affirms has
been exhausted.
—Marina Warner[1]

Historical/critical methods, biblical scholarship, and modern social
phenomenology contribute to the modern feminist critique of Marian
images. The critique, and the current status of women in academics and
in religious ministry, makes for a unique moment in history. In no other
era has it been possible for feminist theologians to establish themselves
as a significant constituency in the dynamic complexity of the Catholic
Church, and therefore to lay claim to women's voice in matters of spirituality. While millenialists proclaim that these are the end times for
human civilization, the energy and potency of the feminist critique
appears to proclaim the "end times" for patriarchal religion as it has been
traditionally practiced. Mary has been a central subject for feminist
deconstructions of Catholicism; however, her role in a rebirth of
Catholic feminist spirituality is not so clear. This conclusion develops a
synthesis of the images of Mary discussed in the previous three chapters.
I review the directions in which Catholic feminists wish to go with

Mary, and I offer a framework for further exploration in the remaking of Mary's role in modern Catholic feminist spirituality.

The Images of Mary: Misogynist Reversals

As a religious social construction, Mary is a moral messenger to the Catholic faithful, with particular significance to women. We have reviewed the origin, development, feminist critique, and moral implications of three key titles of Mary: The Virgin, Mediatrix, and New Eve. For purposes of analysis it was necessary to break down the cult of Mary into these components, although the experienced reality of the Catholic faithful is that these images merge into a single, personified religious icon. While Mary has numerous manifestations, she carries with her a tension-filled conglomeration of her historic imagery and their moral implications.

The conceptualization of Mary as the New Eve connects to her imagery as the Virgin. Sexuality is imposed upon the story of the Fall, tying Mary's exceptional goodness to asexuality. In turn, her intercessory powers are linked to her other images. Mary becomes "Christlike" in her purity and goodness. A leader in the battle of good versus evil, Mary is invested with special powers to help humanity. Each image supports the other, creating an internal logic or consistency. However, a breach in any of these images has the potential to destroy the whole construct. For this reason, the Catholic Church either vigorously defends against or ignores any attack on these images. Gebara and Bingemer succinctly describe the hierarchical and popular attitude toward Mary, which protects her foundational images in what they term as "unthinking submission."

> People do not allow themselves even the slightest critical thought so as to keep their ideal image of Mary intact. If anything touches this image, their whole world comes crashing down . . . they equip themselves with all kinds of defense mechanisms in order to defend the figure of Mary, but at the same time they are defending their own securities, their myths, in an attempt to preserve what they have built up for themselves and perhaps for others . . . this is an image of the woman Mary that has been "retrieved" by a male-centered world, in an attempt to justify and preserve that world.[2]

In a logical and ordered way, Mary's images preserve a gendered ethical code that helps to maintain women's subordinate status within the Catholic Church and in societies for which Catholicism is influential. However, the misogyny is masked by the endearing figure of Mary, the good mother that everyone loves.

If one Marian image appears to be the cornerstone of the others, it would be Mary's virginity. The Church has directed more effort toward developing a theology of Mary's virginity, with the aforementioned minutia of consideration, than any other Marian image. A variety of Catholic moral values flow from Mary's virginity: celibacy, sacrifice, goodness, and perpetual life.

Mary's conglomerative construction also supports Christological constructions. Catholic theology would be drastically altered if Mary had been sexually active, independent, questioning, and unsupportive of "God's plan." Christology requires Mariology as it has evolved. Mary's titles and ideology maintain patriarchal hegemony over the Christian model of womanhood.

> The popes can say Mary is the ideal mother, thus urging contemporary females to stay within their role of mother. They do not say Mary is the ideal business woman, chief executive, career person, athlete, stockbroker, priest or bishop.[3]

Figure 4 expresses the multivariate misogyny in the imagery of Mary, as explored in this book. The images are encircled because Mary is experienced as a whole, but her various "faces" betray sexist ideologies that permeate Catholic theology.

Each title and its related image supports a patriarchal *reversal* of that

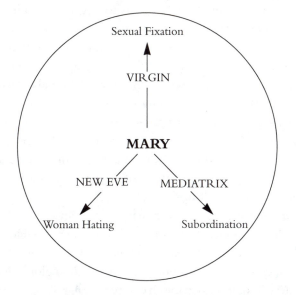

Figure 4: Misogynist Imagery Reversals in the Catholic Doctrines of Mary

image.[4] In common usage, virginity is not usually associated with sexual fixation. Mary as the New Eve is absolutely "good," and therefore would not usually be associated with woman hating. Mary's powerful role as Mediatrix would not usually be associated with perpetuating women's subordinate status. In each case, patriarchal religion achieves a detrimental reversal from a relatively positive title into a negative ideology of gender in the Catholic theology of Mary.

Gail Paterson Corrington is one of many feminist scholars who has observed a pattern of "male inversion of female symbols and myths."[5] The "process of inversion" gives the impression that the appropriated female experience is highly valued. However, in the appropriation process, the actual outcome is a devaluation of the symbols as female experience. Mary exemplifies Corrington's analysis. She is hailed for her virginity; however, her virginity is equated with biological impossibility. Mary is hailed for her sinless nature; however, sinlessness is equated with an acquiescent, submissive, nurturing woman. Mary is hailed as mediatrix, but her power is purely relational and subordinate. In each case, a potentially empowering image for Mary is appropriated by Catholicism into superficial exultation, only to mask an underlying devaluation of women. Whether the term is inversion or reversal, the result is a patriarchal definition of Mary, and, by implication, women, that maintains a system of domination and subordination.

The challenge for feminist theology is to negate such ideologies of gender through new imagery, or to deconstruct the link between existing images and their implications for women. Either the female quasi-deity of Catholicism must be "reimaged," or titles of power, virginity, and goodness must be reinterpreted without detrimental impact upon women. A static Mariology will only find itself increasingly removed from the experience and religious consciousness of women. With reference to Peter Berger's social construction theory introduced in Chapter One, the question is whether feminist theology can provide adequate "legitimations" to save the construct of Mary, or, more importantly, whether feminists even want to save it.

In Chapter Two it became clear that Mary is an essential religious figure in popular, hierarchical, and theological Catholicism. However, the history of the Cult of Mary, detailed in Chapter One, demonstrates that almost every Marian event had a purpose other than to glorify Mary. The rationale for Mariological doctrines has a historical, political, or theological purpose. Further, the images of Mary explored in chapters Three,

Four, and Five served to disempower and contribute to the subordination of women. Given this interrelated data on the Cult of Mary, feminist theologians are faced with a twofold issue. The first is whether Mary is worth saving. This issue revolves around assessing what, if anything, about Mary is redeemable, and to what extent the patriarchal baggage can be removed. Further complicating any attempt at Marian reclamation is the Christian feminist commitment to popular faith. Mary cannot be changed by simply writing an innovative theological treatise. The informed conscience of the Catholic faithful must be appealed to in a nonmanipulative way, in an approach that meets spiritual needs and maintains egalitarian theological vision.

For feminists, the issue of Mary is a microcosm of the larger issue of whether patriarchal religion can and should be redeemed. Feminist and nonfeminist theologians have repeatedly stated that the figure of Mary is a distinguishing feature of Catholicism. If "as Mary goes so goes the Church," what if Mary cannot be redeemed? Can feminists reconcile themselves within Catholicism, or is feminism by definition post-Catholic?

Els Maeckelberghe reflects on how to approach reinterpretations of Mary in *Desperately Seeking Mary: A Feminist Appropriation of a Traditional Religious Symbol*. Maeckelberghe argues that a "new" image of Mary is not an appropriate response for feminist theologians, for two reasons. First, theologians should not be in the business of creating theology. The role of the theologian is to assist the faith community in its interpretation of religious symbols. Maeckelberghe wishes to center the authority for interpretations of Mary squarely upon the community. In addition, she insists that "new" images of Mary violate the concept of religious symbolism. Mary exists within the Catholic story; therefore, any reinterpretation must spring from that story. A new Mary cannot exist outside of the tradition.[6]

While I agree with Maeckelberghe's conclusions, I have some concerns about her rationale. Male theologians have historically exploited popular Marian piety to develop imagery that was useful to patriarchy. Solidifying papal power, subordinating women, maintaining moral controls—all are outcomes of historical Mariology to which Maeckelberghe alludes in her analysis. I would argue that given the misogynist use of the Cult of Mary in the past, feminist theologians have a moral obligation to use their training to take an assertive leadership role in reinterpreting Mary. The power and influence of tradition and the hierarchy of the Catholic Church does not afford faith communities the time and opportunity for new Marian images to evolve. Feminist theologians need to make available new images for public discourse. I agree with Maeckelberghe that the faith community will ultimately decide which Marian images survive and which do not. I also agree that reinterpretations of Mary need to be in continuity with the Christian story, but again, my reasons differ slightly from Maeckelberghe's. If a "new Mary" could be created outside of Christian boundaries, and it empowered women and met the faith community's spiritual needs, I would welcome it. However, my rationale for salvaging Mary is more pragmatic. Deep below the surface of Mary, there is a subversive power. This power could not be completely entombed in the sublime Mary erected by patriarchal authorities. The underlying power manifests itself by Mary's tremendous popularity—popularity that in many cases outstrips that of Jesus and God. Rather than recreate such a religious entity, if feminist theologians tap into this spiritual power, a great deal of work and consternation will be saved. In addition, it is unlikely that the faith community at large would accept a completely new feminist religious construction. Drawing upon Catholic tradition while eliminating the misogyny associated with the Cult of Mary opens a window of opportunity for a renegotiation of the figure of Mary.

Alternative Approaches to the "Mary Problem"

Many Christian feminists want to forget Mary and concentrate on other issues, such as revising the language used for divinity or recovering women's spirituality. One could argue that this entire investigation has been a rationale for moving beyond Mary. However, deconstruction must occur before a reconstruction is possible. Mary is such a complex religious figure that to attempt any reworking of her image without fully addressing her history is to fail to appreciate her religious potency. Nevertheless, many feminist theologians have argued that Mary is not salvageable. The following are some representative statements:

> *Mary Daly:* The appropriate counter-strategy to the breakdown of the Arch-Image [Mary] is certainly not the reinstatement of the Christian Mary but radical reconnection with the Archimage [the Great Original Witch].[7]

> *Kari Borresen:* To make Mary a model for feminists is not only questionable, but absurd, if the essential ecclesiological and Mariological

connection between femininity and subordination is ignored or not known.[8]

Marina Warner: Mary cannot be a model for the New Woman . . . it is more likely that like Ishtar, the Virgin will recede into legend.[9]

Daphne Hampson: There is nothing whatsoever upon which Mariology could be built! It is a castle in the sky, a male construction of an earlier age, for which there exists no possible basis.[10]

Naomi Goldenberg: It would be far better for women to contemplate the images of the great goddesses behind the myth of Mary than to dwell on the man-made image of Mary herself.[11]

Given Mary's history and her use as a tool of the Church against women, it is easy to sympathize with the frustration expressed by these authors. However, I reject the strategy of ignoring Mary because she is either irrelevant or unrecoverable. Two primary reasons drive this conclusion. The first is a defensive concern for the efforts of the women's movement. If women turn their backs on Mary, then she remains, at least at the level of public discussion, under the exclusive control of the hierarchy of the Catholic Church. Given the Church's recent trajectory of entrenchment under orthodox positions, there is no reason to believe Mary will evolve without active attempts at public dialogue by feminist theologians. Because so many Catholic women are consciously or subconsciously affected by the Church, they will continually be bombarded by this model of womanhood. The aggregate effect of stories, rituals, apparitions, biblical readings, and homilies must take some toll on the human psyche, even in the modern context. Feminist theologians have a moral obligation to challenge existing Marian imagery on behalf of Catholic women. This is not to imply that the obligation is to create a reactionary, static, or oppositional image, but they must utilize the best of modern historical critical methods, sociology, and psychology to reveal that the all-male hierarchy of the Catholic Church cannot exclusively interpret Mary.

The second, and related, reason to continue working to reinterpret Mary is that otherwise Catholic feminists will lose a unique opportunity to harness a powerful female image. Even Naomi Goldenberg admits Mary's power,

Mary has a legitimate base of power in the human psyche. Behind her sanitized figure lurk all the great pagan goddesses of the ancient world.[12]

Many authors have pointed out that the hierarchy of the Catholic

Church was not able to fully control the Cult of Mary. There is a trace of subversion in her history. Mary remains empowering to many women. If the delicate balance between the removal of Mary's patriarchal baggage can be achieved while salvaging her empowering aspects, Catholic feminists will have made a great contribution to women's spirituality.

The misogyny in the Cult of Mary has such a complex basis that any modern feminist response to it must be equally comprehensive and complex. While many feminists have commented on the Cult of Mary, and most offer suggestions for change, few have undertaken the burdensome task of developing comprehensive new approaches. The following are four well-developed responses to the challenge of reconstructing Marian images for the modern religious consciousness of Catholic women. Each of the authors is a Catholic feminist theologian to whom I have referred throughout this book. Each also shares the sentiments of Dorothee Solle: "Like many Christians in the liberation movement, I am not ready to surrender Mary to our opponents."[13] These theologians represent a variety of backgrounds. Two are from the United States (Ruether and Johnson), one is from Europe (Halkes), and two collaborate from Latin America (Gebara and Bingemer). They share many common themes that will be adapted into my subsequent recommendations.

Elizabeth Johnson

In the article "Reconstructing a Theology of Mary," Johnson applies "praxis-oriented theology" to the Cult of Mary to shed light on a new theology of Mary.[14] Praxis-oriented approaches to theology view the mission of the Church as critically concerned with the reign of God on Earth, or what is sometimes referred to as "realized eschatology." The Christian message is given new expression in how it addresses and counters unjust social structures. Theological concerns and social morality are united. Johnson does not provide an explicit, comprehensive rationale for applying praxis-oriented theology to Mary, but the application fits well with the feminist concern for Catholic women's alienation from Mary.

Praxis-oriented theology is intimately concerned with the lived experience of the faith community, particularly those who are oppressed by social structures. The feminist critique of Mary is that she has become increasingly distanced from women's experience and that she serves to perpetuate a sexist religious ideology. Johnson's use of praxis-oriented theology is an attempt to transcend the alienation and find an emancipatory Marian theology.

The concepts of "memory," "narrative," and "solidarity" are central to praxis-oriented theology. Christianity is a collection of significant, dangerous memories that are told in a dynamic narrative form. Narrative serves to re-create the community while the community tells the story anew to each generation of believers. The community forms a solidarity among its members in their common goals and vision.[15] It is in the context of memory, narrative, and solidarity that Johnson believes a useful approach to Mary may emerge:

> Awareness of solidarity with Mary in a community of faith which remembers and tells unsettling stories, of which hers is one, may well be an effective rubric with which to begin and to situate an understanding of Mary within praxis-oriented theology.[16]

Johnson cites five memories of Mary, told in the Catholic tradition, with which modern believers can find solidarity.

1. *As a poor member of the people.* While specific facts about Mary are nil, circumstantial evidence indicates that Mary of Nazareth was probably of low estate and a member of the working poor. As such, Mary serves as a source of solidarity with the vast poor and oppressed of today.

2. *As an outsider.* Johnson cites the odd genealogy in Matthew's infancy narrative demonstrating that Mary is of questionable background. She is also controversial because of her mysterious pregnancy.[17] Despite these challenges, Mary is the most prominent woman in Christian history. Johnson finds this to be an empowering concept for "outsiders"—the disenfranchised, the nonmainstream, who must battle for personal dignity.

3. *As a victim of violence.* All mothers who have lost children to violence can empathize with Mary's pain. Her anguish provides energy to those who seek peace and the end of political violence.

4. *As a prophet of justice.* Johnson interprets Mary's "Magnificat" as a proclamation of liberating justice. She is a living example that God's spirit can work through unlikely candidates to heal the oppressed.

5. *As a woman.* When sociopolitical oppression is combined with sexism, women become "the oppressed of the oppressed." Mary lived in an extremely patriarchal society. Women can feel solidarity with Mary when they face gender-based oppression.[18]

While I agree with Johnson's collection of recoverable imagery of Mary, particularly those that reflect and value woman's experience, I am concerned about placing too much emphasis upon continuity with the tradition. While reinterpreting scripture that is two thousand years old and has questionable historical accuracy appears legitimate and desirable, reinterpreting recent Catholic pronouncements is a more difficult task. In her concluding remarks, Johnson states that the dogmas of the Immaculate Conception and the Assumption, respectively, can celebrate victory over unjust power structures and the creation of a new heaven and earth. This is a contrived method of "saving" these documents. The infancy narratives of the gospels are of unknown origin and unknown specific intent. The Church documents of the Immaculate Conception (1850) and the Assumption into Heaven (1954) are of known origin, authorship, and intent. To reinterpret these is to wholly deny their explicit problematic (misogynist?) aspects. Johnson's analysis, as usual, is thoughtful, comprehensive, and helpful to the discourse concerning Mary among Catholic feminists. However, her praxis-oriented approach to Marian theology runs the risk of continuing misogynist themes if "new Mariology" retains too much of what underlies traditional Mariology. An element of self-criticism and admission of historical error will be included in an effective Mariology seeking to redress past mistakes that have hurt women.

Catharina Halkes

European feminist theologian Catharina Halkes, like Johnson and Ruether, chooses to address the challenges of the Cult of Mary directly rather than ignore Mary altogether. "It is because of a deep sense of solidarity or sisterhood that I do not want simply to let go of Mary."[19] Halkes empathizes with those who reject Mary because she, too, recognizes the alienation created by Mary's religious imagery. However, Halkes acknowledges the critical juxtaposition of Mary between feminism and Catholicism. She offers five themes as to why Mary must be dealt with earnestly by feminist theologians.[20]

1. *Set Mary Free.* Because Mary has come to represent women, leaving her behind would hurt all women. Mary must be set free from patriarchal stereotyping, just as women must be freed from such discrimination.

2. *Criticize Concepts of Mary.* Marian images need to be fully analyzed in all their complexity, and they must be exposed for their detrimental effects upon women.

3. *Infuse Women's Experience.* Halkes is concerned that male theologians continue to write about Mary without including women's voices and experience.

4. *Ecumenical Mary.* Rather than simply viewing Mary as a stumbling block to Christian ecumenism, she should be a path by which feminist theology enters the dialogue.

5. *Mary and the Church.* Mary can be used by feminist theology to expose the ambivalent nature of the Catholic Church's attitude toward women.

Halkes clearly states that her contribution to the feminist discussion of Mary is merely an interim report on an important feminist theological project. Her insights into an approach to the Cult of Mary are relatively nonspecific, but thematically correlate closely with my own. My only concern, and this may be due to the brevity of her article, is that Halkes, while hinting at the greater implications for the Catholic Church, does not address how Catholicism might have to change to accommodate a new Mariology. It is questionable whether a significantly altered Mary would come about without fundamental changes in Christology, and therefore the entire religion. This idea will be further pursued at the end of this chapter.

Rosemary Radford Ruether

Rosemary Radford Ruether coined the term "Liberation Mariology" in her alternative to traditional Mariology. Ruether seeks an understanding of Mariology that can clearly act as a witness against sexism as a sin and eliminate patriarchally determined definitions of the spiritual male and female.[21] These definitions create a gendered, essentialist determinism that not only falsely differentiates male and female but serves to create a hierarchy between the sexes. "Mariology becomes a liberating symbol for women only when it is seen as a radical symbol of a new humanity freed from hierarchical power relations, including that of God and humanity."[22] Sexism is but one evil of the "culture of domination and subjugation," and is related to all other forms of subordination. Mary can symbolically break the cycle of subordination for all humanity.

Ruether turns to the Gospel of Luke to find her "foundational text" for liberation Mariology. Mary is portrayed as freely choosing to say "yes" to the angel that appears to her. Mary does not consult Joseph, nor is her consideration tied to what is best for her husband. She makes human salvation possible as both subject and object. She is not a mere vessel of

God's incarnation, but she cooperates with it. Mary participates in the liberating grace of God. Like Johnson, Ruether uses the language of liberation theology to support a new interpretation of Mary. For example, Mary represents God's "preferential option for the poor" in Ruether's sociopolitical exegesis of the Gospels.[23] Ruether takes Mariology beyond a means of freeing women from subjugation and extends the idea to all subjugated peoples.

While there is a great need for feminist theologians to reverse sexist interpretations of the bible, Ruether's approach raises several concerns. First, there is the pervasive problem of the inconsistent application of modern biblical criticism and hermeneutics. Biblical scholars indicate that the infancy narratives probably never occurred as narrated, although this does not mitigate the power and significance of these stories. It does create problems for modern theologians, however. The approach I favor is to acknowledge that the infancy narratives express the faith of the early Christians without necessarily reflecting factual data. This is an important notation to make in order to avoid a historical personification of the myth. A feminist reinterpretation of Mary's role in Luke that takes biblical scholarship into greater consideration would rephrase Ruether's exegesis. In the legends told in early Christianity, Mary had a key role to play in bringing about God's salvation. Early Christians thought so highly of Mary that the fate of human redemption hung on her response to God's call.

I am also concerned about the limited and tenuous basis for Ruether's development of liberation Mariology. Mary is such a vaporous figure in scripture that using her few appearances as a basis for a more instrumental figure has questionable force. Ruether only discusses the single scene in Luke because there is little else upon which to base liberation Mariology. I believe it is more useful to develop Mary as a symbol, somewhat independent of scripture, since that is what the tradition of the Cult of Mary has done. In fairness, Ruether does discuss Mary as a symbol of the Church, the oppressed, and humanity. Chapter Six of *Sexism and God-Talk: Toward a Feminist Theology* is titled "Mary as Symbolic Ecclesiology: Repression or Liberation?" However, further amplification of what, if any, scripture can be used as a basis is needed. Although my critique is aimed at greater clarification and precision of Ruether's argument, her project as a whole is vital to new understandings of Mary. She recognizes that renegotiating Marian imagery is not just essential for redefining women's roles but is also central to redefining hierarchical relationships. I will incorporate these sentiments into the ultimate ramifications of Mary for Catholicism in the last section of this chapter.

Ivone Gebara and Maria Clara Bingemer

Writing from the perspective of Latin-American feminist liberation theology, Gebara and Bingemer apply the liberation model favored by Ruether and Johnson to the Cult of Mary. In *Mary, Mother of God, Mother of the Poor*, Gebara and Bingemer attempt to draw upon underlying themes in hierarchical and popular Catholicism, resulting in an anthropological foundation that is, "unifying, realist, and pluridimensional." The authors describe four transformations that must take place if Marian imagery is to be empowering in the modern religious consciousness.[24]

1. *From a Male-Oriented to a Human-Centered Anthropology.* The authors recognize that the historical theology of Mary reflects a projection of male experience through the hierarchy of the Church. For the Cult of Mary to be made "whole" or "human centered," the inclusion of women's experience must take place.

2. *From a Dualistic to a Unifying Anthropology.* The spirit-material dualism that permeates Catholic theology and affects gender considerations needs to be unified rather than stratified. This mandate is consistent with liberation theology's concern for realized eschatology, or the kingdom of God as experienced on earth.

3. *From an Idealist to a Realist Anthropology.* Related to #3, this theme concerns the Church's creation of an objective reality beyond human attainment. The authors wish to balance the subjective and objective by transforming ideal religious concepts into concepts that are not static but are defined by history and cultural setting. Mary is therefore not locked into medieval categories but allowed to evolve into an empowering religious symbol in each age.

4. *From a One-Dimensional to a Pluri-dimensional Anthropology.* This transformation critiques a "consecrated male-centered vision" and replaces it with appreciation for a multitude of human manifestations. The implication for Christian women is that singular constructs of Mary (Virgin, Mediatrix, New Eve) do not dominate to the exclusion of other imagery.

I have already discussed the contributions of Gebara and Bingemer to the new approaches to Mary, including their highlighting of "process" and "pluralism" in religious symbolism. Recognizing that time and place inform theological understanding, the authors continually return to historical critical methods. Furthermore, they recognize that religious beliefs are pluralistic. Even in a particular historical setting, no religious manifestations are universally empowering or appealing. Gebara and Bingemer acknowledge the power of a multifaceted religious symbol such as Mary. However, they believe that the pluralism should be rooted in popular experience, not hierarchical need.

I applaud the anthropological transformations suggested by Gebara and Bingemer, however, like Halkes, the authors fail to take their recommendations to a natural conclusion. Anthropological shifts cannot be recommended for Mary and not be applied to Jesus. Once again, the discussion of overall implications for Catholicism is avoided.

Towards New Marian Imagery

I concur with a statement by theologian John McKenzie: "If a new Mariology is to be formed, it will be formed by women."[25] This is not to say Mary "belongs" to women any more than Jesus "belongs" to men. However, analysis of history reveals that men, more than women, have dictated the theology and imagery of Jesus and Mary. The modern situation is one of feminist emergence from sexist structures and ideas. Were we to exist in a world in which men and women were equally sensitive to the male and female aspects in themselves, then both sexes could participate in the reformation of Marian imagery. However, women, and particularly feminist theologians, are now throwing off the yoke of a misogynist history and therefore need the opportunity to lay claim to their own spirituality, symbols, and rituals. Gender balance and integration must be part of the vision, lest the Christian feminist movement merely see its objectives as oppositional.

Given the above statement, why am I, a male trained in the Christian tradition, offering propositions for discussion in the negotiation of Marian imagery? The answer stems from theories of social construction. Concepts of "male" and "female" are socially constructed rather than biologically determined. A feminist consciousness is open and available to men and undeveloped in some women. For example, Carol Gilligan does not make an absolute observation about gender with regard to the ethic of care. While women predominantly use an ethic of care, and men predominantly use an ethic of justice, crossover does happen. Gender is not an absolute determinant of behavior or moral deliberation, although the "binary language" of "boys versus girls" receives a great deal of popular press.[26] In my opinion, the same is true for a feminist consciousness. Many feminists have expressed a desire to include men in the women's movement, provided that they, "have come to understand the evils of patriarchy, the injustice that has been done to women, and the way that has distorted all social relations."[27] Even an earlier Mary Daly invited men "who have been able to hear women's new words and accept these as an invitation to break out of the archetypal circle and face nothingness" to share in the struggle.[28] I characterize myself as a profeminist male, and I believe it is possible for men to participate in this discussion. Nevertheless, as a male, and therefore a member of the privileged gender in this society, I must enter the discussion humbly. I cannot speak for women's experience except through empathy, and therefore I cannot offer definitive solutions. What follows is propositional.

Catholic feminist literature reveals a number of themes that should, in my view, be included in a reworking of Marian imagery. An overriding theme is the need to reduce religious alienation. Mary's constructed imagery is out of touch with women's experience. It is losing ground as a traditional means of power *over* women, and its empowering aspects *for* women are overshadowed by its misogynist aspects. Religious constructions, by nature, reify a given set of images, norms, and morality that are historically and socially determined. These constructions can and do evolve as Mary has evolved. However, Marian imagery and its implications for women have not kept pace with the social consciousness of the faith community. Catharina Halkes expresses concern over the process of creating gender-tied religious symbols in Jesus and Mary, and its detrimental impact upon women.

> Women are bound to this procedure and even normalized by it. New and really evocative symbols can no longer be experienced. Christ and Mary themselves are reduced to the level of rigid principles and Mary can no longer provide vital impulses making women critical.[29]

Concepts of the inherent evil and weakness of women, the valorization of virginity, and the second-class status of women are being widely challenged. Reinterpreting Marian images is therefore a moral project. Alienation is experienced as a failed moral identification because much of the moral message of Mary is medieval. The evolution of moral understanding in so many aspects of society makes the alienation between women and Mary understandable. All of the following themes reflect proposals for a new imagery that not only mitigates Marian alienation but returns Mary to a spiritual source of strength and empowerment.

1. *A Reflection of Women's Experience.* Mary should be a source of validation for women, not a tool of vilification. The humanization of Mary requires her removal from her pedestal and the ending of her role as the great exception among women. A full range of humanity needs to flow through Mary including emotions, sexuality, failures, and successes.

2. *A Critical-Historical Approach to Mary.* Mary must be recognized as a symbol. The symbol's personification facilitates religious imagination, but it has no historical basis. No factual claims concerning Mary's character can be made. If Mary is conceptualized as a symbol-in-process and not as a historical entity, religious reification that leads to religious alienation can be further avoided. Historical-critical methods and human spirituality do not have to be at odds.

3. *Greater Plurality.* One of the difficulties with the traditional images of Mary is that some women have not been able to identify with her idealized womanhood. What does the traditional Mary have to say to sexually active women, lesbians, rape victims, outspoken women, or women leaders? As the keeper of Catholic moral hegemony, Mary was more often used to punish rather than support these women. For this reason, I must agree with Gebara and Bingemer in envisioning images of Mary that are more inclusive and less rigidly defined. In Chapter Two, it was established that Mary has been fundamentally a moral, religious figure. Arguing for greater plurality in Marian imagery does not ethically paralyze Mary. However, the morality that flows from her should not divide people along hierarchical stratifications. Given numerous worldwide manifestations of Mary (i.e. the Black Madonnas, Our Lady of Guadalupe, Our Lady of the Snows, Star of the Sea), the concept of plurality holds a great deal of continuity with the Catholic tradition.

4. *Continuity and Discontinuity with the Past.* I have argued for the reinterpretation rather than the vanquishing of Mary, and therefore believe that new imagery should be continuous with the past. However, I advocate limitations on the continuity that are perhaps less in keeping with Catholic tradition than that which some of the Catholic feminists advocate. As mentioned earlier, I distinguish between reinterpretation of biblical texts and dogmatic tradition. The biblical texts are so amorphous when it comes to Mary that, within historical-critical reason, they are ripe for feminist reinterpretation. However, some Catholic dogmatic pronouncements are too vivid in their theological rationale to simply reinterpret. For example, as demonstrated in Chapter Three, it is far from conclusive that Mary was a lifelong virgin, as the Catholic Church teaches. A feminist reinterpretation of scrip-

ture is possible, given what we know about textual formation. There is enough ambiguity to warrant alternative exegesis. However, when it comes to the infallibly pronounced dogma of the Assumption of Mary's body into heaven, knowledge of the author, the political environment, the theological environment, and the purpose of the document is all available. To propose a feminist reinterpretation of this dogma into something apart from the spirit/material dualism that permeates Catholic theology and the Cult of Mary is to deny known historical data. The theological courage to state that there has been progress, or further insight, or new revelation, is warranted in such a case. What was true for Catholics in the nineteenth century does not necessarily work today. The Church has evolved on many fronts: there is no reason to believe that the Cult of Mary cannot evolve past historically determined dogmas.

5. *Eliminate Gendered Construction.* Traditionally, the personification of Christ and God as male and Mary as female has caused a sex-based religious imagery and stratification as discussed in Chapter Four.[30] The projection of gender-oriented attributes—God as active, stern judge and Mary as passive, nurturing protector—contributes to dualistic ontological essentialism. Male and female are conceptualized as opposites rather than understood as sharing human nature. Such a construction hurts both men and women, since sex-typing limits their roles and behaviors. Men have benefited from this arrangement, yet they have also been kept from participating in the entire range of human experience. Ideally, Mary should be an empowering, liberating religious symbol for both men and women. Mary should not be a model solely for either gender, just as neither God nor Jesus should have gender-exclusive religious significance.

An Interim Proposition: "Mary, Everywoman"

I would like to propose yet another title for Mary as an interim model for new Marian imagery that seeks to liberate and empower Catholic women: "Mary, Everywoman." This title reflects continuity with the past. The name "Mary" is retained as an acknowledgment that there is continuity in this Christian tradition. The title "Everywoman" represents a reversal of traditional Marian titles. It is not an exultant adulation expressing an extreme quality. "Everywoman" reflects the fact that this is a symbol in dynamic existence with lived human experience.

Mary, Everywoman is also a symbol-in-process. As human consciousness progresses, so will this symbol. Definitive descriptions of Mary fail to recognize the historical evolution that takes place within religious symbols.

The attempt here is not to write a definitive new Marian theology or a new Liberation Theology. As Maeckelberghe states, such a definition is the task of the interpretive community. What is offered is the moral horizon or the contours of what new Marian imagery would look like. What follows is a proposal for new Marian image drawn from feminist theologians and left for the "magisterium of the people," particularly women, to clarify.

Just as three images of the traditional Mary were examined for their misogynist undertones, I would like to propose three images of "Mary, Everywoman" drawn from feminist themes. These images attempt to reverse the negative construction of Mary while retaining the positive. "Empowerment" and "liberation" are the goals for these images. Mary as "Mary-Woman," "Mary-Mother," and "Mary-Sister" are images drawn from the daily experience of the faithful. Rather than uphold impossible, sacred images, the attempt is to elevate common experience to the sacred.

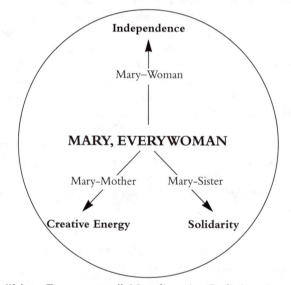

Figure 5: "Mary-Everywoman": Nonalienating Religious Imagery of Mary

Mary-Woman

"Mary-Woman" reflects the goddess-like power in every woman. In *The Goddess in Everywoman: A New Psychology of Women*, Jean Shinoda Bolen employs the goddesses of Greek mythology to describe how paradigms of women's behavior are analogous to goddesses ruling their lives.[31] Bolen's analysis includes both descriptive and normative reflections on the power and behavior of women. Her ultimate message is one of hope, because women do not have to be ruled by these goddesses. Women can choose to be heroines of their own lives by not acquiescing to the attempts at paternalistic control directed at them in society.

> Women need to become choicemaker-heroines instead of being passive, or victim-martyrs, or pawns moved around by other people or circumstances. Becoming a heroine is an enlightening new possibility for women who have been inwardly ruled by vulnerable goddess archetypes.[32]

Bolen's approach to psychological empowerment mitigates personal alienation by shifting the locus of control from the external to the internal. Women can choose to write their own life stories. Applying this theme to feminist spirituality, new approaches to images of Mary should be returned to the control of women, rather than left in the control of an all-male hierarchy. In order to be effective, the breaking down of present religious constructions must also be accompanied by a challenge to power relationships.

"Mary-Woman" praises the female gender in a holistic manner. Not limited to a particular sexuality or social position, Mary-Woman embodies the story of all women. It is significant to an image of Mary that is not viewed in light of a relationship, particularly to a man.[33] Mary's traditional images of virginity, mediator, and absolute goodness have been viewed in relation and subordination to her son. "Mary-Woman" is a suggested image of Mary that is not dependent on others for its power.

Mary-Sister

Sisterhood is a neglected theme in Catholic history, but is a powerful metaphor for religious orders and political movements. Mary-Sister is the embodiment of the power and spirit that comes with women in relationship to other women. Women's communities, organizations, and friendships have accomplished great feats in history. Mary-Sister is an image that celebrates sisterhood. This image takes a nonhierarchical perspective and supports concepts from feminist theory such as "a web of relationships" or "centrarchy," which do not depend upon subordination and domination.

Mary Hunt provides useful background to the image of "Mary-Sister" in her exploration of the ethical and theological significance of friendship. While she admits that friendship is not female exclusive, it is her paradigmatic approach to theology. Just as "liberation" is a new lens through which to view theology for a better understanding of praxis-oriented theology, "friendship" is Hunt's new lens.

> I suggest that friendship, beginning with the kinds of friendships
> that women have with one another, whether sexually explicit or
> not, is paradigmatic of the unity of theory and practice that femi-
> nists live out.[34]

According to Hunt, women's friendships are a revelatory human experience capable of informing women about themselves, one another, the
natural order, and the divine. Naming women's friendships as a primary
revelatory experience is significant because it counters traditional
approaches that attempt to define women in relation to men. Hunt
describes friendships as "the central relation experience for women."
These friendships are often "closer" than the friendships women have
with male lovers and husbands. In developing her historical basis for a
theology of friendship, Hunt uses the biblical story of Mary and her
cousin Elizabeth as an example of the underlying tradition of female
friendships.[35] Hunt demonstrates that there are available resources to
construct a theology of sisterhood containing a Marian image at its core.

Many Catholic communities of women already bear the name of Mary
(i.e., the Immaculate Heart of Mary Community). However, Mary-Sister
does not invoke Mary as an ultimate model of faith to be emulated by
community members. Mary-Sister exists in the gathering of women and
in what they share and can accomplish. This is not an essentialist image;
women simply cannot gather and form community. However, many
women, as an oppressed group in society, do share common experiences of
sexism, lowered status, harassment, "ageism," and "looksism." Mary-Everywoman is not an attempt to create a monolithic woman. The feminist
movement is dealing with issues of race and class layered upon issues of
gender, and new Marian images must also deal with these issues. Catholic
women do not come in one color, and neither can Mary. Sisterhood is
powerful not just because of commonalties but because of pluralism.

Mary-Mother

This image has much in continuity with the Christian tradition and
popular devotion. Mary can be a spirited great mother who is in harmony with all great mothers named and unnamed in history, including the
great Mother-Goddess of the pre-Christian era. As explored in Chapter
Four, the experience of divine motherhood is rooted in human civilization's oldest known forms of religion. In their exhaustive study of
goddess figures, Anne Baring and Jules Cashford note numerous and
almost exclusively female deity figures found in archaeological excava-

tions of ancient civilizations. Their conclusion is that these societies found a significant symbolic link between a woman's potential for birth and the creative power of nature.

> The mystery of the female body is the mystery of birth, which is also the mystery of the unmanifest becoming the manifest in the whole of nature. This far transcends the female body and woman as carrier of this image, for the body of the female of any species leads through the mystery of birth to the mystery of life itself.[36]

Mary as mother is a link to the tradition of honoring female creative power. Rather than being dichotomous with Eve, Mary-Mother shares the creative power of motherhood with her.

Mary-Mother can also find connection to the efforts of modern ecofeminists. Appropriations of the term "Gaia" among ecofeminists is a reference to the Greek Earth-Goddess. Rosemary Radford Ruether opposes the simple juxtaposition of a female "Gaia" to the male "god." However, Ruether believes an alternative "Gaia" tradition can provide insights into a theology for healing the earth.[37] Mary-Mother imagery can identify with Mother-Earth imagery in an interconnected environmental spirituality.

Mary-Mother is not an attempt to define all women as mothers as has been the case in the Catholic tradition (with the exception of religious orders). However, all women have had mothers, real or surrogate, and therefore can have some understanding of the maternal relationship. What is most important for this image is the creative power and potential of women.

What is Missing?

Mary, Everywoman does not have an explicit image of sexuality. This serves a number of purposes. It is an attempt to mitigate the traditional woman = sexuality association that the Cult of Mary perpetuates. As discussed in Chapter Three, the sexual fixation of the Catholic Church has played a limiting function in the lives of both men and women, and cost the Church much of its moral credibility in modern society. Removing sexuality from Mary lessens the significance of any one sexual orientation. Therefore, another purpose of these omissions is to end the reification of particular lifestyles such as celibacy. If Mary is portrayed as exhibiting any particular sexual orientation (i.e. Virgin Mary), it becomes valorized over all others.[38] In Chapter Three, it was demonstrated that

Mary was not merely a virgin but a heterosexual virgin. This becomes an oppressive, divisive image for a religious figure of such prominence.

While sexuality is removed in Mary, Everywoman, a key feminist theme is also missing: the end of sex-typed imagery. Therefore, this imagery does not fit the fifth theme of my own rubric. Mary, Everywoman is clearly female and female directed. It is for this reason that Mary, Everywoman is an interim symbol-in-progress. The religious consciousness of the Catholic faithful is not ready to break down the sex-typed construction of a male Christ and a female Mary. This deconstruction is a worthy objective for men and women to be more sensitive to the masculine and feminine in each. However, the reality of religious imagery is that it is not prepared for such androgyny, and therefore requires an interim symbol.

Ultimate Implications

If Mary is liberated from the traditional roles and images, can Jesus and God remain the same? The answer is, of course, no, but history reveals that change does not have to represent a fatal threat to Christianity. In every age, Mary, Jesus, and God were imagined and portrayed differently, reflecting the social consciousness of the time. Mariology is so important to the systematic theology of Catholicism that the departures from tradition suggested by feminists will involve evolution of other images. The feminist critique of Mary parallels the feminist critique of Catholicism. The three images discussed in this book brought forth a mandate for change in sexual morality, power structures, and definitions of good and evil. However, Mary represents the position of the official teaching of the Church. The same critiques and recommendations for change could just as easily be focused upon Catholicism. Institutional religious change does not come easily. The Second Vatican Council divided Catholics into factions that never reconciled. Further change will also be divisive.

Green's hypothesis about the morality of religion is significant to a feminist mandate that Catholicism must change. If religion is fundamentally about defining morality, and that morality is called into question, then that religion must also be called into question. Catholic feminists do not wish to destroy the Catholic Church. Spirituality, moral discourse, community, and continuity with the past are all part of what feminists want religion to be. However, they are unwilling to give up dignity, freedom, and voice to save the Church. Catholic feminists merely seek to reclaim their Church. Schussler Fiorenza reflects these sentiments:

> Rather than to abandon Christian faith and community as inherent-
> ly oppressive to women, we seek to reclaim the power of Christian
> faith and community for the liberation and wholeness of all, women
> and men.[39]

To survive as a "vital" religion of credible moral significance, the Catholic Church must adapt to feminist consciousness.

The distinction between Catholic and post-Christian feminism is exemplified in Rosemary Radford Ruether's review of Daphne Hampson's *Theology and Feminism*. Hampson's work is a thoroughgoing critique and rejection of Christianity as a religion that cannot escape its misogynist history. She finds the Christian concept of God to be an extension of the male ego. God is a distant, self-sufficient, nonrelational absolute power. The reification of the power-distance of God serves to legitimize hierarchical relationships among humans. Christ reinforces the idea of a distant deity because Jesus is a male incarnation. Males can be identified with God exclusively. Hampson finds this structure of relationships to be morally unjust. Her conclusion is that Christianity is not salvageable.[40] Ironically, Ruether finds Hampson's argument in agreement with Christian orthodoxy.[41] Hampson has accepted the hierarchical Church's definition of Catholicism as the singularly correct one. Such an approach ignores the dynamics of Catholicism discussed in Chapter Two of this book. Ruether agrees with Hampson's fundamental critique, and has written similar critiques herself. However, Ruether, like other Catholic feminists, refuses to let the hierarchy of the Church be the exclusive, defining body of Catholicism. Ruether rejects Hampson's conclusion because it assumes that rejecting Christianity is the only solution for feminists. Ruether refuses to see Catholicism as singularly oppressive, and she acknowledges the countertraditions that bring hope to modern religious feminists. To make her case, Ruether turns to Mary:

> At the cross and at the tomb, it is the women followers of Jesus who
> are the faithful remnant and first witnesses of the resurrection,
> commissioned to take the "good news" back to the cowardly and
> traitorous male disciples huddled in the upper room. It is a woman,
> Mary, who represents the redeemed community that is lifted up, as
> the mighty are put down from their thrones by God's transforming
> work in history. It is the women disciples, as well as Mary, who are
> among those filled with the Spirit at Pentecost, designated as shar-
> ing in the renewed prophetic spirit.[42]

Notes

Introduction

1 Barbara Corrado Pope, "Immaculate and Powerful: The Marian Revival in the Nineteenth Century," in *Immaculate and Powerful: The Female in Sacred Image and Social Reality*, ed. Clarissa Atkinson, Constance Buchanan, and Margaret Miles, (Boston: Beacon Press, 1985), 197.

2 For example, Andrew Greeley, *The Catholic Myth: The Behavior and Beliefs of American Catholics*, 252 (New York: Charles Scribner's Sons, 1990), and Rosemary Radford Ruether, *Sexism and God-Talk: Toward A Feminist Theology* (Boston: Beacon Press, 1983), 80–81.

3 Elizabeth Johnson, "The Marian Tradition and the Reality of Women," *Horizons*, 1 December 1985, 135.

4 Anthony Giddens, *Sociology* (Cambridge: Polity, 1989), 464.

5 Hilda Graef, *Mary: A History of Doctrine and Devotion*, vol. 1 (New York: Sheed and Ward, 1963), 318.

6 According to Graef, Luther viewed Mary as a "pathetic young girl without intrinsic sanctity or merit." In Luther's words, "O blessed Virgin and Mother of God, how utterly nothing and despised you have been." Hilda Graef, *Mary: A History of Doctrine and Devotion*, vol. 2, (New York: Sheed and Ward, 1965), 7–8.

7 Rosemary Radford Ruether, *New Woman, New Earth* (New York: Seabury Press, 1975), 51–52.

Chapter 1

1 Els Maeckelberghe, "Mary: Maternal Friend or Virgin Mother," in *Concilium: Motherhood: Experience, Institution, Theology,* ed. Anne Carr and Elisabeth Schussler Fiorenza, no. 206 (1989): 121

2 Els Maeckelberghe, *Desperately Seeking Mary: A Feminist Appropriation of a Traditional Religious Symbol* (Kampen, The Netherlands: Kok Pharos, 1991), 89–91.

3 Maria Kassel finds a connection between the psychological idealization of mother-hood and conservative Catholicism. A type of "harkening back" accompanies a Marian devotion that is easily romanticized with a view to one's own mother, or at least a notion of idealized motherhood. This harkening-back process often has become confused with a longing for a return to religious tradition. The symbols have been mixed enough to equate a devotion to Mary with conservative Catholicism rooted in the past. Maria Kassel, "Mary and the Human Psyche Considered in the light of Depth Psychology," in *Concilium: Mary in the Churches,* ed. Hans Kung and Jurgen Moltmann, no. 168 (October 1983): 74–82.

4 Mary is also a part of the Muslim tradition and appears in the Qur'an. Chapter 19 of the Qur'an describes her conception and delivery of Jesus. See Denise Lardner Carmody, *Mythological Woman: Contemporary Reflections on Ancient Religious Stories* (New York: Crossroad, 1982), 109–113; and Neal Robinson, "Jesus and Mary in the Qur'an: Some Neglected Affinities," *Religion* no. 20 (1990): 161–75.

5 See, for example, David Wright, ed., *Chosen By God: Mary in Evangelical Perspectives,* (London: Marshall Pickering, 1989); Sue Monk Kidd, "Going Back for Mary: A Protestant's Journey," *Daughters of Sarah* (October 1991): 28–31; Alvin Horst, "Mary in Current Theology: A Lutheran View," *Currents in Theology and Mission* (October 1988): 412–17; as well as several articles in *Concilium: Mary in the Churches* (October 1983).

6 Rosemary Radford Ruether, "Women's Difference and Equal Rights in the Church," *Concilium: The Special Nature of Women?* (December 1991): 12.

7 E. Ann Matter, "The Virgin Mary, A Goddess?," *The Book of the Goddess,* ed. Carl Olson (New York: Crossroad, 1990), 91.

8 Stephen Benko, *The Virgin Goddess: Studies in the Pagan and Christian Roots of Mariology* (New York: E.J. Brill, 1993), 4.

9 Joseph Grassi, *Mary, Mother and Disciple: From the Scriptures to the Council of Ephesus* (Wilmington, DE: Michael Glazier, 1988), 127. See also Michael Carroll, *The Cult of the Virgin Mary: Psychological Origins* (Princeton: Princeton University Press, 1986), 41–48.

10 Benko, *The Virgin Goddess: Studies in the Pagan and Christian Roots of Mariology,* 171–72.

11 Geoffrey Ashe, *The Virgin: Mary's Cult and the Re-Emergence of the Goddess* (London: Arkana, 1985), 151.

12 St. Epiphanius of Salamis translated in Benko, *The Virgin Goddess: Studies in the Pagan and Christian Roots of Mariology,* 171.

13 Benko, *The Virgin Goddess: Studies in the Pagan and Christian Roots of Mariology,* 174.

14 Vasiliki Limberis, *Divine Heiress: The Virgin Mary and the Creation of Christian Constantinople* (London: Routledge, 1994), 120.

15 Mary Daly, *Pure Lust: Elemental Feminist Philosophy* (Boston: Beacon Press, 1984), 76.

16 Ruether, *New Woman, New Earth,* 50.

17 Mary Condren, *The Serpent and the Goddess: Women, Religion, and Power in Celtic Ireland* (San Francisco: HarperSan Francisco, 1989), 55.

18 Ibid., 161.

19 Carl Olson, *The Book of the Goddess, Past and Present*, 1–2.

20 Pamela Berger, *The Goddess Obscured: Transformation of the Grain Protectoress from Goddess to Saint* (Boston: Beacon Press, 1985), 89–91.

21 E. Ann Matter, "The Virgin Mary: A Goddess?," 80–81.

22 Naomi Goldenberg claims that modern Marian power stems from the pre-Christian Goddess: "Mary derives her power in the fact that she compels minds and hearts from the vestiges of these vibrant Goddesses she was supposed to replace." Naomi Goldenberg, *Changing of the Gods: Feminism and the End of Traditional Religion* (Boston: Beacon Press, 1979), 75.

23 The passages that Mary appears in the canonical scriptures are: Gal 4:4; Mk 3:19–21, 3:31–45, 6:3; Mt 1:2, 12:46–50; Lk 1:5–2:52, 8:19–21, 11:27–28; Acts 1; Jn 2:1–11, 19:25–27.

24 Elizabeth Johnson, "The Symbolic Character of Theological Statements About Mary," *Journal of Ecumenical Studies* (spring 1985): 312.

25 Bruce Malina, "Mother and Son," *Biblical Theology Bulletin*, 19, no. 4 (October 1989): 54.

26 Ibid., 317.

27 Karl Rahner, *Mary, the Mother of the Lord* (New York: Herder and Herder, 1963), 83.

28 Ashe, *The Virgin: Mary's Cult and the Re-Emergence of the Goddess*, 3.

29 John Shinners, "The Cult of Mary and Popular Belief," in *Mary, Woman of Nazareth* (New York: Paulist Press, 1989), 163–64.

30 The term "deliver" is used in the context of the plea, "deliver us from danger." The translation of the Greek, "rysai," or "deliver," is the same form used in the prayer, the Our Father, indicating the potency of Mary's intercession. Michael O'Carroll, *Theotokos: A Theological Encyclopedia of the Blessed Virgin Mary* (Collegeville, MN: Michael Glazier Books, 1982), 336.

31 Raymond Brown, et al., *Mary in the New Testament: A Collaborative Assessment by Protestant Roman Catholic Scholars* (Philadelphia: Fortress Press, 1978), 253.

32 Ashe, *The Virgin: Mary's Cult and the Re-Emergence of the Goddess*, 196.

33 Carroll, *The Cult of the Virgin Mary: Psychological Origins*, 75.

34 There is some evidence that this Marian title existed as early as the third century. It may have been an adaptation of the Egyptian title, "Mother of God," given to Isis. O'Carroll, *Theotokos: A Theological Encyclopedia of the Blessed Virgin Mary*, 342.

35 Nestorius, *Reply to Proclus* (429 C.E.). Quoted in *The World Treasury of Religious Quotations*, ed. Ralph Woods (New York: Cromwell, 1953), 684.

36 Marina Warner, *Alone of All Her Sex: The Myth and the Cult of the Virgin Mary* (New York: Vintage Books, 1976), 65.

37 Benko, *The Virgin Goddess: Studies in the Pagan and Christian Roots of Mariology*, 257.

38 In *Divine Heiress*, Limberis argues that the Council of Ephesus was a key moment in history for Christianity and for Mary. Through Mary, pagan religions, still operative in the fourth century, became symbolically Christianized through the declaration of Mary as *Theotokos*. Constantinople, the new center of the Roman Empire and Christianity, became a catalyst for the transformation of Mary from a secondary figure in Christianity to a central role, as manifested in hymns, art, and ritual.

39 Anne Baring and Jules Cashford, *The Myth of the Goddess: Evolution of an Image* (London: Viking, 1991), 551.

40 Warner, *Alone of All Her Sex: The Myth and the Cult of the Virgin Mary*, 147.

41 Amaury de Riencort, *Sex and Power in History* (New York: McKay, 1974), 218.

42 Warner, *Alone of All Her Sex: The Myth and the Cult of the Virgin Mary*, 183.

43 Ivone Gebara and Maria Clara Bingemer, *Mary: Mother of God, Mother of the Poor* (New York: Orbis, 1987), 128, 131.

44 Virgil Elizondo, "Mary and the Poor: A Model of Evangelising," in *Concilium: Mary in the Churches*, ed. Hans Kung and Jurgen Moltmann, no. 168 (1983): 59.

45 Evelyn P. Stevens, "Marianismo: The Other Face of Machismo in Latin America," in *Female and Male in Latin America: Essays*, ed. Ann Pescatello (Pittsburgh: University of Pittsburgh Press, 1973), 89–101.

46 Rosemary Radford Ruether, *Sexism and God-Talk*, 170–73.

47 Karen Armstrong, *The Gospel According to Woman: Christianity's Creation of the Sex War in the West* (New York: Anchor Books, 1986), 104.

48 Riencort, *Sex and Power in History*, 250–52. See also Chapter 5 of Carolyn Merchant, *The Death of Nature: Women, Ecology and the Scientific Revolution* (San Francisco: Harper & Row, 1980).

49 Francis Sullivan, *Magisterium: Teaching Authority of the Church* (New York: Paulist Press, 1983), 18. Elisabeth Schussler Fiorenza critiques interpretations of "Magisterium," such as Sullivan's, because these definitions fail to recognize that women are excluded from participation in the teaching authority of the Church because of their gender. Schussler Fiorenza, "Claiming Our Authority and Power," in *Concilium: The Teaching Authority of the Believers*, ed. Johannes–Baptist Metz and Edward Schillebeeckx, no. 180 (1985): 53.

50 The Immaculate Conception has been a source of ongoing confusion for lay Catholics. It is sometimes assumed to be a feast day dedicated to the conception of Jesus, but is actually a celebration of Mary's conception untouched by original sin. Adding to the confusion is the Church's choice of liturgical text for the feast day (Lk 1:26–38), which ironically describes Jesus' conception. Shawn Madigan, "Do Marian Festivals Image 'That Which the Church Hopes to Be'?," *Worship*, 65 (May 1991): 196.

51 There is no evidence that the early Christians believed in Mary's sinless nature. Berhard Lohse, *A Short History of Christian Doctrine: From the First Century to the Present* (Philadelphia: Fortress Press, 1978), 201.

52 Maeckelberghe, *Desperately Seeking Mary: A Feminist Appropriation of a Traditional Religious Symbol*, 98.

53 Previous attempts to advance this dogma had been rejected. Benko, *The Virgin Goddess: Studies in the Pagan and Christian Roots of Mariology*, 204.

54 Mary Daly finds the timing of this dogma of the Immaculate Conception of Mary (1854) and the beginning of the modern feminist movement at the historical meeting at Seneca Falls, New York in 1848 more then coincidental. As the Church moved toward the greater use of Mary as a model of Church orthodoxy, extolling the virtues of a level of purity unattainable by human women, the beginnings of organized resistance by women foreshadowed polar social forces. Daly, *Pure Lust*, 102.

55 Nicholas Perry and Loreto Echeverria, *Under the Heel of Mary* (London: Routledge, 1988), 115.

56 Pope, "Immaculate and Powerful," 182.

57 Perry and Echeverria, *Under the Heel of Mary*, 121.

58 Maeckelberghe, *Desperately Seeking Mary: A Feminist Appropriation of a Traditional Religious Symbol*, 98.

59 John Dwyer, *Church History: Twenty Lectures of Catholic Christianity* (New York: Paulist, 1985), 339.

60 Justo Gonzalez, *A History of Christian Thought* (Nashville: Abingdon Press, 1975), 362.

61 Richard McBrien, *Catholicism* (San Francisco: HarperSan Francisco, 1994), 887.

62 Warner, *Alone of All Her Sex: The Myth and the Cult of the Virgin Mary,* 1103–104.

63 Gebara and Bingemer, *Mary: Mother of God, Mother of the Poor,* 114.

64 Lohse, *A Short History of Christian Doctrine,* 213.

65 Madigan, "Do Marian Festivals Image 'That Which the Church Hopes to Be'?," 203.

66 Warner, *Alone of All Her Sex: The Myth and the Cult of the Virgin Mary,* 86.

67 Ashe, *The Virgin: Mary's Cult and the Re-Emergence of the Goddess,* 208.

68 Madigan, "Do Marian Festivals Image 'That Which the Church Hopes to Be'?," 203.

69 O'Carroll, *Theotokos: An Encyclopedia of the Blessed Virgin Mary,* 55–56.

70 Pope Pius XII quoted in McBrien, *Catholicism,* 1102.

71 Baring and Cashford, *The Myth of the Goddess: Evolution of an Image,* 553.

72 Graef, *Mary: A History of Doctrine and Devotion* 1: 152.

73 The Second Vatican Council gave little attention to women in the conciliar documents. Ruether, "The Place of Women in the Church," in *Modern Catholicism,* ed. Adrian Hastings (New York: Oxford University Press, 1991), 260.

74 The biblical movement—a call for theological grounding in the message of the bible and in particular the gospels—should not be confused with the increased significance of biblical scholarship that attempts to apply historical critical methods to better understand the authorship, message, and audience of the books of the bible. Biblical scholarship tends to be an ally of feminist theology because it demystifies the sacred texts. The biblical movement, when devoid of sound scholarly approaches, can be used to turn back the clock for women.

75 Kari Borresen, "Mary in Catholic Theology," in *Concilium: Mary in the Churches,* ed. Hans Kung and Jurgen Moltmann, no. 168 (1983): 53.

76 O'Carroll, *Theotokos: A Theological Encyclopedia of the Blessed Virgin Mary,* 351–56.

77 Kari Borresen finds the bishops' writing on Mary to be a confusion of Christotypical and ecclesiatypical approaches. Written only 14 years after the declaration of the Assumption (the culmination of Mary's acquisition of divinity) the bishops attempt to define a nonexultant, limited role for Mary, yet slip in some areas, such as her role in salvation, to give her certain Christlike qualities. Borresen, "Mary in Catholic Theology," 53.

78 *The Dogmatic Constitution on the Church,* ed. Walter Abbott, translated in *The Documents of Vatican II* (New Jersey: New Century Publishers, 1966), 94–95.

79 Anne Carr, "Mary in the Mystery of the Church: Vatican Council II," in *Mary According to Women,* ed. Carol Frances (Kansas City: Leaven Press, 1985): 10–16.

80 Michael Novak, *The Open Church* (New York: MacMillan, 1964), 177.

81 Quoted in Stephen Benko, *Protestants, Catholics, and Mary* (Valley Forge: Judson Press, 1968), 90.

82 Stefano De Fiores, "Mary in Postconciliar Theology," vol. I of *Vatican II: Assessment and Perspectives Twenty-Five Years After,* ed. Rene Latourelle (New York: Paulist Press, 1988), 474.

83 On November 7, 1980, Pope John Paul II stated that feminism ran counter to women's true vocation as mothers. Daly, *Pure Lust,* 56.

84 On March 24, 1984, Pope John Paul II knelt at a statue of Our Lady of Fatima in a crowded St. Peter's square and dedicated the entire planet to the Immaculate Heart of Mary. Perry and Echeverria, *Under the Heel of Mary,* 1.

85 Uta Ranke-Heinemann, *Eunuchs for the Kingdom of Heaven* (New York: Doubleday, 1990), 347.

86 O'Carroll, *Theotokos: A Theological Encyclopedia of the Blessed Virgin Mary,* 384.

87 Peter Hebblethwaite, "Bullet that Wounded Pope Landed in Fatima Afore Him," *National Catholic Reporter*, 24 May 1991, 7–8.

88 Perry and Echeverria, *Under the Heel of Mary*, 287.

89 Rosemary Radford Ruether, "John Paul II and the Growing Alienation of Women from the Church," in *The Church in Anguish: Has the Vatican Betrayed Vatican II?* (San Francisco: Harper & Row, 1986), 280.

90 Daly, *Beyond God the Father*, 81.

91 Peter Berger and Thomas Luckmann, *The Social Construction of Reality: A Treatise in the Sociology of Knowledge* (New York: Anchor Books, 1966), 129.

92 Ibid., 60–62.

93 Mary is such an important icon that often great lengths are taken to "legitimize" her role in the face of certain alienation. The examples of this are numerous. In the "Liturgy for Mothers" that circulated between the eleventh and sixteenth centuries, Mary is invoked repeatedly as the "consoler of women in labor." Given the ancient Catholic belief that Mary experienced no pain in childbirth, Mary's role as consoler represents a rather contrived legitimation. However, the need of the faithful overcame the obvious stumbling block. Emilie Amt, *Women's Lives in Medieval Europe: A Sourcebook* (New York: Routledge, 1993), 97.

94 Peter Berger, *The Sacred Canopy: Elements of a Sociological Theory of Religion* (New York: Anchor Books, 1969), 29.

95 Ibid., 85.

96 John McKenzie, "The Mother of Jesus in the New Testament," in *Concilium: Mary in the Churches*, ed. Hans Kung and Jurgen Moltmann, no. 168 (1983): 9.

97 Mary Daly, *Beyond God the Father* (Boston: Beacon Press, 1973), 35–36.

98 See Daly's analysis of the Sado-Ritual Syndrome in *Gyn/Ecology: The Metaethics of Radical Feminism* (Boston: Beacon Press, 1978), 130–33.

99 Daly, *Gyn/Ecology*, 87.

100 Maeckelberghe, *Desperately Seeking Mary: A Feminist Appropriation of a Traditional Religious Symbol*, 1–3.

101 Rosemary Radford Ruether, "Women's Difference and Equal Rights in the Church," *Concilium: The Special Nature of Women?* (December, 1991): 16.

102 Ruether, *Sexism and God-Talk: Toward a Feminist Theology*, 15.

103 Recent statistics indicate that mass attendance for women had begun to decline in the early 1990's. Charles Davis speculates that the issue of ordination and lack of decision-making ability for women has contributed to this decline. Charles Davis, "Catholics Will Give When Church Moves Into Future," *National Catholic Reporter*, 12 February 1993, 13.

104 Ashe, *The Virgin: Mary's Cult and the Re-Emergence of the Goddess*, vii.

105 Elisabeth Gossman, "The Construction of Women's Difference in the Christian Theological Tradition," *Concilium: The Special Nature of Women?*, ed. Anne Carr and Elisabeth Schussler Fiorenza, no. 218 (December, 1991): 53–54.

106 Catharina Halkes, "Mary and Women," in *Concilium: Mary in the Churches*, ed. Hans Kung and Jurgen Moltmann, no. 168 (1983): 67.

Chapter 2

1 Perry and Echeverria, *Under the Heel of Mary*, 313.

2 Felicium Foy, ed., *The Catholic Almanac 1991* (Huntington, Ind.: Our Sunday Visitor, 1991), 364.

3 The rosary is an outgrowth of Marian piety of the middle ages. The concept of

beads of prayer was borrowed from eastern religions and introduced to Christianity in the eleventh century. A full rosary consists of 150 "Hail Marys" prayed in multiples of ten with meditation on a single mystery in the life of Jesus or Mary (for example, the Annunciation), separated by an "Our Father" and the doxology of the Church. They are usually recited in cycles of 50, with meditation on one of the three mystical categories: the sorrowful, the joyful, and the glorious mysteries. Warner, *Alone of All Her Sex: The Myth and the Cult of the Virgin Mary*, 306–307.

4 After World War II, a number of rosary-centered organizations developed in the United States. The most popular and lasting of these organizations is the Blue Army of Our Lady of Fatima. Founded in 1947 by Fr. Harold Colgan and John Haffert, the organization was formed to counter the "red army" of communism. Members pledge to wear a scapular and pray the rosary daily. At its height in the 1950s, the organization claimed 10,000,000 members worldwide. Today, the Blue Army continues to send magazines and newsletters concerning the spiritual dimension of the struggle with communism, despite the fall of the Soviet Union. Perry and Echeverria, *Under the Heel of Mary*, 252–53.

5 The following are the feast days of Mary celebrated in the United States Catholic Church: Immaculate Conception (Dec. 8), Mary, Mother of God (Jan. 1), Our Lady of Lourdes (Feb. 11), Annunciation (March 25), Visitation (May 31), Our Lady of Mt. Carmel (July 16), Dedication of St. Mary Major (Aug. 5), Assumption of Mary (Aug. 15), Queenship of Mary (Aug. 22), Nativity of Mary (Sept. 8), Our Lady of Sorrows (Sept. 15), Our Lady of the Rosary (Oct. 7), Presentation of Mary (Nov. 21), Immaculate Heart of Mary (Saturday after Corpus Christi).

6 Luis Maldonado, "Popular Religion: Dimensions, Levels and Types," in *Concilium: Popular Religion*, ed. Norbert Greinacher and Norbert Mette, no. 186 (1986): 6.

7 Officially recognized Marian appearances: Rue du Bac, Paris, France, 1830; La Salette, France, 1846; Lourdes, France, 1858; Pontmain, France, 1870; Fatima, Portugal, 1917; Beauraing, Belgium, 1932–33; Banneux, Belgium, 1933.

8 Pope, "Immaculate and Powerful," 173, 187.

9 E. Ann Matter, "The Virgin Mary: A Goddess?," 91. Between 1928 and 1971, the Vatican received 210 reported sightings of Mary. O'Carroll, *Theotokos: A Theological Encyclopedia of the Blessed Virgin Mary*, 47; and Malina, "From Isis to Medjugorje: Why Apparitions?," *Biblical Theology Bulletin*, 19, no. 4 (1989): 83.

10 McBrien, *Catholicism*, 1107.

11 12 million faithful visit Our Lady of Guadalupe each year, and 4.5 million visit Lourdes annually. Carroll, *The Cult of the Virgin Mary: Psychological Origins*, xii.

12 John R. Shinners, "The Cult of Mary and Popular Belief," in *Mary, Woman of Nazareth*, ed. Doris Donnely, (New York: Paulist, 1989), 161–62.

13 Benedict Ashley, *Theologies of the Body: Humanist and Christian* (St. Louis: Pope John Center, 1985), 538.

14 Andrew Greeley, *The Mary Myth* (New York: Seabury Press, 1977), 23–48.

15 Greeley, *The Catholic Myth: The Behavior and Beliefs of American Catholics*, 244–45.

16 Andrew Greeley and Mary Greeley Durkin, *How to Save the Catholic Church* (New York: Viking, 1984), 1.

17 Greeley, *The Catholic Myth: The Behavior and Beliefs of American Catholics*, 7.

18 Charles Curran, *American Catholic Social Ethics: Twentieth-Century Approaches* (Notre Dame: University of Notre Dame Press, 1982), 13.

19 Greeley, *The Catholic Myth*, 129.

20 Rosemary Radford Ruether, "Women-Church: Emerging Feminist Liturgical Communities," in *Concilium: Popular Religion*, ed. Norbert Greinacher and Norbert Mette, no. 186 (1986): 53.

21 A 1993 open letter published by the Women's Ordination Conference at the time of the Pope's visit to Denver, Colorado was consistent with ecclesial language, but with an ironic purpose. Mary's name was invoked as instrumental in the origination of the incarnation, the argument being that women have always played instrumental roles in the Church and should therefore be allowed to serve as priests.

22 Shinners, "The Cult of Mary and Popular Belief," 178.

23 Schussler Fiorenza, "Feminist Theology as A Critical Theology of Liberation," 616.

24 Walter Abbott, *Constitution of Divine Revelation,* in Walter Abbott, ed. *The Documents of Vatican II,* 117.

25 Evolution of official Catholic thought can be demonstrated in a number of areas. See John T. Noonan Jr., *The Scholastic Analysis of Usury* (Cambridge: Harvard University Press, 1957) and *Contraception: A History of Its Treatment by the Catholic Theologians and Canonists* (Cambridge: Belknap Press, 1986).

26 Many Catholic theologians considered to have achieved scholarly excellence have been censored in varying degrees by Rome because of their dissent from official Church teaching. The list includes John Courtney Murray, Yves Congar, Hans Kung, Edward Schillebeeckx, Leonardo and Clodovis Boff, Charles Curran, Matthew Fox, and Gustavo Gutierrez.

27 Baring and Cashford, *The Myth of the Goddess: Evolution of an Image,* 553.

28 According to Richard McBrien, the Marian dogmas are an essential part of a Catholic identity. "A [Catholic] person might, for example, reject these definitions [the Immaculate Conception and the Assumption of Mary] precisely because they are papal actions. . . . A person might also reject any place for Mary in the Christian dispensation and the Catholic tradition. Such views would effectively disengage one from the Catholic tradition and the community which embodies it." McBrien, *Catholicism,* 1104.

29 For example, in the infamous Ratzinger Report, a type of state of the Church report from a neoconservative perspective, the key appointee of the Pope, the prefect of the Congregation for the Doctrine of the Faith, wrote of Mary as the remedy for all heresies. The chief heresy in this context was liberation theology. Perry and Echeverria, *Under the Heel of Mary,* 288.

30 The analysis of Barbara Hilkert Andolsen finds that Catholic social teaching has a strong gender bias that leaves women's work out of the equation for social justice. Barbara Hilkert Andolsen, "A Woman's Work is Never Done: Unpaid Household Labor as a Social Justice Issue," Women's Consciousness, ed. Barbara Hilkert Andolsen, Christine Gudorf, and Mary Pelauer (New York: Winston Press, 1987), 3.

31 Ibid., 6.

32 Pope Leo XIII, *Rerum Novarum,* in *Justice in the Marketplace,* ed. David Byers (Washington D.C.: United States Catholic Conference, 1985), 32.

33 Pope Pius XI, *Quadragismo Anno,* ed. Byers, 65.

34 Andolsen, "Women's Work is Never Done," 8.

35 Pope John XXIII, *Pacem in Terris,* ed. Byers, 158.

36 Abbott, *Pastoral Constitution on the Church in the Modern World,* 207.

37 Pope Paul VI, *Octogesima Adveniens,* ed. Byers, 230.

38 Pope John Paul II, *Laborem Exercens,* ed. Byers, 323.

39 Andolsen, "Women's Work is Never Done," 13.

40 Lisa Cahill, "Current Theology: Notes on Moral Theology: 1989, Feminist Ethics," in *Theological Studies,* no. 5, (1990): 58; and Catharina Halkes, "Mary in My Life," in Edward Schillebeeckx and Catharina Halkes, *Mary: Yesterday, Today and Tomorrow,* (New York: Crossroad, 1993), 77–78.

41 John Paul II, *On the Dignity and Vocation of Women, Mulieris Dignitatem* (Washington, D.C.: United States Catholic Conference, 1988), 64.

42 John Paul II, *The Mother of Redemptoris Mater*, 101.

43 Walter Burghardt, "The Role of the Scholar in the Catholic Church," in *Moral Theology: Challenges for the Future*, ed. Charles Curran (New York: Paulist Press, 1990), 19.

44 Bernhard Haring, "The Role of the Catholic Moral Theologian," *Moral Theology: Challenges for the Future*, ed. 32–33.

45 Adapted from Carol Christ, "Symbols of Goddess and God in Feminist Theology," *The Book of the Goddess, Past and Present*, 238.

46 Anne E. Carr, *Transforming Grace: Christian Tradition and Women's Experience* (San Francisco: Harper and Row, 1988), 95.

47 Pamela Dickey Young, *Feminist Theology/Christian Theology: In Search of Method* (Minneapolis: Fortress Press, 1990), 20.

48 Ruether, *Sexism and God-Talk: Toward A Feminist Theology*, 15.

49 Elisabeth Schussler Fiorenza, *Bread Not Stone* (Boston: Beacon Press, 1984), 13.

50 Ruether, *Sexism and God-Talk: Toward A Feminist Theology*, 20.

51 Ibid., 37–45.

52 Elizabeth Johnson, *She Who Is: The Mystery of God in Feminist Theological Discourse* (New York: Crossroad, 1992), 29–30.

53 Elaine Storkey, "The Significance of Mary for Feminist Theology," *Chosen by God: Mary in Evangelical Perspectives*, 184–85.

54 Ruether, *Sexism and God-Talk*, 12–13.

55 Elisabeth Schussler Fiorenza, *In Memory of Her* (New York: Crossroad, 1990), 146.

56 Ronald Green, *Religion and Moral Reason* (New York: Oxford University Press, 1988), xi.

57 Lisa Cahill, "Current Theology: Notes on Moral Theology: 1989, Feminist Ethics," in *Theological Studies*, no. 51, (1990): 50.

58 Ibid., 62.

59 David Tracy quoted in Cahill, "Current Theology: Notes on Moral Theology: 1989, Feminist Ethics," in *Theological Studies*, no. 51, (1990): 63.

60 Green, *Religion and Moral Reason*, 3.

61 Margaret Farley, "New Patterns of Relationship: Beginnings of a Moral Revolution," in *Introduction to Christian Ethics: A Reader*, ed. Ronald Hamel and Kenneth Himes (New York: Paulist Press, 1989), 76.

62 Carroll, *The Cult of the Virgin Mary: Psychological Origins*, 59.

63 Ibid., 88–89.

64 Ibid., 49–74.

65 Els Maeckelberghe, "Mary: Maternal Friend or Virgin Mother?," in *Concilium: Motherhood: Experience, Institution, Theology*, ed. Anne Carr and Elisabeth Schussler Fiorenza, no. 206 (1989): 123.

66 Nancy Chodorow, *The Reproduction of Mothering: Psychoanalysis and the Sociology of Gender* (Berkeley, University of California Press, 1978), 111–129.

67 Maeckelberghe, "Mary: Maternal Friend or Virgin Mother?," 124.

68 Sandra Zimdars-Swartz, Encountering Mary: From La Salette to Medjugorje (Princeton: Princeton University Press, 1992), 19.

Chapter 3

1 Alexander A. DiLella, who authors the commentary for Sirach in *The Jerome Biblical Commentary*, refers to this passage as the climax of the author Ben Sira's misogyny. It reflects the sexism of the era, including the notion that childlessness was always women's fault and that avoidance of sexual sin was also a women's sole responsibility. The passage also reveals the view that women—especially nonvirginal women—were considered dangerous. DiLella, "Sirach," in *The New Jerome Biblical Commentary* ed. Raymond Brown, Joseph Fitzmyer, and Roland Murphy (Englewood Cliffs, New Jersey: Prentice Hall, 1990), 507.

2 While the significance of Greco-Roman attitudes toward virginity is also relevant to this discussion, for the purposes of this paper, the focus will be the Jewish norms of the period as developed in the Hebrew Scriptures. Peter Brown emphasizes the difference between the social view of virginity in the Greco-Roman tradition and that found in the Judeo-Christian tradition. The Vestal Virgins of Rome and the protectoresses of Greece served as social exceptions that reinforced marriage and child bearing. As will be discussed further, in the Judeo-Christian tradition, virginity became the primal state of humanity, and the zenith of womanhood. In each culture, virginity served a different social value system. Peter R. L. Brown, *The Body and Society: Men, Women and Sexual Renunciation in Early Christianity* (New York: Columbia University Press, 1988), 8–9.

3 Carol Ochs, *Behind the Sex of God: Toward a New Consciousness—Transcending Matriarchy and Patriarchy* (Boston: Beacon Press, 1977), 68, 73.

4 Baring and Cashford, *The Myth of the Goddess: Evolution of an Image*, 548.

5 Elizabeth Clark and Herbert Richardson, *Women and Religion: A Feminist Sourcebook of Christian Thought* (San Francisco: Harper and Row, 1977), 26.

6 Joseph Blenkinsopp, "Deuteronomy," in *The New Jerome Biblical Commentary*, 94.

7 From a biological standpoint, the virginal standard of a broken and thus bloody hymen is of problematic validity because of physiological differences amongst women. For a concise review of hymen myths see Jennifer Gonnerman, "Your Hymen: The Inside Story," *On the Issues* (summer, 1995), 60.

8 Blenkinsopp, "Deuteronomy," 105.

9 The same section in Deuteronomy demonstrates the social attitude about rape. If a man raped a betrothed women who did not cry out for help, then both parties were stoned to death. Only if a betrothed women could not cry for help was the man punished by death. Nonbetrothed women who were raped had to be married by the perpetrator, who also had to pay a sum to the woman's father. The woman paid the double penalty of being raped and having to marry the rapist (Deut. 22:22–23:1)! The tone of these laws was one of correcting a property violation against the father or husband and not correcting injustice directed at women. The legal victim was the male because compensation was directed toward him.

10 L. William Countryman, *Dirt, Greed and Sex: Sexual Ethics in the New Testament and Their Implications for Today* (Philadelphia: Fortress Press, 1988), 157.

11 Family lineage and ownership of women was such an important theme of biblical culture that Deuteronomy 25:5–10 provides instruction on what brothers who keep their "real" property together should do if one of them dies. The surviving brother was to marry the widow and conceive children to keep the property within the family. This law disintegrated after women began to acquire the right of inheritance. Blenkinsopp, "Deuteronomy," 105.

12 There was a shift to a higher valorization of virginal religious orders for women with the rise of Christianity in the fourth century C.E.

13 Countryman, *Dirt, Greed and Sex*, 159.

14 Biblical texts such as Deuteronomy may represent an accurate picture of law and moral standards but may not realistically portray the actual practices of society. Historically, legal approbations are *reactive* to social behavior. The implication is that the existence of such laws meant that there were probably adulterers, rapists, and women who were sexually active, which created the need for legal restrictions.

15 Gebara and Bingemer, *Mary: Mother of God, Mother of the Poor*, 101.

16 Other traditions surrounding the miraculous birth of Jesus included that it was a painless birth for Mary and that there was no afterbirth. Ranke-Heinemann, *Eunuchs for the Kingdom of Heaven*, 342.

17 Barbara Walker, *The Woman's Encyclopedia of Myths and Secrets* (San Francisco: Harper and Row, 1983), 605; and Jerome Neyrey, "Maid and Mother in Art and Literature," *Biblical Theological Bulletin*, 19 no. 4, (October 1989): 65–75.

18 I have omitted the canonical gospels of John and Mark because the authors of these texts do not reveal that they had any knowledge of Mary's tradition of virginity. Bruce Malina concludes that without the synoptic tradition, Mary would not have been remembered at all. Malina, "Mother and Son," 55.

19 Modern biblical scholarship is applied in the treatment of the gospel texts. Biblical scholarship posits a layered origin of the gospels. The first layer is Jesus' actual words in parables and aphorisms. The second layer is the remembrance of the disciples concerning early Christians in their discourse on the disciples and Jesus. The third layer is the community of early Christians in its discourse on the disciples and Jesus. Finally, the fourth layer includes the early Christian communities' reflection on themselves and upon the preceding layers. These layers began in oral form and eventually assumed the written form we have today, but only the fourth layer of discourse is extant. The significance of this approach is the amount of filtering, in terms of time and intermediaries, that separate current readers of the bible from what can be called "eyewitness accounts"—if there were any. In some cases, possibly such as the infancy narrative, it is questionable whether anyone witnessed the events or whether they even occurred. The origins of such passages may have been theological rather than historical. Brown, et al., *Mary in the New Testament*, 9–12.

20 In the marriage process of this era, a man and a woman were betrothed or promised to each other prior to the bride being brought into the husband's house. Although there is some confusion in the terminology used in the gospels, Mary probably conceived during the betrothal period. Even if Mary did enter Joseph's house, there is no claim that the two had sexual relations. Brown, et al., *Mary in the New Testament*, 83.

21 All gospel translations, both canonical and noncanonical, are the Scholars Version, taken from *The Complete Gospels*, ed. Robert J. Miller (Sonoma, CA: Polebridge Press, 1992).

22 The earliest dated canonical gospel, Mark, is virtually silent about Mary, and contains no infancy narrative. Mark provides a great deal of evidence that Mary was not perpetually a virgin because of later offspring.

23 There is evidence that the earliest surviving manuscript of the gospel of Matthew may have been altered to make the virgin–birth story plausible. Baring and Cashford, *The Myth of the Goddess: Evolution of an Image*, 564.

24 Brown, et al., *Mary in the New Testament*, 92.

25 Jane Schaberg, *The Illegitimacy of Jesus: A Feminist Theological Interpretation of the Infancy Narratives* (New York: Crossroad, 1990), 70.

26 John Meier, "The Brothers and Sisters of Jesus in Ecumenical Perspective," *Catholic Biblical Quarterly*, no. 54 (1992): 9.

27 Ochs, *Behind the Sex of God*, 73.

28 While family lineage was extremely important to the Hebrews, it appears odd to include a genealogy for someone who supposedly has no blood relationship to his "father" (Jesus to Joseph). Ranke-Heinemann, *Eunuchs for the Kingdom of Heaven,* 30.

29 Miller, *The Complete Gospels,* 122.

30 Brown, et al., *Mary in the New Testament,* 153.

31 Miller, *The Complete Gospels,* 323.

32 It should be noted that the *Infancy Gospel of James* is not the only New Testament apocrypha to mention Mary's virginity. Other texts include the *Sibylline Oracles, the Ascension of Isaiah,* and *the Odes of Solomon.* Schaberg, 190–92. *The Infancy Gospel of James* was more popular in the eastern church then in the west. Ranke-Heinemann, *Eunuchs for the Kingdom of Heaven,* 343.

33 Benko, *The Virgin Goddess,* 202.

34 Ibid., 196.

35 Miller, *The Complete Gospels,* 374.

36 Two of the unique features of this account of the birth of Jesus are the use of a midwife and the birth in a cave.

37 Rosemary Radford Ruether, *Mary—The Feminine Face of the Church* (Philadelphia: Westminster Press, 1975), 55.

38 Brown, et al., *Mary in the New Testament,* 258–59.

39 There are similar motifs in the two birth narratives. The birth of Melchizedek can be found in 2 Enoch 23, which is dated to the first century C.E. Schaberg, 189–90. Melchizedek was a priest-king legendary figure alluded to several times in the Hebrew scriptures (including Genesis 14: 18–20). There are a number of similarities between the myths surrounding Melchizedek and Jesus. John McKenzie, *Dictionary of the Bible,* (New York: MacMillan, 1965), 563.

40 Benko, *The Virgin Goddess,* 203.

41 Elaine Pagels, *The Gnostic Gospels* (New York: Vintage Books, 1979), xxii.

42 Raymond Brown, Carolyn Osiek, and Pheme Perkins, "Early Church," in *New Jerome Biblical Commentary,* 1351.

43 Pagels, *The Gnostic Gospels,* xix.

44 Barbara MacHaffie, *Her Story: Women in Christian Tradition* (Philadelphia: Fortress Press, 1986), 32.

45 Pagels, *The Gnostic Gospels,* 48–53.

46 The Gnostic *Gospel of Mary* [Magdalene], for which perhaps 50 percent is extant, demonstrates the significant role of women in the early Church and their struggle against patriarchal control. Miller, 352.

47 Brown, Osiek, Perkins, "Early Church," 1351.

48 Rosemary Radford Ruether, *Womanguides: Readings Toward a Feminist Theology* (Boston: Beacon Press, 1985), 161.

49 Ruether, *Sexism and God-Talk,* 36.

50 Pagels, *The Gnostic Gospels,* 66–67; and Marvin Meyer, "Making Mary Male: The Categories 'Male' and 'Female' in the Gospel of Thomas," *New Testament Studies* 31 (1985): 564.

51 Pagels, *The Gnostic Gospels,* 53.

52 Brown, Osiek, Perkins, "Early Church," *The New Jerome Biblical Commentary,* 1351.

53 William Phipps, *Influential Theologians on Wo/man* (Washington D.C.: University Press of America), 40.

54 George Tavard, *Woman in Christian Tradition* (Notre Dame: Notre Dame Press, 1973), 112.

55 While Jerome may have held a twisted view of Christian womanhood, Peter Brown argues that Jerome treated the minds of men and women equally in the rigors of studying and understanding the Christian message. Peter Brown, *The Body and Society*, 368–69.

56 Armstrong, *The Gospel According to Woman: Christianity's Creation of the Sex War in the West*, 64.

57 Phipps, *Influential Theologians on Wo/man*, 49.

58 St. Jerome, "Against Helvidius on the Perpetual Virginity of Mary," quoted in Phipps, *Influential Theologians on Wo/man*, 49.

59 Peter R. L. Brown, *The Body and Society*, 383.

60 According to Phipps, "Jerome's distortions of the original Judeo-Christian sexual ethic also shed light on the acid stream of misogyny which has polluted church tradition. . . . As a self-appointed apostle of virginity, Jerome was guilty of clever but crass manhandling of Scripture. . . . Jerome's perverse treatment lent credence to the old saw of cynics that anything can be proved by shrewd students of scripture." From *Influential Theologians on Wo/man*, 54–55.

61 Arthur Droge and James Tabor, *A Noble Death: Suicide and Martyrdom Among Christians and Jews in Antiquity* (San Francisco: HarperSan Francisco, 1992), 178.

62 Schussler Fiorenza, *In Memory of Her*, 68.

63 While Ruether's purpose in this analysis is significant to Christian feminism, it is not a unique conclusion. The Protestant tradition has long regarded Jesus as having biological brothers and sisters, and thus has denied the post partum virginity of Mary. Meier, "The Brothers and Sisters of Jesus in Ecumenical Perspective," 1.

64 Another traditional Catholic apologetic originated by Epiphanius is to declare the brothers and sisters of Jesus to be stepchildren of Mary through a previous marriage of Joseph. Meier, 21.

65 Rosemary Radford Ruether, "The Collision of History and Doctrine: The Brothers of Jesus and the Virginity of Mary," *Continuum* 7. no. 1(winter–spring 1969): 95.

66 Brown, et al., *Mary in the New Testament*, 65–67.

67 Meier, "The Brothers and Sisters of Jesus in Ecumenical Perspective," 21.

68 John McKenzie, "The Mother of Jesus in the New Testament," in *Concilium: Mary in the Churches*, ed. Hans Kung and Jurgen Moltmann, no. 168 (1983): 6.

69 Ruether, "The Collision of History and Doctrine: The Brothers of Jesus and the Virginity of Mary," 99–100.

70 Miller, *The Complete Gospels*, 6.

71 Brown, et al., *Mary in the New Testament*, 153.

72 For further discussion of the factual nature of the infancy narratives see Brown, *Mary in the New Testament*, 12–14. The two infancy narratives are dramatically different as is the *Infancy Gospel of James*. They contain many historical inaccuracies of chronology and events and do not necessarily "fit" the body of literature with which they are associated.

73 Uta Ranke-Heinemann, *Putting Away Childish Things: The Virgin Birth, the Empty Tomb, and Other Fairy Tales You Don't Need to Believe to Have a Living Faith* (San Francisco: HarperSan Francisco, 1994), 40–44.

74 Brown, *Mary in the New Testament*, 261.

75 Ron Cameron, ed., *The Other Gospels: Non-Canonical Gospel Texts* (Philadelphia: Westminster Press, 1982), 163–64.

76 This text has been used to argue that Jesus was illegitimate, as well as to substantiate the fatherhood of Joseph. The contradiction here is that the illegitimacy theme runs counter to the interests of a gospel intended as a Christian apologetic glorifying Jesus. Ibid., 168.

77 Schaberg, *The Illegitimacy of Jesus*, 32–33.

78 Ibid., 66.

79 Ibid., 72–73.

80 Ibid., 138.

81 Ibid., 141.

82 "... my lowly status" is sometimes read "... his handmaid's lowliness."

83 Schaberg, *The Illegitimacy of Jesus*, 100.

84 Ibid., 98.

85 Brown, et al., *Mary in the New Testament*, 141.

86 McBrien, *Catholicism*, 542.

87 Carroll, *The Cult of the Virgin Mary: Psychological Origins*, 90–96.

88 Elizabeth Castelli, "Virginity and its Meaning for Women's Sexuality in Early Christianity," *Journal of Feminist Studies in Religion* 2, no. 1, (spring 1986): 78.

89 Key documents and creeds affirming Mary's virginal conception of Jesus include: The Apostle's Creed (unknown date), The Nicene Creed (325 C.E.), the Nicene-Constantinopolitan Creed of the first Council of Constantinople (381 C.E.), the Athansian Creed (end of the fifth century), the Fourth Lateran Council (1215 C.E.) and the Second Council of Lyons (1274 C.E.). McBrien, *Catholicism*, 542.

90 There have been enduring hypotheses implying that Jesus did indeed marry. Ranke-Heinemann, *Eunuchs for the Kingdom of Heaven*, 44.

91 Miller, *The Complete Gospels*, 372.

92 Warner, *Alone of All Her Sex: The Myth and the Cult of the Virgin Mary*, 69.

93 Carroll, *The Cult of the Virgin Mary: Psychological Origins*, 88.

94 Warner, *Alone of All Her Sex: The Myth and the Cult of the Virgin Mary*, 70.

95 Kari Vogt, "'Becoming Male': One Aspect of an Early Christian Anthropology," in *Concilium: Women, Invisible in Church and Theology*, ed. Elisabeth Schussler Fiorenza and Mary Collins, no. 182, (1985): 72–81.

96 Ruether, *Sexism and God-Talk: Toward a Feminist Theology* (1983): 248.

97 Miller, *The Complete Gospels*, 322.

98 Antiquity scholar Marvin Meyer chooses to interpret this passage in the wider scope of the liberation tradition found in the Gospel of Thomas. According to Meyer, the gender hierarchy described was an inevitable part of the social setting. Meyer, "Making Mary Male: The Categories 'Male' and 'Female' in the Gospel of Thomas," 570.

99 Mary Daly, *The Church and the Second Sex* (Boston: Beacon Press, 1968), 248.

100 Modern scholars do not find Ephesians 4:13 as gender-bound as did the church fathers. It is now translated as intending to find perfection in maturity or adulthood. Paul Kobelski, "Ephesians," in *The New Jerome Biblical Commentary*, 889.

101 In an ironic twist of history, in the early church women suffered illness in fasting to please men with their lack of femininity, and in the modern era women suffer illness by fasting to please men with their slender femininity.

102 MacHaffie, *Her Story*, 45–49.

103 *Odes to Solomon* translated in Schaberg, *The Illegitimacy of Jesus*, 192.

104 Rene Laurentin, "Holy Mary," in *Concilium: Models of Holiness*, ed. Christian Duquoc and Casiano Floristan, no. 129, (1979): 62.

105 Elizabeth Clark, "Ascetic Renunciation and Feminine Advancement: A Paradox of Late Ancient Christianity," *Anglican Theological Review* 63 (1981): 240–57. Rosemary Ruether, "Mothers of the Church: Ascetic Women in the Late Patristic Age," *Women*

of Spirit: Female Leaders in the Jewish and Christian Traditions, ed. Ruether and Eleanor McLaughlin, 93–94.

106 Castelli, "Virginity and its Meaning for Women's Sexuality in Early Christianity," 85.

107 Ibid., 63.

108 Ibid., 87–88.

109 David R. Shumway, *Michel Foucault* (Boston: Twayne, 1989), 144.

110 Catharina Halkes, "Mary in My Life," in Edward Schillebeeckx and Catharina Halkes, *Mary: Yesterday, Today and Tomorrow*, 59.

111 Armstrong refers to this as the "Christian neurosis," *The Gospel According to Woman*, 4.

112 John Paul II, *On the Dignity and Vocation of Women, Mulieris Dignitatem* (1988): 74–79.

113 Catharina Halkes objects to the Pope's use of Mary as a model for Catholic women in this text because: 1. The universalization of religious imagery is dangerous to a diverse faith community. 2. Religious imagery should not be used to enforce norms and values. Catharina Halkes, "Mary in My Life," in Edward Schillebeeckx and Catharina Halkes, *Mary: Yesterday, Today and Tomorrow*, 77.

114 Janice Capel Anderson, "Mary's Difference: Gender and Patriarchy in the Birth Narratives," *Journal of Religion* (April 1987): 198.

115 The Pope uses "essentialist" arguments in describing womanhood as motherhood. Gregory Baum, "Bulletin: The Apostolic Letter Mulieris Dignitatem," in *Concilium: Motherhood, Experience, Institution and Theology*, ed. Anne Carr and Elisabeth Schussler Fiorenza no. 206 (1989): 147.

116 Mary Hunt, *Fierce Tenderness: A Feminist Theology of Friendship* (New York: Crossroad, 1991), 52.

117 Schussler Fiorenza, "Feminist Theology as Critical Theology of Liberation," 622–23.

118 Ibid., 623.

119 Adrienne Rich, "Compulsory Heterosexuality and Lesbian Experience," *Signs* (summer 1980): 631–60.

120 Carmody, *Mythological Woman*, 92.

121 Daly, *Gyn/Ecology: The Metaethics of Radical Feminism*, 85.

122 Beverly Harrison, *Making the Connection: Essays in Feminist Social Ethics,* ed. Carol S. Robb (Boston: Beacon Press, 1985), 130.

123 Ranke-Heinemann, *Eunuchs for the Kingdom of Heaven*, 342.

124 Daly, *The Church and the Second Sex*, 162.

125 Ruether, *Sexism and God-Talk: Toward a Feminist Theology*, 144.

126 Harrison, *Making the Connection*, 144.

127 Audre Lorde, "Uses of the Erotic," *Weaving the Visions: New Patterns in Feminist Spirituality*, ed. Judith Plaskow and Carol Christ (San Francisco: Harper and Row, 1989), 208–209.

128 Carter Heyward, *Touching Our Strength: The Erotic as Power and the Love of God* (San Francisco: Harper and Row, 1989), 3.

129 This notion of God as lover is not entirely new, although it opposes the current trajectory of mainstream Christianity, and particularly Catholicism. There has been considerable attention given to this subject. One example is Andrew Greeley's concept of God which includes Mary as the feminine face of God, and as a passionate lover. *The Catholic Myth: The Behavior and Beliefs of American Catholics*, 286.

130 Heyward, *Touching Our Strength*, 5.

131 Carroll, *The Cult of the Virgin Mary: Psychological Origins*, 223–24.

132 *Vatican Declaration on Sexual Ethics*, (Huntington, IN: Our Sunday Visitor, 1975), 10.

133 Ibid., 12.

134 Pope Paul VI, *On the Regulation of Birth, Humanae Vitae* (Washington, DC: National Council of Bishops, July 25, 1968), 10.

135 *Decree on the Appropriate Renewal of the Religious Life,* in Abbott, *The Documents of Vatican II,* 565.

136 *Vatican Declaration on Sexual Ethics,* 12.

137 John Phillips, *Eve: The History of an Idea* (San Francisco: Harper and Row, 1984), 145.

138 See Chapter 7 of *The Making of Moral Theology: A Study of the Roman Catholic Tradition* (Oxford: Clarendon Press, 1987) by John Mahoney. The author chronicles how change on the issue of artificial contraception was thwarted by conservative efforts and a concern to maintain historical consistency.

139 National Conference of Catholic Bishops, *Behold Your Mother: Woman of Faith, A Pastoral Letter on the Blessed Virgin Mary* (Washington D.C.: United States Catholic Conference, 1973): 19.

140 In Karen Armstrong's analysis of Second Testament views on sexuality, she actually finds Paul more lenient then Jesus, but attributes this to the fact that Paul's letters predate the gospels. She finds an increasing restrictive view of sex, but not as prohibitive as the later writings of the Church fathers. *The Gospel According to Women,* 14.

141 *The Dogmatic Constitution on the Church* in Abbott, *The Documents of Vatican II,* 71–72.

142 John Paul II, *The Christian Family in the Modern World, Vatican Council II: More Post Conciliar Documents* ed. Austin Flannery (New York: Costello, 1982), 827.

143 Ruether, *Sexism and God-Talk,* 144–45.

144 This moral dualism also reflects the mind/body distinction found in Catholic theology.

145 Susan Power Bratton, *Six Billion and More: Human Population Regulation and Christian Ethics* (Louisville: John Knox Press, 1992), 199.

146 Joseph Gallagher, "Rome's Birth Control Conceptions Flunk Real World Test," *National Catholic Reporter* (4 September 1992): 6.

147 A nationwide survey conducted by Twenty-Third Publications indicates that the percentage of Catholics who "trust" priests, particularly in areas in which accusations of child molestation have occurred, is low. For example, in a parish in which there is a reported charge against a priest, only 44 percent of respondents believed that priests could be trusted. Even in unaffected diocese, only 59 percent report trusting their priests. This is a far cry from the sacrosanct Catholic view of priests in the past. *Los Angeles Times,* "Reports of Sex Abuse Erode Trust, Confidence in Clergy, Study Finds," 5 September 1992, sec. B4.

148 Phillips, *Eve: the History of An Idea,* 142.

149 In the goddess cults of Ishtar, Asherah, and Aphrodite, which preceded Christianity, a holy virgin was not a physical virgin but simply unmarried. These women dispensed grace through a variety of means, including sexual relations. Barbara Walker interprets *The Infancy Gospel of James* to indicate that Mary was a "holy Virgin." Walker, 1049.

150 Halkes, "Mary in My Life," in Edward Schillebeeckx and Catharina Halkes *Mary: Yesterday, Today and Tomorrow,* 75.

151 Daly, *Beyond God the Father,* 84.

Chapter 4

1 Daly, *Beyond God the Father,* 83.

2 Armstrong, *The Gospel According to Woman,* 82.

3 The number of titles historically given Mary for her role in human salvation are numerous. While Mediatrix is the most popular, other titles include Reparatrix, Auxilatrix, Adjutrix, and Co-redemptrix.

4 McBrien, *Catholicism*, 11–13.

5 Baring and Cashford, *The Myth of the Goddess: Evolution of an Image*, 553.

6 Pope, "Immaculate and Powerful," 195.

7 Raymond Brown, *Biblical Reflections on Crises Facing the Church* (New York: Paulist Press, 1975), 96–97.

8 Brown, et al., *Mary in the New Testament*, 183–87.

9 Even the Bishops of the Second Vatican Council allude to the significance of Mary at the Wedding Feast at Cana where, "moved by pity . . . her intercession brought about the beginning of miracles by Jesus the Messiah." Abbott, 89.

10 Brown, et al., *Mary in the New Testament*, 193.

11 Pheme Perkins, "Mary in Johannine Traditions," *Mary, Woman of Nazareth: Biblical and Theological Perspectives,* ed., Doris Donnelly (New York: Paulist Press, 1989): 111.

12 O'Carroll, *Theotokos: A Theological Encyclopedia of the Blessed Virgin Mary*, 97.

13 Fulton J. Sheen, *Life of Christ* (New York: Image Books, 1977), 76–77.

14 John Paul II, *The Mother of the Redeemer, Redemptoris Mater*, 44–46.

15 Grassi, *Mary, Mother and Disciple*, 123.

16 Elizabeth Johnson, "Mary as Mediatrix," *The One Mediator, The Saints, and Mary: Lutherans and Catholics in Dialogue VIII*, ed. H. George Anderson, J. Francis Stafford, and Joseph A. Burgess (Minneapolis: Augsburg, 1992), 311.

17 Grassi, *Mary, Mother and Disciple*, 125–126.

18 O'Carroll, *Theotokos: A Theological Encyclopedia of the Blessed Virgin Mary*, 239.

19 Cyril of Alexandria quoted in O'Carroll, *Theotokos: A Theological Encyclopedia of the Blessed Virgin Mary*, 113.

20 Elizabeth Johnson, "Mary as Mediatrix," 312.

21 O'Carroll, *Theotokos: A Theological Encyclopedia of the Blessed Virgin Mary*, 156.

22 Germanus of Constantinople translated in O'Carroll, *Theotokos: A Theological Encyclopedia of the Blessed Virgin Mary*, 156.

23 Warner, *Alone of All Her Sex: The Myth and the Cult of the Virgin Mary,* 322.

24 O'Carroll, *Theotokos: A Theological Encyclopedia of the Blessed Virgin Mary*, 341.

25 Warner, *Alone of All Her Sex: The Myth and the Cult of the Virgin Mary,* 323.

26 O'Carroll, *Theotokos: A Theological Encyclopedia of the Blessed Virgin Mary*, 341.

27 Warner, *Alone of All Her Sex: The Myth and the Cult of the Virgin Mary,* 325.

28 Matter, "The Virgin Mary, A Goddess?," 86.

29 McBrien, *Catholicism*, 1086.

30 Elizabeth Johnson, "Mary as Mediatrix," 313.

31 Elizabeth Johnson, "Mary and the Female Face of God," 509.

32 In actuality, Aquinas wrote relatively little on Mary's role in salvation. He was more concerned about arguing that she had not been born free from original sin.

33 O'Carroll, *Theotokos: A Theological Encyclopedia of the Blessed Virgin Mary*, 344.

34 McBrien, *Catholicism*, 876.

35 O'Carroll, *Theotokos: A Theological Encyclopedia of the Blessed Virgin Mary*, 84.

36 Warner, *Alone of All Her Sex: The Myth and the Cult of the Virgin Mary,* 296.

37 O'Carroll, *Theotokos: A Theological Encyclopedia of the Blessed Virgin Mary*, 228.

38 Elizabeth Johnson, "Mary as Mediatrix," 315.

39 Elizabeth Johnson, *She Who Is*, 129.

40 O'Carroll, *Theotokos: A Theological Encyclopedia of the Blessed Virgin Mary*, 242.

41 "Proceedings of the International Mariological Congress" (1950) 1: 234.

42 Quoted in Elizabeth Johnson, "Mary as Mediatrix," 320.

43 *The Dogmatic Constitution of the Church*, in Abbott, *The Documents of Vatican II*, 86.

44 Elizabeth Johnson, "Mary as Mediatrix," 323.

45 Sandra Zimdars-Swartz defines an apparition as "a specific kind of vision in which a person or being not normally within the visionary's perceptual range appears to that person, not in a world apart as in a dream, and not as a modification of a concrete object as in the case of a weeping icon or moving statue, but as a part of the environment, without apparent connection to verifiable visual stimuli." *Encountering Mary*, 4.

46 Occasionally, Mary's apparitions depict a vengeful side of Mary that does not tolerate disrespect. For example, a fifteenth-century legend described a man who doubted Mary's power and subsequently had his tongue shrivel up. Shinners, "The Cult of Mary and Popular Belief," 172–73.

47 Zimdars-Swartz, *Encountering Mary*, 6.

48 Malina, "From Isis to Medjugorje: Why Apparitions?," 83.

49 Zimdars-Swartz, *Encountering Mary*, 8.

50 Carroll, *The Cult of the Virgin Mary: Psychological Origins*, 134–40.

51 Shinners, 176–77; and Malina, "From Isis to Medjugorje: Why Apparitions?," 80.

52 Pope, "Immaculate and Powerful," 181.

53 Baring and Cashford, *The Myth of the Goddess: Evolution of an Image*, 405.

54 Daly, *Pure Lust*, 193.

55 Catharina Halkes, "Mary and Women," in *Concilium: Mary in the Churches*, ed. Hans Kung and Jurgen Moltmann, no. 168 (1983), 68.

56 Patricia Aburdene and John Naisbitt, *Megatrends for Women* (New York: Villard Books, 1992), 253–58.

57 Eleanor Rae and Bernice Marie-Daly, *Created in Her Image: Models of the Feminine Divine* (New York: Crossroad, 1990), 47.

58 Carr, *Transforming Grace*, 134.

59 Elizabeth Johnson, *She Who Is: The Mystery of God in Feminist Theological Discourse*, 4.

60 Ruether, *Sexism and God-Talk*, 47.

61 Carol Christ, "Why Women Need the Goddess: Phenomenological, Psychological, and Political Reflections," in *Womanspirit Rising: A Feminist Reader in Religion*, ed. Carol Christ and Judith Plaskow, 277–86.

62 Carol Christ, "Symbols of Goddess and God in Feminist Theology," in *The Book of the Goddess Past and Present*, 244.

63 Schussler Fiorenza, "Feminist Spirituality, Christian Identity, and Catholic Vision," 139.

64 Benko, *The Virgin Goddess*, 265.

65 Schussler Fiorenza, "Feminist Spirituality, Christian Identity, and Catholic Vision," 138.

66 Daly, *Pure Lust*, 93.

67 Matter, "The Virgin Mary: A Goddess?," 94.

68 Greeley, *The Catholic Myth*, 254.

69 Ibid., 4.

70 Ibid., 62.

71 Ibid., 244.

72 Rose Romano, "The Virgin Mary and Feminist Spirituality: Experiences of an Italian Catholic," *Daughters of Sarah*, vol. 17, no. 5 (fall 1991), 41.

73 Ruether, *New Woman/New Earth*, 17.

74 Ibid., 152.

75 Ibid., 153–154.

76 Ben Kimmerling, "Mary, Mary Quite Contrary," *The Furrow* (May 1988), 282.

77 Elizabeth Johnson, "The Marian Tradition and the Reality of Women," 134.

78 Dorothy Solle, "Meditation on Luke 1:46–55," in *Women in a Strange Land*, ed. Clare Fisher (Philadelphia: Fortress Press, 1975), 79.

79 Nel Noddings, *Women and Evil* (Berkeley: University of California Press, 1989), 66.

80 Ruether, "The Feminine Nature of God: A Problem in Contemporary Religious Life," in *Concilium: God As Father?*, ed. Metz and Schillebeeckx (1981), 63.

81 Harrison, *Making the Connection*, 141.

82 Schussler Fiorenza, "Claiming Our Authority and Power," 51.

83 A pragmatic reason for allowing women's ordination may alter the Church hierarchy's position more quickly than feminist rationale or ethics—a priest shortage. The worldwide shortage and aging of priests may force the Church to accept women priests and/or married priests before it is "theologically ready." Charles Davis cites a U.S. Catholic Conference estimate that the number of priests in the U.S. will decline by 40 percent between 1996 and 2005 despite a rising Catholic population. Charles Davis, "Catholics Will Give When Church Moves into Future," *National Catholic Reporter* (12 February 1993): 13.

84 The defense of an all-male priesthood based upon Mary's nonpriesthood goes as far back as the fourth century, to Epiphanius of Salanis. The existence of such a defense would indicate that the controversy over women's ordination finds its origins in the early Church. Robert Kress, *Whither Womankind? The Humanity of Women* (St. Meinrad, IN: Abbey Press, 1975), 237.

85 McBrien, *Catholicism*, 778.

86 Elisabeth Schussler Fiorenza believes that to prevent tokenism and assimilation into the male hierarchical system, perhaps women should become bishops first and only later be ordained priests. "Feminist Theology as a Critical Theology of Liberation," 619.

87 Carr, *Transforming Grace*, 52.

88 Richard McBrien points out that the Church routinely allows for the innovations made in the first centuries of the Church (such as the priesthood). However, time is a relative perspective. McBrien believes if humanity makes it to the year 20,000, certainly the first 2,000 years will be considered formative. Richard McBrien, *Report on the Church* (San Francisco: HarperSan Francisco, 1992), 121.

89 The translation of Giorgio Otranto, "Notes on the Female Priesthood in Antiquity" is found in Mary Ann Rossi, "Priesthood, Precedent, and Prejudice: On Recovering the Women Priests of Early Christianity," *Journal of Feminist Study of Religion*, 7, no. 1 (Spring 1991): 84.

90 Karen Jo Torjesen, *When Women were Priests: Women's Leadership in the Early Church and the Scandal of their Subordination in the Rise of Christianity* (San Francisco: HarperSan Francisco, 1993), 55–59.

91 O'Carroll, *Theotokos: A Theological Encyclopedia of the Blessed Virgin Mary*, 122.

92 Raymond Brown, *Biblical Reflections on Crises Facing the Church*, 54.

93 Winsome Munro, "Women Disciples: Light from Secret Mark," *Journal of Feminist Studies in Religion* (spring 1992), 57.

94 Susan Brooks Thistlethwaite, "Every Two Minutes: Battered Women and Feminist Interpretation," in *Weaving the Visions: New Patterns in Feminist Spirituality*, ed. Judith Plaskow and Carol Christ, 309.

95 Kress, *Whither Womankind?*, 237–38.

96 Episcopal Bishop John Spong writes, "Perhaps it has not yet occurred to the bishop of Rome that Jesus did not choose any Polish males to be disciples either, but this did not exclude the Polish boy Karol Wojtyla, who became John Paul II." *Born of a Woman* (San Francisco: HarperSan Francisco, 1992), 7.

97 Paul Jewett, *The Ordination of Women* (Grand Rapids, MI: Eerdmans, 1980), 35; and Rosemary Radford Ruether, "Ordination: What is the Problem?," *Women and Catholic Priesthood,* ed. Anne Marie Gardner (New York: Paulist Press, 1976) 31.

98 Ruether, "John Paul II and the Growing Alienation of Women from the Church," 282–283.

99 Elizabeth Johnson, "The Maleness of Christ," 115.

100 Ruether, "Ordination: What is the Problem?," 30.

101 Margaret Farley, "Moral Imperatives for the Ordination of Women," in *Women and the Catholic Priesthood: An Expanded View*, ed. Anne Marie Gardner (New York: Paulist Press, 1976), 40.

102 Carr, *Transforming Grace,* 57.

103 Farley, "Moral Imperatives for the Ordination of Women," 46.

104 McBrien, *Report on the Church*, 135.

105 For example, John Paul II in *On the Dignity and Vocation of Women*, clearly states the fundamental equality of the sexes (pp. 6–7). Official statements fail to recall that the Church has historically fought women's rights including suffrage. Ruether, "Women's Difference and Equal Rights in the Church," 14.

106 Ibid., 57.

107 Ruether, "The Place of Women in the Church," 265.

108 Ruether, "Women's Difference and Equal Rights in the Church," 15.

109 Rosemary Radford Ruether, "Is Feminism the End of Christianity? A Critique of Daphne Hampson's *Theology and Feminism*," *Scottish Journal of Theology*, vol. 43, 392–93.

110 Hans Urs von Balthasar, "The Marian Principle," *Communio*, no. 15 (spring 1988): 122.

111 Ibid., 130.

112 Ibid., 127.

113 Ibid., 129.

114 Schussler Fiorenza, "Feminist Spirituality, Christian Identity, and Catholic Vision," 147.

115 Elisabeth Schussler Fiorenza, "Breaking the Silence, Becoming Visible," in *Concilium: Women Invisible in Church and Theology*, ed. Elisabeth Schussler Fiorenza and Mary Collins, no. 182 (1985), 9.

116 Schussler Fiorenza, "Feminist Theology as a Critical Theology of Liberation," 623.

117 Pope John Paul II quoted in John Thavis, "Pope: Reject 'extreme' feminism," *National Catholic Reporter* (16 July 1993), 7.

118 John Mahoney, *The Making of Moral Theology: A Study of the Roman Catholic Tradition*, 46–47.

119 There are theologians who argue that Catholic moral theology has always tried to contextualize acts. This contextualization has been recently named "proportionalism," and is exemplified in doctrine such as "the principle of double effect," in which

a forced choice of the lesser of two evils may morally justify a given action. Proportionalism remains a somewhat controversial topic, as it is not an official position of the Church, and there may be some significant applications, such as in sexual ethics, in which its use is inconsistent. See Bernard Hoose, *Proportionalism: The American Debate and its European Roots* (Washington D.C.: Georgetown University Press, 1987).

120 McBrien, *Catholicism*, 839.

121 In terms of gender orientation, while both men and women consider both care and justice orientations within the process of moral reasoning, each sex settles upon a single orientation for the final decision. Men exhibit a high propensity for an ethic of justice, while women exhibit a high propensity for an ethic of care. Carol Gilligan, "Moral Orientation and Moral Development," in *Women and Moral Theory*, ed. Eva Feder Kittay and Diana T. Meyers (Savage, Maryland: Rowan and Littlefield, 1987), 25. For the purposes of discussing a generalized, gender-based difference in moral orientation, empirical absolutes are not as essential as the symbolic association of moral orientation with gender. Barrie Thorne, *Gender Play: Girls and Boys in School* (New Brunswick, NJ: Rutgers University Press, 1993), 105.

122 Berger, *The Sacred Canopy: Elements of a Sociological Theory of Religion*, 122.

123 For example, Catholic social teaching has upheld the right to property; however, in a hierarchy of rights, this right to property can be abrogated by the superior human right to subsistence.

124 Seyla Benhabib, "The Generalized and the Concrete Other: The Kohlberg-Gilligan Controversy and Moral Theory," *Women and Moral Theory*, ed. Eva Feder Kittay and Diana T. Meyers, 158.

125 Gilligan, *In A Different Voice*, 100.

126 Rosemarie Tong, *Feminist Thought: A Comprehensive Introduction* (Boulder, CO: Westview Press, 1989), 162–63.

127 Elizabeth Gould Davis in *The First Sex* (New York: Penguin, 1972) argues that Christianity would not have been popularly accepted in many areas had it not been for the inclusion of a female care tradition (pp. 243–46).

128 Gilligan, "Moral Orientation and Moral Development," 24.

129 Ibid.

130 Warner, *Alone of All Her Sex: The Myth and the Cult of the Virgin Mary*, 288–89.

131 Zimdars-Swartz, *Encountering Mary*, 247.

132 John Paul II, *The Mother of the Redeemer* (Washington, D.C.: United States Catholic Conference, 1987), 80.

133 Simone de Beauvoir, *The Second Sex* (New York: Vintage Books, 1952), 160.

134 Catholic tradition contains a tremendous corpus of works that reinforce the role of men as the heads of the family. For example, John Chrysostom, writing in the late fourth century, described women being saved from the "vainglory" of civic life by men who married them. Women were to be molded by husbands in a manner comparable to that of a monastery. Peter Brown, *The Body and Society*, 312–13.

135 Gregory Smith, "Mary and Mother's Work," *The Mother: Heart of the Home* (St. Meinrad, IN: Grail Publications, 1955), 57–58.

136 See Paul Harrington, *Women's Sublime Call* (Boston: Daughters of St. Paul, 1964). This is only one example of a deluge of Catholic literature on the "women problem."

137 Elizabeth Johnson, "Marian Tradition and Reality of Women," 124.

138 Mary Gordon, "Coming to Terms with Mary," *Commonweal*, (15 January 1982), 11.

139 See Nancy Chodorow, *The Reproduction of Mothering: Psychoanalysis and the Sociology of*

Gender; Miriam Johnson, *Strong Mothers: Weak Wives* (Berkeley: University of California Press, 1988); Diane Ehrensaft, *Parenting Together* (Chicago: University of Illinois Press, 1990); Sara Ruddick, "Maternal Thinking," in *Rethinking the Family* ed. Barrie Thorne, Marilyn Yalom, and Lynne Segal, (Boston: Northeastern University Press, 1992); *Is the Future Feminist,* (New York: Peter Bedrick Books, 1987); and Carole Pateman, *The Sexual Contract* (Stanford: Stanford University Press, 1988).

140 Valerie Charlton quoted in Lynne Segal, *Is the Future Feminist?: Troubled Thoughts On Contemporary Feminism,* 14.

141 Gebara and Bingemer, *Mary: Mother of God, Mother of the Poor,* 37.

142 Ruether, "Women's Difference and Equal Rights in the Church," 17.

Chapter 5

1 Daly, *Beyond God the Father,* 65.

2 A related theme for the New Eve is the further subjugation of women into secondary roles within relationships in a pattern consistent with the discussion of the previous chapter. Eve was the "helpmate" of Adam. The male role of Adam is active and creative, while Eve is secondary. Christ as the "New Adam" assumes the male role, while Mary, "The New Eve" is given the female, supportive role. In the words of Kari Borresen, this typology seems to "transpose the androcentric system from the order of creation into the order of redemption." Borresen, "Mary in Catholic Theology," 50.

3 Elizabeth Johnson, "Marian Tradition and the Reality of Women," 121.

4 Ruether, *Woman Guides,* 38. Ruether provides several example of pre-Christian creation stories of the Goddess.

5 Eamon R. Carroll, *The Mother of Christ* (New York: The Mission Society, 1962), 18–19.

6 The Vulgate Bible was St. Jerome's Latin translation of the bible completed in 383 C.E. While the sources were good and Jerome was as well-prepared to make the translations as anyone could be in that era, it is not considered a scholarly critical text by modern standards. Subsequent careless copying also contributed to numerous errors. Adding to the problems of critical exegesis was the declaration by the Council of Trent that the Vulgate was the "authentic" text to be used in the Church. However, in 1943, in the encyclical *Divino Afflante Spiritu,* Pope Pius XII clarified that biblical scholarship was free to pursue the most historically accurate texts. McKenzie, *The Dictionary of the Bible,* 916–18.

7 Warner, *Alone of All Her Sex: The Myth and the Cult of the Virgin Mary,* 246.

8 O'Carroll, *Theotokos: A Theological Encyclopedia of the Blessed Virgin Mary,* 371.

9 Phillips, *Eve: The History of an Idea,* 139.

10 Richard Clifford and Roland Murphy, "Genesis," in *Jerome Biblical Commentary,* 12.

11 O'Carroll, *Theotokos: A Theological Encyclopedia of the Blessed Virgin Mary,* 140.

12 Burghardt, "Mary in Western Patristic Thought," 113.

13 Phillips, *Eve: The History of an Idea,* 133.

14 Stephen Benko finds the late date of the association of Mary with Revelation 12 to be a result of the competition between Christian and non-Christian belief systems. Benko speculates that Christians avoided allusion to the non-Christian terminology evident in Revelation 12. Only after the triumph of Christianity in the fifth century could explicit connections between Mary and Revelation 12 flourish. *The Virgin Goddess,* 136.

15 Phillips, *Eve: The History of an Idea,* 138–39.

16 Geoffrey Ashe uses the lack of evidence to substantiate Mary's title as the "New

Eve" as a an indication of a hidden history of the Church. Admitting that his analysis is speculative, Ashe believes a forceful Marian movement, such as that of the Collyridians, perpetuated the divinity of Mary. This movement merged with "mainstream" Christianity at the time of the Council of Ephesus, thus explaining the Marian title "Theotokos" that was proclaimed at the Council. Ashe fails to find any documented support for the adoption of the title "Theotokos." The notion of Mary as the New Eve, or an equal partner of Jesus, would have been a part of this suppressed movement. While Ashe's conjecture requires additional archaeological and biblical proof before it attains widespread support, such a historical suppression is consistent with the feminist movement and women's spirituality in Christian history. The lack of documented historical development of Mary's title as the New Eve is remarkable, considering the extent of support for other Marian images. Ashe, *The Virgin: Mary's Cult and the Re-Emergence of the Goddess*, 125–26, 195.

17 Armstrong, *The Gospel According to Woman*, 312.

18 Elizabeth Sarah describes the first creation narrative as linear and hierarchical, with Adam as the "apex of creation," while the second account of creation is centered upon the earth. Elizabeth Sarah, "The Biblical Account of the First Woman: A Jewish Feminist Perspective," *Women's Voices: Essays in Contemporary Feminist Theology* ed. Teresa Elwes (London: Marshall Pickering, 1992), 55.

19 Warner, *Alone of All Her Sex: The Myth and the Cult of the Virgin Mary*, 178.

20 In 1 Tim 2:13, Eve and the story of the Fall were invoked by the author (probably not Paul) to reinforce the subordinate role of women in the early Church. Apparently, women were taking significant preaching and leadership positions that required reprimanding. Robert A. Wild, "The Pastoral Letters," in *The Jerome Biblical Commentary*.

21 Gossman, "The Construction of Women's Difference in the Christian Theological Tradition," 50.

22 According to legend, the source of contention between Adam and Lilith was sexual position. Adam essentially desired Lilith to assume the "missionary position," while Lilith desired to be on top. The hierarchy of sexual positioning has been of significant concern in both the early Muslim and Christian traditions. Women's sexual subordination has been a reflection of a gendered understanding of cosmology. Walker, *The Woman's Encyclopedia of Myths and Secrets*, 541–42. See also footnote in Daly, *Gyn/Ecology*, 85.

23 Baring and Cashford, *The Myth of the Goddess: Evolution of an Image*, 510–11.

24 Carmody, *Mythological Woman*, 92.

25 Judith Plaskow, "The Coming of Lilith: Toward a Feminist Theology," in *Womanspirit Rising: A Feminist Reader in Religion*, 206–207.

26 Phillips, *Eve: The History of an Idea*, 16.

27 Ibid., 90–91.

28 Ibid., 91–92.

29 Ibid., 96–97.

30 Elizabeth Johnson, "The Marian Tradition and the Reality of Women," 122.

31 The early Church developed divergent concepts of Eve. One was the Eve/Mary parallel, discussed at length here. The other was the Church/Eve parallel. This notion arose from the idea that Eve was formed from Adam's rib and the Church was formed from the pierced side of the dying Christ. These two themes eventually merged, beginning in the fourth century, as Mary was likened to the Church. Borresen, "Mary in Catholic Theology," *Concilium: Mary in the Churches*, ed. Hans Kung and Jurgen Moltmann, 50.

32 Ruether, *Sexism and God-Talk*, 166.

33 Benko, *The Virgin Goddess*, 236.

34 Phipps, *Influential Theologians on Wo/man*, 143.

35 Phillips, *Eve: The History of an Idea*, 135.

36 John Shelby Spong asserts it was necessary that the Church fight and then ignore the teaching of evolution not just because it contradicted Genesis but because it threatened the basis for original sin and the logic that supported Christological and Mariological soteriology. If there was no historical event of the Fall, and therefore no original sin, for what purpose did Jesus die? Spong, *Born of A Woman*, 217.

37 Warner, *Alone of All Her Sex: The Myth and the Cult of the Virgin Mary,* 60–61.

38 Ruether, *Sexism and God-Talk*, 168.

39 O'Carroll, *Theotokos: A Theological Encyclopedia of the Blessed Virgin Mary*, 211.

40 Justin Martyr, *Apology*, 2, 5:3.

41 Justin Martyr, *Dialogus cum Tryphone*, 709–12, translated in Walter Burghardt, "Mary in Western Patristic Thought," *Mariology* 1, ed. Juniper-Carol (Milwaukee: Bruce, 1955), 111.

42 O'Carroll, *Theotokos: A Theological Encyclopedia of the Blessed Virgin Mary*, 188.

43 Burghardt, "Mary in Western Patristic Thought," 112–13.

44 Burghardt, "Mary in Eastern Patristic Thought," 90.

45 Walter Burghardt, "Mary in Eastern Patristic Thought," in *Mariology* 2, ed. Juniper Carol (Milwaukee: Bruce, 1957), 90.

46 McBrien, *Catholicism*, 444.

47 This early-third-century passage is perhaps the most often-quoted statement regarding the culpability of women as the ancestors of Eve. The notion of women as "the Devil's Gateway" became a much sermonized title of patriarchal zealotry against women. Tertullian blames women even for the death of Jesus at the close of this quote. While this is quite a damnation, one wonders what Christianity would be if Jesus had not been martyred. Walker, *The Woman's Encyclopedia of Myths and Secrets*, 290.

48 St. Augustine quoted in O'Carroll, *Theotokos: A Theological Encyclopedia of the Blessed Virgin Mary*, 140.

49 Graef, *Mary: A History of Doctrine and Devotion*, vol. 2, 56–60.

50 Benko, *The Virgin Goddess*, 205.

51 Frederick Jelly, "The Roman Catholic Dogma of Mary's Immaculate Conception," in *The One Mediator, The Saints and Mary,* ed., H. George Anderson, J. Francis Stafford, and Joseph A. Burgess (Minneapolis: Augsburg, 1992), 273.

52 Lawrence Everett, "Mary's Death and Bodily Assumption," in *Mariology*, 2, ed. Juniper-Carol (Milwaukee: Bruce, 1957), 488–89.

53 Gebara and Bingemer, *Mary: Mother of God, Mother of the Poor*, 115–16.

54 Avery Dulles, "The Dogma of the Assumption," *The One Mediator, The Saints and Mary*, ed. George Anderson, Francis Stafford, and Joseph Burgess (Minneapolis, Augsburg, 1992), 288.

55 Abbott, *The Documents of Vatican II*, 88.

56 National Conference of Catholic Bishops, *Behold Your Mother Woman of Faith*, 16.

57 Noddings, *Women and Evil*, 5.

58 Daly, *Beyond God the Father*, 47.

59 In 1975, after Mary Daly had evolved to a post-Christian perspective, she returned to her 1968 work, *The Church and the Second Sex,* to write a new introduction in which she discussed her own shift in opinion concerning the myth of the Fall. She described the Fall as a reversal of historical and biological fact that is fundamental to

patriarchal religion. According to Daly, no amount of reform or modernization will alter such a dynamic. It is for these reasons that Daly a post-Christian, and rejects reform movements. Daly, *The Church and the Second Sex*, 22.

60 Kim Chernin, *Reinventing Eve: Modern Woman in Search of Herself* (New York: Harper and Row, 1988), 149.

61 Walker, *The Woman's Encyclopedia of Myths and Secrets*, 288–91.

62 Pagels, *The Gnostic Gospels*, 66.

63 Translated in Pagels, *The Gnostic Gospels*, 31.

64 For extended treatments of the noncanonical Myths of Eve, besides Walker, see Philips, Chapter 10; and Baring and Cashford, *The Myth of the Goddess: Evolution of an Image*, Chapter 13.

65 See Raymond Brown and Raymond Collins, "Canonicity," in *Jerome Biblical Commentary*, 1034.

66 Ibid., 1041.

67 Walker, *The Woman's Encyclopedia of Myths and Secrets*, 291.

68 Simone de Beauvoir, *The Second Sex,* 159.

69 Baring and Cashford, *The Myth of the Goddess: Evolution of an Image*, 503.

70 Augustine's formulation of original sin and concupiscence in relation to the story of Adam and Eve exemplifies of how sex, and Eve, became associated with the fundamental immorality of humanity found in Catholic doctrine. Concupiscence represents human desire to take pleasure in human creatures rather than in God. According to Augustine, every act of sex is associated with concupiscence. Therefore, every child is born out of the concupiscence of his or her parents. Sex is the means for transferring original sin down through the generations, in Augustine's theology. Adam and Eve committed a sin of disobedience. However, in paradise they may have had sex without sinning. Their sex would not have involved physical pleasure but would have been mere bodily function for the purpose of procreation. After the Fall, concupiscence crept into their sexuality, and any further sex was sinful. As contrived as Augustine's explanation of original sin appears, more difficult to take seriously is his argument that, prior to the Fall, any sexual activity Eve had with Adam would not have violated her intact hymen. Armstrong, *The Gospel According to Woman*, 35, 155.

71 Mary Evans, *Woman in the Bible* (Chicago: Paternoster Press, 1983), 19.

72 Baring and Cashford, *The Myth of the Goddess: Evolution of an Image*, 504–508.

73 Daly, *Beyond God the Father*, 96.

74 Chernin, *Reinventing Eve*, xvi.

75 Gebara and Bingemer, *Mary: Mother of God, Mother of the Poor*, 99.

76 Phyllis Trible, "Eve and Adam: Genesis 2–3 Reread," in *Womanspirit Rising: A Feminist Reader in Religion*, 75–76; and Gossman, 52–53.

77 Trible, "Eve and Adam: Genesis 2–3 Reread," 79.

78 Trivka Frymer-Kensky, "Women," in *Harper's Bible Dictionary*, ed. Paul Achtemeier (San Francisco: Harper and Row, 1985), 1140.

79 Trible, "Eve and Adam: Genesis 2–3 Reread," 80.

80 Trible's interpretation is somewhat controversial among feminist biblical scholars because she exonerates the texts as authentically liberationist and fails to recognize the patriarchal nature of the authors. See Ilana Pardes, *Countertraditions in the Bible: A Feminist Approach* (Cambridge: Harvard University Press, 1992), 21.

81 Elizabeth Cady Stanton, *The Woman's Bible: The Original Feminist Attack on the Bible* (New York: Arno Press, 1975), 24–26.

82 Pardes, *Countertraditions in the Bible*, 14.

83 Noddings, *Women and Evil*, 3.

84 Daly, *Beyond God the Father*, 45.

85 Ibid., 68.

86 Kassel, "Mary and the Human Psyche Considered in the Light of Depth Psychology," 77.

87 Goldenberg, *Changing of the Gods*, 75.

88 Kassel, "Mary and the Human Psyche Considered in the Light of Depth Psychology," 77.

89 Noddings, *Women and Evil*, 6.

90 Elizabeth Johnson, *She Who Is: The Mystery of God in Feminist Theological Discourse*, 252.

91 Barbara Welter, "The Cult of True Womanhood: 1820–860," *American Quarterly* (1966): 152.

92 Noddings, *Women and Evil*, 229–45.

93 Warner, *Alone of All Her Sex: The Myth and the Cult of the Virgin Mary*, 254.

94 Marilyn French cites research indicating that 28 percent of all couples admit physical violence has occurred in their marriage. However, the true rate of violence directed at women in a family might be as high as 50 percent. A man beats a women every four seconds in the United States, and four women die from a man's beating every day. Marilyn French, *The War Against Women* (New York: Summit Books, 1992), 187.

95 Schussler Fiorenza, "Breaking the Silence–Becoming Visible," *Concilium: Women— Invisible in Theology and Church*, no. 182 (1985): 6–7.

96 Margaret Miles, "Violence Against Women in the Historical Christian West and In North American Secular Culture: The Visual and Textual Evidence," in *Shaping New Vision: Gender and Values in American Culture*, ed. Clarissa Atkinson, Constance Buchanan, and Margaret Miles (Ann Arbor, MI: UMI Research, 1987), 27.

97 See also Elisabeth Schussler Fiorenza and Mary Shawn Copeland, eds., *Concilium: Violence Against Women*, (1994).

98 Demosthenes Savramis, *The Satanizing of Woman: Religion Versus Sexuality*, (New York: Double Day, 1974), 64.

99 Joanne Carlson Brown and Rebecca Parker, "For God So Loved the World?," in *Christianity, Patriarchy and Abuse: A Feminist Critique*, ed. Joanne Carlson Brown and Carole Bohn, (Ann Arbor, MI: UMI Research, 1987), 3.

100 Daly, *Gyn/Ecology*, 231.

101 Polly Young-Eisendrath and Demaris Wehr, "Individualism and Reasonable Violence Against Women," *Christianity, Patriarchy and Abuse: A Feminist Critique*, ed. Joanne Carlson Brown and Carole Bohn, (Ann Arbor, MI: UMI Research, 1987), 118–23.

102 Ibid., 127.

103 Thistlethwaite, "Every Two Minutes," 305.

104 A booklet produced by the Women's Education Institute titled "Violence Against Women: A Curriculum for Empowerment" addresses how clergy may actually aid violence against women through the use of biblically based religious rationalization, pages 11, 14.

105 Linda Gordon, *Heroes of Their Own Lives: The Politics and History of Family Violence* (New York: Penguin Books, 1988), 251, 286.

106 Adrienne Rich documents the Catholic Church's vehement opposition to the use of anesthesia in reducing women's pain in childbirth during the middle of the nineteenth century. "The lifting of Eve's curse seemed to threaten the foundations of patriarchal religion; the cries of women in childbirth were for the glory of God the

Father. An alleviation of female suffering was seen as "hardening" society, as if the sole alternative to the *mater delorosa*—the eternally suffering and suppliant mother as epitomized by the Virgin—must be the Medusa whose look turns men to stone." If women did not suffer in childbirth, somehow Catholic theological order would be overturned. Adrienne Rich, *Of Woman Born: Motherhood as Experience and Institution* (New York: W.W. Norton, 1976), 168.

107 Miles, "Violence Against Women in the Historical Christian West and in North American Secular Culture: The Visual and Textual Evidence," 21.

108 Ibid.

109 Brown and Parker, "For God So Loved the World?," 12–13.

110 Rita Nakishima Brock, "Dusting the Bible on the Floor: A Hermeneutics of Wisdom," in *Searching the Scriptures: A Feminist Introduction*, ed. Elisabeth Schussler Fiorenza, (New York: Crossroad, 1993), 66.

111 Elizabeth Johnson, *She Who Is: The Mystery of God in Feminist Theological Discourse*, 253.

112 Edward Schillebeeckx, *Mary, Mother of the Redeemer* (New York: Sheed and Ward, 1964), 111.

113 Ruether, "The Western Religious Tradition and Violence Against Women in the Home," in *Christianity, Patriarchy and Abuse: A Feminist Critique*, 32.

114 Ibid., 34.

115 Miles, "Violence Against Women in the Historical Christian West and in North American Secular Culture: The Visual and Textual Evidence," 22.

116 Ruether, "The Western Religious Tradition and Violence Against Women in the Home," 35–38. See also Chapter Six of Daly, *Gyn/Ecology*.

117 Rich, *Of Woman Born*, 114–15.

118 Karen Horney, *Feminine Psychology* (New York: W.W. Norton, 1967), 113.

119 Ruether, "The Western Religious Tradition and Violence Against Women in the Home," in *Christianity, Patriarchy and Abuse: A Feminist Critique*, 31.

120 Minouche Kandel, "Women Who Kill Their Batterers Are Getting Battered in Court," *Ms.* July/August 1993 (88–89).

121 Leonardo Boff, *The Maternal Face of God: The Feminine and Its Religious Expressions* (San Francisco: Harper and Row, 1987), 116.

122 Kathleen Barry as quoted in Young-Eisendrath and Wehr, "Individualism and Reasonable Violence Against Women," in *Christianity, Patriarchy and Abuse: A Feminist Critique*, 126.

123 Elizabeth Johnson, "Marian Tradition and the Reality of Women," 124.

124 Daly, *Gyn/Ecology*, 111.

125 Ibid., 133.

126 For example, see Daly's critique of sociologist Peter Berger in Chapter One. Mary Daly, *Beyond God the Father*, 35–36.

127 Daly, *Pure Lust*, 104.

128 Zimdars-Swartz, 31.

129 Ibid., 266.

130 Ibid., 76.

131 Ibid., 87.

132 Ruether, "The Western Religious Tradition and Violence Against Women in the Home," in *Christianity, Patriarchy and Abuse: A Feminist Critique*, 40.

Chapter 6

1 Warner, *Alone of All Her Sex: The Myth and the Cult of the Virgin Mary,* 338.

2 Gebara and Bingemer, *Mary: Mother of God, Mother of the Poor,* 8.

3 Bruce Malina, "Mother and Son," *Biblical theology Bulletin,* 19, no. 4 (October 1989): 54.

4 Mary Daly refers to the reversal of image and meaning as a "strategy of the Sadosociety" in its effort to mask underlying misogyny. Daly, *Pure Lust,* 67–68.

5 Gail Paterson Corrington, "The Milk of Salvation: Redemption by the Mother in Late Antiquity and Early Christianity," *Harvard Theological Review,* 82, no. 4, (1989): 407.

6 Maeckelberghe, *Desperately Seeking Mary,* 149.

7 Daly, *Pure Lust,* 94.

8 Borresen, "Mary in Catholic Theology," 54.

9 Warner, *Alone of All Her Sex: The Myth and the Cult of the Virgin Mary,* 338–339.

10 Daphne Hampson, *Theology and Feminism* (Oxford: Basil Blackwell, 1990), 73.

11 Goldenberg, *Changing of the Gods,* 76.

12 Ibid., 75.

13 Dorothee Solle, *The Strength of the Weak: Toward a Christian Feminist Identity* (Philadelphia: Westminster, 1984), 47.

14 Elizabeth Johnson, "Reconstructing a Theology of Mary," 69.

15 Ibid., 77.

16 Ibid., 81.

17 Elizabeth Johnson does not directly allude to illegitimacy theories suggested in Chapter Three and articulated by Jane Schaberg. However, Johnson's contention would be further bolstered by these theories because single mothers have a long tradition of being considered outside the mainstream of society.

18 Ibid., 81–85.

19 Halkes, "Mary and Women," 66. Halkes updates this analysis in "Mary in My Life," 59.

20 Ibid., 66–67.

21 Ruether, *Sexism and God-Talk: Toward a Feminist Theology,* 152.

22 Ruether, *New Woman/New Earth,* 58.

23 Ruether, *Sexism and God-Talk: Toward a Feminist Theology,* 153–57.

24 Gebara and Bingemer, *Mary: Mother of God, Mother of the Poor,* xi, 1–12.

25 McKenzie, "The Mother of Jesus in the New Testament," 10.

26 Barrie Thorne's analysis of the research on sex/gender differences in child development reveals wider differences within a gender than between genders. Nevertheless, research that focuses upon difference receives more popular attention. Thorne concludes that gender differences are found not so much in observable behavior but in symbolic dimensions of experience. Thorne, *Gender Play: Girls and Boys in School,* 104–105.

27 Rosemary Radford Ruether, "Patriarchy and the Men's Movement: Part of the Problem or Part of the Solution?," in *Women Respond to the Men's Movement: A Feminist Collection,* ed. Kay Leigh Hagan, (San Francisco: Pandora, 1992), 14.

28 Daly, *Beyond God the Father,* 169.

29 Halkes, "Mary and Women," 69.

30 Feminist theologians, in their criticism of gender in trinitarian figures, do not wish

to deny that Jesus was male (although much has been written in opposition to viewing God as male). Concern exists when gender garners a salvific significance, or, in the case of priesthood, gender is essential for emulation of Christ. Elizabeth Johnson states the critique succinctly: "good news is stifled when Jesus' maleness, which belongs to his historical identity, is interpreted as being essential to his redeeming Christic function and identity. The Christ functions as a religious tool for marginalizing and excluding women." Elizabeth Johnson, "The Maleness of Christ," 108.

31 Jean Shinoda Bolen, *The Goddess in Everywoman: A New Psychology of Women* (New York: Harper and Row, 1984), 15.

32 Ibid., 281.

33 While the image of "Mary-Woman" values independence rather then relationship, the intent is not to deny relationality. For example, "Mary-Woman" can still be in continuity with Carol Gilligan's model of moral orientation.

34 Hunt, *Fierce Tenderness: A Feminist Theology of Friendship*, 4.

35 Ibid., 75–91.

36 Baring and Cashford, *The Myth of the Goddess: Evolution of an Image*, 8.

37 Rosemary Radford Ruether, *Gaia and God: An Ecofeminist Theology of Earth Healing* (San Francisco: HarperSan Francisco, 1992), 4.

38 It could be just as damaging for women to replace a universalized patriarchal image of Mary with a universalized feminist image of Mary. See discussion in Goldenberg, 76–77.

39 Schussler Fiorenza, "Claiming Our Authority and Power," 51–52.

40 Daphne Hampson, *Theology and Feminism*, 162.

41 Rosemary Radford Ruether, "Is Feminism the End of Christianity? A Critique of Daphne Hampson's *Theology and Feminism*," *Scottish Journal of Theology* vol. 4, 391.

42 Ibid., 394.

Index

—A—

Adam and Eve, 125, 134, 135, 202n. 2, 205n. 70; as defining Christian morality 137–144. *See* Lilith; Eve

Aeiparthenos, 15

alienation, 36,114; of Mary from women's experience, 70, 87, 153, 164, 171, 175, 186n. 93; and religious construction, 5, 26, 166, 172; and religious mystification, 146; and sin, 143; *See* mystery

Ambrose, St., 73, 74, 133

analogical imagination, 2, 106

apparitions,16, 20, 25, 198n. 45; and Mary's popularity, 33–35; and Mary's power, 100, 101; and physical abuse, 154; *See* Fatima; Lourdes

Apocalypses of the Virgin, 95

Aquinas, Thomas, St., 97, 113, 116, 197n. 32

asceticism, 62, 64, 71, 73

Ashe, Geoffrey, 11, 14, 27

Assumption of Mary, 79, 87, 166, 173, 185n 77, 187n. 32; history of, 19, 20; and New Eve, 135, 136

asymmetrical family relationships, 106, 113, 115, 119, 121

atonement theology, 127, 134, 135

Augustine, St., 19, 116, 135, 205n. 70

—B—

Beauvoir, Simone de, 120, 140

Behold Your Mother Woman of Faith, 136

Benko, Stephen, 11, 12, 60, 105, 135

Berger, Peter, 24–26, 29, 66, 111, 116, 138, 160

Bernard, St. of Clairvaux, 96, 97, 103
biblical scholarship, 20, 47, 65–68, 99, 110, 157, 168
Bingemer, Maria Clara, 142, 158, 164, 169, 170, 172
Blue Army, 37, 101, 187n. 4
Bridget, St. of Sweden, 16
Brigit, St. of Ireland, 12
Brown, Raymond, 92, 93, 110, 112

—C—
Call to Action, 37
Calvin, John, 97
Cana, marriage feast at, 91–93, 197n. 9
Carroll, Michael, 14, 50, 71, 81, 101
Catholic doctrine, 17, 82, 200n. 119, 205n. 70
celibacy: and Mary, 24, 79, 159, 177; as masochism, 50; valorization of, 71, 81, 83, 84
Chalcedon, Council of, 15
Christology: and biblical movement, 21; "high," 70; and Mariology, 10, 12, 15, 19, 47, 49, 93, 167
Christotypical, Mary as, 7, 15, 185n. 77
Collyridians, 11, 12, 203n. 16
compulsory heterosexuality, 74, 75, 86
contraception, 73, 78, 81, 83, 85, 196n. 138
cult of Mary: and Catholic social teaching, 40; as female element in Catholicism 105; fluidity of, 31; history of, 1–7, 9–11, 13, 14, 16, 17, 21–24, 97, 102; and ordination, 113; and popular Catholicism, 35, 36; and psychoanalysis, 50, 81; as religious construction, 24–27; and sexuality, 56, 75, 78, 80, 147
Cyril of Alexandria, St., 94

—D—
Daly, Mary, 3; on Adam and Eve, 125, 138, 141, 144; on American gynecology, 148; on Catholic sexual ethics, 80, 86, 87; on men in

women's movement, 171; as post-Christian, 123; on power of Mary, 89, 102, 105; and sado-ritual syndrome, 152–154; on virginal conception of Jesus, 78
deconstruction, of Marian imagery, 7, 138, 162, 178
Deiparae Virginis, 20
Deuteronomy, Book of, 55
dissent, 39, 44
Divino Afflante Spiritu, 21
divorce, 55
Dogmatic Constitution of the Church, 22, 23
dualism: body/soul, 72, 76, 196n. 144; in ethical approaches, 115; gendered, 105–107, 132; good/evil, 126, 128, 137, 138, 142–147, 152–155; *See* Eve/Mary parallel

—E—
ecclesiatypical, Mary as, 7, 100, 106
empowerment, of women, 73, 104, 150, 175
Enoch, Book of, 132, 192n. 39
Ephesus, Council of, 14, 15, 94, 183n. 39, 203n. 16
Ephraem, St. of Syria, 93, 135
Epiphanius, St., 11, 129, 137, 193n. 64, 199n. 84
Epistle of Pope Gelasius, 109
erotic, power of, 80
eschatology, 79, 169
ethic of care, 115, 117, 119, 170, 201n. 121
ethics of Mariology, 1, 87, 115–117, 119, 170
Eve: basis for violence against women, 146–156; ethical implications of, 143–146, 206n. 106; feminist analysis of, 138–143; in formulation of New Eve, 14, 125–129; myth development of, 130–137, 203n. 31, 204n. 47, 205n. 50; subordinate to Adam, 202n. 2

Eve/Mary parallel, 5, 17, 125, 127, 135–140, 143–147, 153–155, 203n. 31

evil: and Eve, 128–139, 141–147, 153; of sexism, 112; of sexuality, 87; of women, 5, 104, 108, 126

externalization, 25, 27

—F—

Fall of humanity, 64, 129–135, 139, 141–144, 146, 150, 158, 203n. 20, 204nn. 36, 59, 205n. 70

father ineffective families, 71

Fatima, apparition at, 23, 154

female friendships, 87, 175, 176

feminine nature, 75

feminism: and Catholicism, 166, 185n. 83; and critique of patriarchy, 38, 81, 138; and dual parenting, 121; and morality, 48–51, 147; as post-Christian, 161; and the Vatican, 41, 114, 120; and women's experience, 46

feminist theologians: divergent approaches of, 45; and the goddess, 168; goals of, 47, 104; and ordination, 109; as redefining theology, 144, 157, 161–163, 170, 174; and sexual ethics, 65, 66

Fiorenza, Elisabeth Schussler: on feminist theology, 38, 123, 178; on the goddess, 105; on hermeneutics, 46, 47; on historical criticism, 65; on women's ordination, 114; on violence against women, 147; on virginal motherhood, 76, 77

Fourth Lateran Council, 15, 194n. 89

—G—

Gebara, Ivone, 142, 158, 164, 169, 170, 172

Genesis, book of, 126, 127, 130–132, 134, 139–142, 192n. 39, 104n. 36

Germanus of Constantinople, 94

Gilligan, Carol, 115–118, 170

Gnosticism, 62, 63, 65–67, 139, 192n. 46

God: as all powerful, 145; of heterosexuality, 76; and justice, 118, 119; as male, 102, 104, 107, 108, 111, 121, 131, 173, 179; and relationship to Mary, 15, 18, 49, 89, 94–96; See revelation of God

Goddess: assimilation into Mary, 11–13, 60, 71; Eve as, 139, 142; Mary as, 6, 36, 39, 56, 102–107; spirituality, 15, 16, 19, 27, 55, 81, 90, 174–176, 196n. 149

golden age of Mary, 20, 98, 110

Graef, Hilda, 7,

Grain Protectoress, 13

Greeley, Andrew, 2, 35, 36, 105, 106,

Green, Ronald, 48, 49, 178

Guadalupe, Our Lady of, 16, 33, 172, 187n. 11

—H—

Halkes, Catherina, 28, 74, 86, 102, 164, 166, 167, 170, 171

Hebrew Scriptures, 55, 58, 115

hierarchy of Catholic Church: all male, 79–81, 108–110, 121–123, 167, 169, 175, 199n. 83; and apparitions, 101; conservative nature of, 10, 44, 84, 179; and popular Catholicism, 15, 106; teachings of, 17, 21, 27

hieros gamos, 135

Hildegard of Bignen, 28

historical criticism, 65, 66, 71, 138

homosexuality, 80, 81, 85

householders, 110

Humanae Vitae, 82

hymen, 23, 55, 133, 153, 190n. 7, 205n. 70

hyperdulia, 39

—I—

illegitimacy of Jesus, 68, 69, 193n. 76, 208n. 17

Immaculate Conception, 17–20, 33,

39, 47, 98, 135, 166, 184n. 50, 187n.
5, 188n. 28
Ineffablis Deus, 18
infallibility, papal, 19, 82
Infancy Gospel of James, 57, 60–62, 65,
192n. 32, 193n. 72, 196n. 149
infancy narratives, 57, 59–61, 67, 68,
132, 166, 168, 193n. 72
innocence, valorization of, 55, 149,
150
intercession of Mary, 90, 93–97, 101,
115, 117, 119, 183n. 30, 197n. 9
internalization, 25, 26, 153
Irenaeus, 14, 127, 134, 136

—J—
Jerome, St., 4, 57, 63–67, 72, 127, 137
Jesus Christ: and Mary's influence
over, 91–95, 155; and salvation, 15,
19, 114, 134, 204n. 36; and siblings,
4, 61,66, 67, 70; *See* illegitimacy of
Jesus; atonement theology
John, Gospel of, 61, 62, 66, 67, 91, 92,
110
John Paul II, Pope: on Mary, 23, 75,
93, 120, 185n. 84; on virginity, 84;
on women's roles, 4, 24, 42, 43,
114, 185n. 83; *See Laborem Exercens;*
Mulieris Dignatatem; Redemptoris
Mater
John XXII, Pope, 41, 42
John XXIII, Pope, 41, 42
Johnson, Elizabeth: on feminist theology, 47; on nature of God, 2, 104,
145, 150; on nature of women, 3,
121, 152; on theology of Mary, 13,
98, 100, 125, 164–166
Justin Martyr, St., 127, 133

—L—
Laborem Exercens, 42, 43
Leo XIII, Pope, 41, 92
liberation Mariology, 106, 107, 167,
168, 188n. 29
liberation theology, 106, 169

Lilith, 131, 154, 203n. 22
Lourdes, apparition at, 34, 187n. 7
Luke, Gospel of, 57, 59–61, 67, 69,
107, 110, 126, 129, 136, 167, 168
Luther, Martin, 7, 97, 181n. 6

—M—
machismo, 16, 50
magisterium, 17, 38, 174
Magnificat of Mary, 69, 107, 165
Mariology: and apparitions, 34, 35:
basis for, 6, 7, 153; feminist reinterpretation of, 33; impact of Vatican
II on, 23; "low," 5; *See* cult of Mary;
liberation Mariology
Mark, Gospel of, 58, 66, 67, 191n. 22
marriage: biblical understandings of,
55, 56, 58, 61, 190n. 11, 191n. 20;
Paul on, 71; St. Jerome on, 64;
versus virginal life, 73, 75, 84; and
violence, 206n. 94
martyrdom of women, 72, 149
Mary, Everywoman, 5, 173–178
Mary-Mother, 176, 177
Mary-Sister, 175, 176
Mary-Woman, 174, 175, 209n. 33
Matthew, Gospel of, 57–61, 66–69,
165
mediation: in Catholic theology, 90,
102; of Mary, 44, 91–94, 97–99,
100, 101, 108, 114, 115, 119, 120,
137, 155
middle ages, Mary in, 13, 17, 95, 96
misogyny: in construction of Mary, 26,
74, 147, 159, 162, 164; in Genesis,
140; in Gnosticism, 63; of John Paul
II, 24
modernism, 40, 65, 101
moral theology: and Christian
feminists, 3, 74; Mary as a tool of,
49, 57; as mediation, 44; and
relational ethics, 115–117, 200n.
119
motherhood: in Hebrew scriptures, 56,
126, 142; of Mary, 5, 14, 87, 93, 94,

106, 120, 122; pre-Christian understanding, 176; and virginity, 43, 53,
69, 75–78, 82; as woman's nature,
44, 119, 151, 182n. 3, 195n. 115
Mulieris Dignitatem, 43
mystery: in Catholic theology, 17, 70,
86, 100, 103; of Mary's life, 13;
potential manipulation of, 145,
146; of women's bodies, 177
mythology, 77, 131, 132, 174

—N—
natural law, 41, 76, 116, 117
Nestorius, 14, 44
Nicaea, Council of, 53

—O—
objectification, 25, 51
Odes to Solomon, 73
ordination, women's: Catholic
arguments against, 109, 186n. 103,
199n. 83; and connection to
goddess spirituality, 5, 102, 106;
feminist support for, 111–114; *See*
hierarchy of the Catholic Church;
priesthood; Women's Ordination
Conference
Origen, 19, 44, 63, 68, 73
original sin: and Augustine, 116, 205n.
70; and the Fall of Humanity, 131,
141, 148; and Hebrew scriptures,
132; and Mary, 17–19, 184n. 50,
197n. 32, 204n. 36; *See* Fall of
humanity

—P—
Panarion, 11
parenting, 7, 43, 90, 115, 121
*Pastoral Constitution of the Church in the
Modern World*, 42
patriarchy, 108, 151, 155, 161, 171
Paul VI, Pope, 15, 23, 42
Philip, Gospel of, 63
Pius IX, Pope, 18–20
Pius X, Pope, 19–21, 41, 98, 136

Pius XI, Pope, 19–21, 41, 98, 136
Pius XII, Pope, 19–21, 98, 136
pluralism, 46, 62, 170, 176
popular Catholicism, 31–33, 35–38,
101, 105, 169
pornography, 80
priesthood: and discipleship, 110; and
loss of credibility, 85; and women,
11, 89, 102, 108–112, 114, 199nn.
83, 84; 209n. 30

—Q—
Quadragisimo Anno, 41

—R—
Redemptoris Mater, 23, 43
reification: definition of, 25, 48; of
heterosexuality, 76; of hierarchy,
176; of male experience, 111; of
virginity, 55, 66; of women's inferiority, 138; *See* social construction,
theory of
Rerum Novarum, 41, 42
revelation of God, 21, 34, 80, 82, 90,
173
Revelation, Book of, 126, 129, 130,
202n. 14
reversals, patriarchal, 120, 155, 160,
173, 204n. 59
rosary, 33, 186n. 3, 187n. 4
Ruether, Rosemary Radford: on feminine aspect of God, 106, 177; on
feminist liturgical movements, 36,
46; on Jesus' siblings, 4, 66, 67, 70;
on John Paul II, 24; language for
God, 104; renegotiating Marian
imagery, 3, 26, 167–169; on significance of Mary, 2, 79, 84; on
violence against women, 150, 151

—S—
Schaberg, Jane, 3, 4, 68, 69, 70, 71
Sergius, Pope, 12
sexual activity: biblical understandings
of, 56, 196n. 140; Catholic Church

view on, 75, 76, 81, 83–85, 205n.
70; Gnostic view on, 62; and death,
79; social construction of, 74
Sirach, Book of, 54, 189n. 1
sisterhood, 131, 166, 175, 176
Sixtus IV, Pope, 18
social construction, theory of: definition of, 24, 25; and gender, 71, 170;
and implications for Mariology, 27,
28, 118, 148, 158
soteriology, 130, 204n. 36
spousal order of Marian virginity, 4, 75
Stanton, Elizabeth Cady, 140, 143
Sub Tuum Praesidium, 14
Supratemporal Marian Principle, 113

—T—
Tertullian, 14, 63, 67, 128, 135, 204n.
47
theologoumenon, 70
Theophilus, story of, 95
Theotokos, 14, 15, 94
Thomas, Gospel of, 72, 194n. 98
Transitus Marie, 19
Trent, Council of, 202n. 6
triple virgin, 57

—V—
Vatican Council, First, 19
Vatican Council, Second: and
Eve/Mary parallel, 136, 137; on
Marian mediation, 98–100, 197n. 9;

on Mary as Mother of God, 15;
significance of, 21
violence, against women, 70, 147–155,
165, 206n. 94, 197n. 9
virgin birth of Jesus, 23, 39, 58, 63, 67,
68, 78, 86
virginity: as becoming male, 72, 73;
biblical understandings of, 54–56
190n. 12; and Catholic theology,
133, 193n. 63; and Gnosticism,
62–64; as independence, 107; and
Infancy Gospel of James, 60, 61, 192n.
32; Mary's perpetual, 4, 15, 66, 67,
70, 148, 159; and Gospel of
Matthew, 57, 58, 191n. 18; and
motherhood, 43, 53, 75, 84
Vulgate Bible, 127, 202n. 6

—W—
Warner, Marina, 95, 119, 127, 157, 163
watcher myth, 132
witchhunts, 16, 48, 151
Woman Church, 37
women's movement, 108, 163, 171
Women's Ordination Conference, 37,
188 n. 21

—Z—
Zimdars–Swartz, Sandra, 51, 100, 119,
154
Zwingli, Ulrich, 97